Howlings from the Pit

OTHER TITLES FROM FALCON PRESS

Joseph C. Lisiewski, Ph.D.
   Israel Regardie and the Philosopher's Stone
   Ceremonial Magic and the Power of Evocation
   Kabbalistic Cycles and the Mastery of Life
   Kabbalistic Handbook for the Practicing Magician

Israel Regardie
   The Complete Golden Dawn System of Magic
   The Golden Dawn Audio CDs
   The Eye in the Triangle
   What You Should Know About the Golden Dawn

Christopher S. Hyatt, Ph.D.
   Undoing Yourself With Energized Meditation & Other Devices
   Radical Undoing: Complete Course for Undoing Yourself (DVDs)
   Energized Hypnosis (book, CDs & DVDs)
   To Lie Is Human: Not Getting Caught Is Divine
   The Psychopath's Bible: For the Extreme Individual
   Secrets of Western Tantra: The Sexuality of the Middle Path

Christopher S. Hyatt, Ph.D. with contributions by
Wm. S. Burroughs, Timothy Leary, Robert A. Wilson, et al.
   Rebels & Devils: The Psychology of Liberation

S. Jason Black and Christopher S. Hyatt, Ph.D.
   Pacts With the Devil: A Chronicle of Sex, Blasphemy & Liberation
   Urban Voodoo: A Beginner's Guide to Afro-Caribbean Magic

Lon Milo DuQuette & Christopher S. Hyatt, Ph.D.
   Aleister Crowley's Illustrated Goetia

Christopher S. Hyatt, Ph.D. & Antero Alli
   A Modern Shaman's Guide to a Pregnant Universe

Antero Alli
   Angel Tech: A Modern Shaman's Guide to Reality Selection
   Angel Tech Talk (CDs)

Peter J. Carroll
   The Chaos Magick Audio CDs
   PsyberMagick

Phil Hine
   Condensed Chaos
   Prime Chaos
   The Pseudonomicon

For up-to-the-minute information on prices and availability, please visit our website at
http://originalfalcon.com

Howlings from the Pit

A Practical Handbook of
Medieval Magic, Goetia & Theurgy

by
Joseph C. Lisiewski, Ph.D.

Introduction & Commentary
by Mark Stavish, M.A.
Founder of the Institute
for Hermetic Studies

Afterword by
David Rankine

THE *Original* FALCON PRESS
TEMPE, ARIZONA, U.S.A.

Copyright © 2011 C.E. by Joseph Lisiewski, Ph.D.

All rights reserved. No part of this book, in part or in whole, may be reproduced, transmitted, or utilized, in any form or by any means, electronic or mechanical, including photocopying, recording, or by any information storage and retrieval system, without permission in writing from the publisher, except for brief quotations in critical articles, books and reviews.

International Standard Book Number: 978-1-935150-45-9
Library of Congress Catalog Card Number: 2010919052

First Edition 2011

Cover by Linda Joyce Franks

The paper used in this publication meets the minimum requirements of the American National Standard for Permanence of Paper for Printed Library Materials Z39.48-1984

Address all inquiries to:
THE ORIGINAL FALCON PRESS
1753 East Broadway Road #101-277
Tempe, AZ 85282 U.S.A.
(or)
PO Box 3540
Silver Springs, NV 89429 U.S.A.
website: http://www.originalfalcon.com
email: info@originalfalcon.com

Dedication

To Bill Heidrick, my old friend and colleague in these matters for the past thirty-two years. Thanks, Bill, for your guidance, direction, and support in these matters most Occult. Without your counsel, I would have been left wanting, indeed.

— Dr. Joseph Lisiewski

Table of Contents

How To Use This Book 9
Introduction by Mark Stavish 10
Chapter One—An Overview of Western Magic 15
Chapter Two—Preparations for Old System Magic Part I 30
Chapter Three—Preparations for Old System Magic Part II 62
Chapter Four—Efficacy: Its Mechanics and Role in Old System Magic 90
Chapter Five—The Theory of Magic 119
Chapter Six—The Practice of Magic 140
Chapter Seven—The Effects of Magic 173
Chapter Eight—Magic, Mysticism & Alchemy 186
Chapter Nine—Questions & Answers 212
Afterword by David Rankine 282

How To Use This Book

You are holding in your hands a strange and intriguing book. It is part formal study, part essays, and part dialogue, such as one would find between a teacher and student. As such it is, as the title states, a handbook, a practical reference guide for the aspiring magician. This format in many ways is ideal, as it allows the reader to carry it with them, and to simply open to almost any page and begin reading and finding something useful for their work or meditation. This is, in short, a modern grimoire of sorts, and you, are the modern heir to this powerful system of magic. However, to get the most out of this work the following guidelines are suggested:

1. Read through the book with a notebook handy, writing down the important points discussed by the author.
2. Organize your notes along the lines of specific areas, such as: Magical Theory, Practice of Evocation, Subjective Synthesis, Medieval Mind, Mysticism, Alchemy, Planetary Cycles, and Kabbalistic Analysis.
3. Carefully place information under each category, and review your notes when reading. As you will see, this is a book that is meant to guide you, and therefore it is meant to be studied and not simply read.
4. Take time to re-write your notes in shorter and shorter form, and to study various sections. By doing this, you will internalize the material presented, make it your own, and thereby be successful in your application of it.

While this book is by no means an academic treatise on magic, designed to be as practical as possible, some additional background information has been deemed essential by the author, hence the copious use of commentary in the form of footnotes. A variety of texts are cited and referred to in addition to those mentioned directly in the text. Readers who wish to further their knowledge of Western occultism are encouraged to study them as part of their program of magical education.

Introduction

When Dr. Lisiewski first asked me to write a commentary and introduction for a book based on his newsletter *Howlings from the Pit: A Journal of Old System Magic, Theurgy and Goetia* I was both pleased and apprehensive. Pleased because when we had first discussed his newsletter several years ago, along with each issue as they appeared, I knew that the material was prepared for both the beginner to ceremonial magic as well as those who have been working in it for a while. *Howlings*, as it came to be called, was originally published quarterly from May 2007 until February 2008. While only four issues were produced, they were massive in size, and followed by equally large weekly postings on Dr. Lisiewski's website which addressed readers' questions between issues and clarified a variety of points within medieval ceremonial magic. The material as presented has been modestly edited to remove redundancies, promotional notations, and personal miscellany.

Those who are familiar with Dr. Lisiewski's works will find this book an invaluable addition to their literary and practical work in not only magic, but also laboratory alchemy, mysticism, and even the more contemporary schools of New Thought, the historical precursor to the New Age Movement. Readers who are not familiar with Dr. Lisiewski's writings will be in for an eye-opening experience, as they may for the very first time, see in print the words of one of the most admired and reviled men in modern magic. Honesty and straightforwardness tends to do that to people's reputations, and honest and straightforward he is. This book also is in many ways a sort of modern grimoire of its own, in that it is the compilation of forty years of occult practices. It is not a cookbook, but like any meaningful text, is aimed first at creating the proper mental climate—or view as it is called—and then from that perspective, undertaking actions (rituals) based on well-formulated thoughts and relationships that will bring about the desired results of the ritual one is performing. I remember decades ago, when I first met Professor

Peter Roche de Coppens, during which he presented me with a signed copy of his then recent book, *The Invisible Temple: The Nature and Use of the Group Mind for Spiritual Attainment* (Llewellyn Publications, 1987). After handing me the book, a book that is like his other works on Christian qabala, an extended "Kabbalistic Analysis" of the various Christian prayers and rites, he said, "Neither God nor the Devil has any use for a lazy man." Those looking for easy enlightenment, or as Lisiewski calls it, "a quick-fix" to life's mundane problems need look elsewhere, for neither will be found within the pages of this book—or any other for that matter. All that is promised herein is work, and from that, results one can actually recognize as having come from an occult operation.

As Lisiewski states in the first chapter of his book *Kabbalistic Cycles & the Mastery of Life*:

> "Ironically, however, these occult laws...are not so easy to manipulate... Why? Because of two operational conditions that reflect back on the laziness and shallowness of the contemporary mind.
>
> The first operational condition is that an effective 'Subjective Synthesis' must be built up within the subconscious (or unconscious) mind of the individual. This all-important concept was rigorously discussed in my first book, *Ceremonial Magic & The Power of Evocation*. The reader would do well to consult a copy of that book, and learn the details of this all-important subjective synthesis state. Suffice to say here that the state of subjective synthesis is that subconscious constellation of beliefs and ideas that govern most of our conscious actions, ideas, and mental perceptions of our personal universe: the outer world we see, act towards and react to, and the inner world of our psychic nature that we are barely conscious of.
>
> When these subconscious beliefs and ideas are structured through our *conscious effort* into a unified whole, each part supporting the other in a particular framework—that is, a given belief about something—the subconscious mind directs the outcome according to those beliefs...what matters is that at some level we *think* and *act* on the supposed existence of these external and internal [occult] influence, treating them with all the respect and

caution we give to any of the physical forces that affect us every day, such as electricity and gravity."[1] (p.19–20)

As stated earlier, I was apprehensive because by ceremonial magic we are not talking what is often passed off today as "Western esotericism" or "ritual magic" but instead, the "old school" Medieval magic of the *grimoires*. These grimoires, or grammars, are in fact little more than the notebooks or outlines of magical operations performed in Europe and appear to have come from within closed corridors of the dominant priesthood itself. This presented a daunting task, as writing commentary required that the reader in fact receive a considerable education in Classical, Medieval and Renaissance magical theories, as well as have them presented in an authentic manner—a manner which differs considerably from modern schools of ritual magic that are mainly derived from the ritual initiations and practices of the Hermetic Order of the Golden Dawn and its offshoots. In addition there was the commentary that has been added to the original text. This commentary, in addition to clarifying certain points, as well as putting them in a historical context, is in many ways a synopsis of the many conversations and emails Dr. Lisiewski and I have had over the years, as well as a reflection of my own 35 years of research and practice in the fields of general esotericism, alchemy and ritual magic. These conversations between Dr. Lisiewski and myself have taken place on a weekly and often daily basis, thereby giving me unique insight into his work and perspective—a perspective that is possibly known only to myself, and his handful of personal students.

Despite the title of this book, and the tone of the articles it includes, it should be clearly stated that Dr. Lisiewski has written extensively on the Golden Dawn system, even being directed by Regardie decades ago to assist in editing a Golden Dawn correspondence course. As a result of this and other work, Lisiewski

---

[1] The second operational law is that we must be rigorous in self-examination, our application of the principals set forth, and our synthesis of various areas of knowledge to break down the artificial boundaries that have been established between the various areas of knowledge since the end of the Renaissance. We must synthesize the various "–ologies" into a whole, and demonstrate the effectiveness of this personal synthesis in our daily life.

(along with many other magicians I have met, but often would not say as much in public) recognized that the Golden Dawn system worked quite well at creating "change" in the consciousness of the operator, but that this change rarely (and often chaotically when it did), bring about any desirable conditions in the physical world. To help others in this work he eventually wrote *The Magician's Handbook*, and additional articles on this topic are included in this book. To be clear on this point: the Golden Dawn and similar based systems of magic were not designed to create change in the material world, and can only do so if specific and definite steps are taken. Privately magicians with whom I have spoken have called this 'flogging the mule' to get the system to work material changes. With Medieval, or Old System Magic, *material changes was its sole and only purpose*. As such, one must use the right tool for the right work. My own comments and methods for making modern kabbalah and magic more effective in the physical world can be found in *Kabbalah for Health and Wellness*.

While it would be impossible to cover every aspect of magic as a running commentary to Dr. Lisiewski's articles, I have tried my best, and hope that it is of genuine and sincere use to readers seeking to avail themselves of "Old System" magic in their desire to better their lives.

Now, here we have hit upon an important point. That is, people undertake magic to better their lives. They perform—or hire others to perform—magical rituals, to move invisible forces so that those forces will have specific and desired impact on the visible world, thereby bringing the operator or their client, tangible material results: love, money, sex, success, fame, better health for herd, beast, or man, you name it, there is an operation for it in one of the old 'grammars' of magic. What is missing in many of the magical texts, and for a series of reasons particular to each compiler of the individual texts, are rituals designed to bring one into communion with God or some kind of profound, but ambiguously described spiritual illumination. This needs to be made clear, because for the most part, ritual magic of the period was clearly an operation or skill aimed at the manipulation of power—power over others as well as the natural environment. If one wanted salvation they had to go to the Mother Church; if it was illumination they sought, then prayer and penance was the time-proven method for attaining it. The paths of collective worship and the path of individual illumination were both (and for many still are) under the direction of the priesthood. Magic, however, even with its apparent roots inside the dark and dank halls of Catholic monasticism, or possibly bureaucratic power grabs, was not, as it appealed directly to a higher power, to God himself and his Holy angels, even if it was to call upon the demons of hell. This stepping over the boundary of what could be controlled by the existing religious-political establishment and what could not was a step many would take, even at the risk of losing their minds in the process, or lives if caught by the civil or religious authorities.

However, it was not always this way, and at different times and in different places, magic was not only part and parcel of the religious establishment, it was also a critical part of daily life. This is nowhere better exemplified than in ancient Egypt, the land considered by many to be the cradle—rightly or wrongly—of the various "Western Esoteric Traditions".

Mark Stavish, M.A.
Director of Studies
Institute for Hermetic Studies
Wyoming, Pennsylvania
20 March 2010

Chapter One

An Overview of Western Magic

Egyptian Magic

An ancient Talmudic proverb states that God divided all of the world's magic into ten parts, of which, Egypt received nine of them, and the remaining one-tenth was divided amongst the rest of the world. As such, it is not surprising that the Hebrew word for magician is derived from the Egyptian one. So deeply ingrained is this belief in Egypt's magical supremacy that nearly every magical legend from the Medieval through Modern eras has sought to show its validity by mentioning Egypt in some form as the source for its greatness and power. Even the 18th Century quasi-Masonic "Egyptian Rite" of Count Alessandro Cagliostro, the premier magical order of its day, had little to do with Egypt, and was in fact, directly connected to the grimoires attributed to King Solomon. Yet, this small detail mattered not to either his supporters or detractors. So great was the call of Egypt, that the words of Hermes eclipsed those of the Greek philosophers and helped give birth to the Italian Renaissance four centuries ago.

The allure of Egypt was, and still is strong, and to attempt to separate her magic and religion into discrete categories is both impossible and meaningless. In fact, among the ancient Egyptians there was no word for religion as we know it, yet there was a distinct and informative one for magic—*heka*—which is often interpreted to mean, "magical power" or a power to compel the gods and goddesses to act on the magician's behalf in the visible and invisible worlds. Through complex ritualistic identification with the various gods and goddesses, the magician in fact acted as a god incarnate and through their own power compelled spirits to act or move as desired.

In *Daily Life of the Egyptian Gods* the authors Dimitri Meeks and Christine Favard-Meeks state:

> "Heka personified, above all, the life force, or *ka*, in action. As such, it is the expression of the kind of knowledge that is proper to each divinity and enables him or her to act on the basis of *sia* [creative, imaginative, and organizing power of deity]... Human beings also dispose of this life force, which makes it possible for them to exist...this heka enables them to communicate with the divine world, which bathes in the same energy. Heka, even permits them, it was believed, to influence the world of the gods. In a religious or ritual framework different from that found in the temples, the use of heka thus made it an approximate equivalent of magic." (p.236–237)

Critical to the magicians of the classical period, as to the yogis of India and others areas of the East, was the notion that this magical power was both a bodily force that resided in the belly, as well as a word or sound, and produced genuine physical manifestations.

> "The kind of knowledge and intelligence that could be articulated and could create resided in the heart, the seat of directing and organizing consciousness. Yet not all intellectual faculties were concentrated there. There was a profounder, more intimate place, the intestines; a special power lay concealed in them, one that drew all its force from the energy of life itself. This energy was called *heka*. To swallow heka was to strengthen and develop this power; to swallow one's own heka was to refrain from putting it to use. Heka was what resulted from giving form to all the energies (ka) one absorbed; it constituted an inward, personal sort of knowledge distinct from the universal or collective type of knowledge... Heka was often directed against one's enemies and served essentially as a means of self-protection... A repository of knowledge bound up with and individual, such as knowledge of a god's real name...heka was rarely transmitted to others, at least not voluntarily.... Consequently, the malignant forces ranged against the gods preferred to attack their hearts and viscera in order to gain complete mastery over the power their victims possessed. To penetrate—as a fly might, for example—the belly of a god was an

easy way to establish oneself in the most intimate part of his being, and acquire a position of domination there." (p.96)

This power to become equal to the gods was the measuring stick of a magician's effectiveness. Magic was even looked upon not as a curse or something to fear outright—although 'good' and 'bad' magic existed—but as a gift from the gods to be appreciated and used to improve daily life, as well as to maintain the harmonies of heaven and earth. It is not surprising then that professional magicians were sought out by all classes of society to act on their behalf. Magic, properly used, maintained order and harmony, and thereby happiness in this world and the next.

> "To become one with the Word was, then, to be removed from all evil. The Word is good and is manifest in the Order of the world. God, as goodness, obeys his own laws, for the Order and the good are identical." (p.77)

The most powerful part of Egyptian magic to survive however, may have been in the idea that a mortal being of flesh and blood can identify with and become one with the gods—the forces of creation. In *The Corpus Hermeticum*, composed during the First through Third Centuries, A.D., demonstrate a powerful early Egyptian influence when we read:

> "19. Consider this yourself. Command your soul to go anywhere, and it will be there quicker than your command. Bid it to go to the ocean and again it is there at once, not as if it had gone from place to place but was already there. Order it to fly up to heaven and it will need no wings, nor will anything impede it, neither the fire of the sun, nor the ether, nor the whirlwind, nor the other heavenly bodies, but cutting through them all it will soar up to the last body. And if you wish to break through all this and to contemplate what is beyond (if there is anything beyond the cosmos), it is in your power.
> 20. See what power you have and what speed! You can do all these things and yet God cannot? Reflect on God in this way as having all within Himself as ideas: the cosmos, Himself, the whole. If you do not make yourself equal to God you cannot understand Him. Like is understood by like. Grow to immeasurable size. Be free from every body, transcend all time. Become eternity and thus you will understand God. Suppose nothing to be impossible for

yourself. Consider yourself immortal and able to understand everything: all arts, sciences and the nature of every living creature. Become higher that all heights and lower than all depths. Sense as one within yourself the entire creation: fire, water, the dry and the moist. Conceive yourself to be in all places at the same time: in the earth, the sea, in heaven; that you are not yet born, that you are within the womb, that you are young, old, dead; that you are beyond death. Conceive all things at once: time, places, actions, qualities and quantities; then you can understand God.

21. But if you lock up your soul in your body, abase it and say: 'I understand nothing; I can do nothing; I am afraid of the sea; I cannot reach heaven; I do not know who I was nor who I shall be.' What have you to do with God? For you cannot conceive anything beautiful or good while you are attached to the body and are evil. For the greatest evil is to ignore what belongs to God. To be able to know and to will and to hope is the straight and easy way appropriate to each that will lead to the Supreme Good. When you take this road this Good will meet you everywhere and will be experienced everywhere, even where and when you do not expect it; when awake, asleep, in a ship, on the road, by night, by day, when speaking and when silent, for there is nothing which it is not.

22. Now do you say that God is invisible? Be careful. Who is more manifest than He? He has made all things for this reason: that through them you should see Him. This is the goodness (*to agathon*) of God; this is His excellence: that He is made manifest through all. Though you cannot see what is bodiless, *Nous* is seen in the act of contemplation, God in the act of creation. These things have been made clear to you Hermes thus far. Reflect on all other things in the same way within yourself and you will not be led astray." (*The Way of Hermes*, Translation by Clement Salaman, et al. p.57–58)

While magic flourished during the Greek occupation of Egypt, even giving rise to the Pythagorean and Neoplatonic traditions, which would fuse with other traditions and become what is now known as Classical Hermeticism, it was during the Roman period that things took a turn for the worse. Roman law forbid magical practices at various times, limiting them along with oracles to state use only. Roman rulers were so afraid of magic, or any spiritual practice that was not officially sanctioned, that two centuries prior to persecuting Christians off and on during the First through Third Centuries, C.E., they murdered followers of Dionysius by the thousands. Here, in Roman occupied Egypt, the beginning of a trend that would continue on into the period when Christianity would be the official religion of the Roman Empire, magic and religion would emerge as separate and distinct entities, with one receiving full state support and the other being forced underground and into the shadows and fringes of society. By 392 C.E., even private worship in one's home was declared illegal in an effort to wipeout the last remaining strongholds of pre-Christian worship—that of the family rites and practices. While the effectiveness of this law was negligible, it demonstrates how far the state would go to control the hearts and mind of the people. In short, Christianity did not conquer Rome as so many theologians have said; it is Rome that conquered Christianity.

Medieval Europe

The early Middle Ages saw not only a collapse of organized social structures as Asiatic barbarian hordes swept across Europe destroying the tottering and decadent remains of the Roman Empire, but also the temporary resurgence of magical practices. This in part was a result of magic being defined by early Church authorities as anything that did not include the power of God the Father, Son, and Holy Spirit as their focal point. So, many pre-Christian practices were 'christened' as it were, and the words, "In the Name of the Father, Son, and Holy Spirit" found themselves appended to a host of rituals and practices that would make many modern churchgoers speechless.

> "Among not only ordinary folk but the privileged of sixth-century France as well, protective spells 'were by custom tied about the neck for health's sake, with exorcistic writings, while around Saint Peter's, they were displayed for sale on Bonifaces' day. The symbol of a fish was one of the popular one's to ward off evil, and gave a shape to amulets not only for the living but to those buried with the dead through the western areas, from pagan time up into twentieth-century Italy and Sicily. In eastern Martyria you could buy stamps to impress a spell on paper, showing a saint to his or her name and the words 'Blessing of....'; or you could buy medico-amuletic armbands for the pilgrim trade inscribed with the five-pointed star (the pentalpha or Solomon's Seal), the lion-headed snake (Chnoubis), the Annunciation or Women at the Tubs, bits of Psalm 90, and so forth—a jumble of mostly Christian but also non-

Christian symbols and words sets long in circulation. A sampling of archeological data of this sort spread across Syria, Palestine and Egypt of the early Byzantine period 'reveals a world thoroughly and openly committed to supernatural healing, and one wherein, for the sake of health, Christianity and sorcery had been forced into open partnership'." (*Christianity & Paganism in the Fourth to Eighth Centuries* by Ramsay Macmullen, p.141)

It was not until the Late Middle Ages, as a result of the Black Death that swept through Europe between 1347 and 1352, killing it is estimated one-third of the population, that magic and witchcraft were persecuted.

What could not be eliminated was absorbed and synthesized into the existing doctrines of the faith, thereby giving Christianity—now in the adolescent or early adulthood stage of its growth—a subconscious connection to its pre-Christian roots both in the Middle East and Europe. This is most powerfully exhibited in the role and reverence given to Jesus' mother Mary.

"These nocturnal voyages [of the witches] represented the vast quantity of phantasmagoria concerning witches and wizards that invaded the imagination of the late Middle Ages. After the thirteenth century, the Sabbat accumulated in its imaginary content a sum of decomposing pagan beliefs and myths that contributed mythical features closely related to the Celtic world. Ever on the lookout for magical beliefs that could serve its needs, the Church tried to divert the suggestive powers contained in pagan myths. It founded a cult to Mary on a site haunted by fairies. The pilgrimage to Notre-Dame-d'Abodance, near Evian, thus places under the authority of the Virgin the ancient powers of Dame Habonde, as we can see through the works of medieval authors, and transferred the powers of the fairy to the Virgin Mary." (*Christianity: The Origins of a Pagan Religion* by Philippe Walter, p.54)

The Cult of the Virgin is by far the most popular and powerful of all the features of both Medieval and modern Catholicism, and constitutes a magical rite par none when examined in light of the use of the rosary as a means of getting assistance from invisible powers in daily affairs. The entire Roman Catholic method of assigning sainthood and the assistance that can be requested and expected from them, constitutes in itself a virtual Christian pantheon. Medals, scapula, relics and blessed objects were the mainstay of Roman Catholic lay Christianity until the middle of the Twentieth Century, and still exhibit a powerful influence in non-European countries where Catholicism dominates, where, in fact, they are de facto magical devices regardless of what church doctrine says on the matter.

This is an important point, for as we shall see, magic, particularly the kind of operative magic discussed in this book, requires and imparts a change in our thinking, in how we experience and understand the workings of the world around us. Dr. Lisiewski calls this 'the Medieval brain change' wherein our perceptions are elevated and heightened to a new level, and the world around us become inhabited with a host of creatures denied, ignored, or rationalized away by the modern world. To become effective at medieval magic, we need to realign our thinking process to that of the Middle Ages, and the more we perform magic, and in particular if we are successful at it, the more our perceptions begin to structure themselves along that period.

Unfortunately for many modern magicians this brain change also requires dealing with the darkest aspect of the Late Medieval psyche, that of the extreme intolerance of the Roman Catholic Church and its persecution of all that was considered heresy through the *Holy Office of the Inquisition*. The Inquisition was officially formed in 1239 and tasked with defending the church from enemies seen and unseen, corporeal as well as spiritual. While the range and authority of the Holy Office varied across time and place, its influence was profound enough to cause deep fear in everyone from royalty to peasant. Among the first victims of the Inquisition was the Italian magician and astrologer Cecco d'Ascoll, who was burned at the stake in 1327 as a heretic. Nearly 500 years later, Count Alessandro Cagliostro, founder of Egyptian Freemasonry, is often referred to as the last prisoner of the Inquisition to die in the Papal fortress of Saint Leo in 1795.

The Renaissance would witness the extremes of religious persecution and a profound flowering of spiritual thought, philosophy, and practice whose impact is felt to this day. The Hermetic Revival would dominate the intellectual scene for centuries and in itself would give birth to the very thing that would strike the death knell for magical philosophies—the Scientific Revolution.

The Modern Period

In *The Golden Thread: The Ageless Wisdom of the Western Mystery Traditions,* Joscelyn Godwin writes:

> "There is an old tradition that at some time during the seventeenth century, the original Brothers of the Rosy Cross left Europe and went to India, to live a more tranquil life there. I take this as a symbolic statement, meaning that the renovation of the whole world heralded in the Rosicrucian manifestos had failed, and that Western civilization was henceforth abandoned to its own devices. The mention of India, however, is curious. Who at that time would have thought of that land as a suitable home for wise men? During the following century, while the Indian subcontinent was being colonized, it pass in the Western imagination for a pit of ignorance and superstition, of untouchables, holy cows, and wife burning. Yet, ironically enough, the next appearance of a spiritual mission to Europe (and, by then, also to America) came precisely from there." (p.133)

By the middle of the Nineteenth Century intellectual elites in Europe were beginning to react to the Industrial Revolution and its impact on traditional, rural, family-based lifestyles. While much of this was an over idealization of a 'simpler age' by people who were themselves removed from the toils of labor either in the countryside or the burgeoning factory sweetshop complexes that became the mainstay of urban employment for nearly a century. This movement would take many forms, but the one which concerns us the most is known as the Occult Revival, which would start in France, and soon spread to Great Britain, Germany, Austria-Hungary, and even the United States and Russia.

In addition, there was the perceived assault upon Western and Christian values, by the first wave of Oriental sages, yogis, Mahatmas and their various legates to arrive in Europe and America. To this end, the European Occult Revival must be understood as very much being a reaction to what was seen as a decline in society, a decline marked by a growing alienation from nature, growing atheistic philosophies and political movements of which Marxism and Communism would be the foremost enemies of tradition, and of course, an assault on society as a whole and its institutions.

The earliest and clearly most influential of the occult writers of this period was Alphonse Louis Constant, better know by his pen name, Eliphas Levi. The son of a French shoemaker, Levi entered the seminary but left before ordination. He entered into socialist politics of the day and penned a work outlining his theory of Christian socialism entitled, *The Bible of Liberty*. Given the climate of the day, Levi eventually served time in prison under charges of instigating insurrection, wherein he encountered the writings of Emmanuel Swedenborg. This would eventually lead him to study the great Renaissance occultists, and Arthur Schopenhauer whose influential thesis of the importance of the will can be found throughout Levi's writings and those of later occultists.

As Levi states in his work, *Transcendental Magic*, "The Great Work is, before all things, the creation of man by himself. That is to say, the full and entire conquest of his faculties and his future; it is especially the perfect emancipation of his will assuring…full power over the Universal Magical Agent. This Agent, disguised by the ancient philosophers under the name of the First Matter, determines the form of modifiable substances and we can really arrive by means of it at metallic transmutation, and the Universal Medicine."

Or as stated by the Egyptian masters, "I became the creator of what came into being. I came into being in the forms of *khepera* coming into being in primeval times… I became the creator of what came into being, that is to say, I produced myself from primeval matter which I made."

Herein is the total summation of the core philosophy that would drive Western magical traditions for the next century and a half. The mainstay of which would be the British magical order known as the Hermetic Order of the Golden Dawn, and from France, the Martinist Order. While radically different in several respects, both movements drew upon the writings of Levi, were deeply influences by the operative magical writings of the Renaissance and Medieval periods that used qabala and astrology as their base, and saw the need for a European-based system of initiation in response to those coming from India. The main difference would be that while not hostile to Christianity, the Golden Dawn was and still is primarily a revival of Egyptian and pagan ideas around a kabbalistic core and a Rosicrucian mythos at its center. Martinism and its various appended bodies and degrees is a statedly Christian order, albeit a mystical one and deemed heretical by the Roman Catholic Church, deeply entrenched in Gnostic tendencies and ideals. What unified them to some lesser degree also, was a quasi Masonic influence, in that among both groups, Freemasons played a major role in shaping the rituals, teachings, and initiations that were undertaken. This structure would in turn be both a blessing and a curse to the Western magical traditions as the original orders would break down and various quarrels and battles for authority and control over who would be the leader of the would be Illuminati.

The Twentieth Century: Age of Aquarius or the End of Tradition?

While the various magical and occult orders of the late Nineteenth to early Twentieth Century provided a detailed body of teachings, practices, and structure of study, they also provided insight into some of the most troubling aspects of human nature. While many see the collapse of these orders as not only inevitable, but also essential for the widespread dissemination of the teachings they provided, the all to human failure of their leaders to act like truly enlightened beings rather than children on a school yard is frustrating to many. This has caused many to question the validity of magic as a means to anything other than insanity and ruin. While in part this is true, it is also simply a sign of the age in which we live. While some see the explosion and flowering of occult philosophies that has taken place over the last century in general, and since the late-1960s in particular, others view it a sign of a degenerate society. Traditionally one learned magic or any occult practice from someone who knew it and practiced it. A lineage or line of teacher-student relationships was developed. To some degree, checks and controls were in place. Even if one had access to the popular books of magic of the 15th or 16th Centuries, they were, as has been pointed out, only outlines of operations. An entire body of cultural knowledge and assumptions was built into them—knowledge and assumptions that have been lost.

While the modern era through first the publishing industry and now the internet has provided the would be magician with more information than he or she could possibly use in a dozen lifetimes, the problems of walking the magical path alone should not be understated.

Francis Israel Regardie, the close friend and personal teacher of Dr. Lisiewski, former secretary to Aleister Crowley, and the man single-handedly responsible for the greatest dissemination of magical knowledge in the Twentieth Century through his published works, warned about the psychological issues that can arise when undertaking magical work. While he saw them as a natural reaction to the newfound energies that magic awakens, it must be stressed that the psychological stresses created by working within the Golden Dawn system are small in comparison to those brought forth by working Old System Magic—the magic of the grimoires. While Regardie advocates psychotherapy as being undertaken concordant with magical operations, Dr. Lisiewski follows the traditional path of advocating the development of a strong prayer life—as we shall see. Both may be right, for as it is written in *The Arbatel, Concerning the Magic of the Ancients*, regarding the preparations required for learning magic states it this way,

> "The SECOND requirement, is that a person should descend into himself, to carefully examine what parts are mortal and…immortal… THIRDLY, in contemplating his immortal soul [consciousness], learn to worship, love and fear [respect] the eternal God… Contemplation of his mortality should lead him to do what he knows will please God, and benefit his neighbor… The SEVENTH requirement for the aspiring magus is the highest degree of justice, namely, he should support nothing which is wicked, unfair, or unjust, **or even entertain such thoughts** [italics added], and thus he will be divinely protected from all evil." (*Arbatel: Concerning the Magic of the Ancients*, Newly translated, edited and annotated by Joseph H. Peterson. Ibis Press, Lake Worth, Florida. 2009. p.80–81)

Here again we can read the words of the *Arbatel*,

> "To your neighbor you owe human kindness, so that those who take refuge in you will be persuaded to honor the Son [individualized power of God]: This is the law and prophets… Truly you

must help your neighbor with the Gifts of God, whether they are spiritual or material goods." (p.25–27)

Let us hold these words to our hearts as we proceed along the pathway of magic, so that we end up find the glorious light we seek, rather than the words of Regardie,

"I sometimes wish in moments of reverie, that Crowley, the O.T.O., Waite and the Golden Dawn would all gently blow away in a cloud and disappear and never be heard from again." (*The Golden Dawn Scrapbook,* by R.A. Gilbert, p.196)

What is a Grimoire?

The word *grimoire* is taken from Medieval French meaning "grammar", or in more modern terms, a sort of handbook, or notebook. The "grammars of magic" are by far among the most important, lasting, and influential books from the medieval period. The purpose of these writings is simple—to summon spirits to do one's bidding. Of this, almost all of the grimoires deal with demonic or *goetic* magic. The word goetia is derived from ancient Greek, and eventually came to meaning a necromancer who called back spirits from the dead, and later simply a magician how could perform a variety of magical acts. Unlike in modern magical operations, the summoning of spirits, be they human or non-human, angelic or demonic, was a key part of classical magic, and that of the Graeco-Egyptian, or early Hermetic systems, as well.

In Medieval Europe goetic magic appears to have been in existence as early as the Eleventh Century, and was composed extensively of monks, priests, and minor clerics who possessed the necessary knowledge of church ritual and Latin to read the texts and perform the rituals. This underground stream of magic within the Roman Catholic Church, as we have shown, would contribute considerably to Hermetic revival of the Renaissance, as well as indirectly to the ritual magic of the Hermetic Order of the Golden Dawn and others. Unlike mystical practices, devotional prayers, or angelic invocations, goetic operations were extremely practical in nature. In addition to obtaining information of all sorts—scientific, prophetic, military, alchemical, or the innumerable secrets of nature—they could also be directed to heal, kill, bring love or discord, wealth or poverty, and anything else that could be imagined. While the "art of summoning spirits" fell into disuse as interest in magic waned from the late Seventeenth Century onward, the art managed to survive in part in folk traditions, most importantly that of German folk magic or *pow-wow*. *The Sixth and Seventh Books of Moses* constitutes one of the most widely and continually used books of magic in existence, and is the heart of German folk traditions. For more information see: *The Sixth and Seventh Books of Moses*, edited by J. Peterson, and *The Red Church* by C. Bilardi.

It is however to Aleister Crowley that most modern magicians look when seeking inspiration in the art of goetia. It also to Crowley that we see the first open statement that the demons of the goetia are not, or at least may not be, independent beings, but instead aspects of the magician's own mind brought forth into operation.

> "...all sense-impressions are dependent on changes in the brain, we must include illusion, which are after all sense-impressions as much as 'realities' are, in the class of 'phenomena dependent on brain-changes.'" Magical phenomena, however, come under a special sub-class, since they are willed, and their cause is the series of 'real' phenomena called the operations of ceremonial magic... These unusual impressions [the tools of the operations of magic] produce unusual brain-changes; hence their summary is of unusual kind. Its projection back into the apparently phenomenal world is therefore unusual. Herein then consists of the reality of the operations and effects of ceremonial magic, and I conceive that...the effects refer only to those phenomena which appear to the magician himself... The spirits of the Goetia are portions of the human brain. Their seals therefore represent methods of stimulating or regulating those particular spots... The names of God are vibrations calculated to establish:...general control of the brain...control over the brain in detail...control of one special portion [of the brain]." (*The Greater Key of Solomon*, translated by S.L. MacGregor Mathers, Samuel Weiser, Inc., York Beach, ME. p.16–17)

With this statement, Crowley set in motion a theory that would begin to dominate the magical community of the Twentieth Century—that demons are simply projections of one's own mind, and with that, see changes in the way goetic magic was performed. Magical circles made of chalk and paint would be replaced with one's visualized by the magician. Divine Names set down for centuries would be replaced by one's of the magician's own choosing. Traditional implements mentioned in the grimoires, and whose detailed directions for construction were considered imperative for success, would be replaced with those of the Golden Dawn or done away with altogether. For if demons were simply in one's own mind, then they could be addressed within the confines of one's own mind, and rituals modified as needed, or done away with entirely. While this makes perfect sense, it also seems that along with making goetic magic more accessible to a wider range of potential users, it also made it less reliable and unstable at best. The notorious "Sling-Shot Effect" appears to be in many ways partially a result of ignoring the directions given and choosing to attempt to perform goetic magic as almost a free form of self-expression rather than a specific ritual with a purpose. While there are many magicians who claim success in this mode of working, there are also many who claim or remain silent regarding their failures. To find the reason for this, we need look no further than to the French mage, Eliphas Levi:

> "...human will when without works is dead, or at any rate is only a vague desire... An imagination is not a realized thing, it is only a promised something, while an act is a reality... All ceremonies, consecrations, ablutions, and sacrifices are prayers in action, and are symbolic formulas; and they are the most potent prayers because they are translations of words into action...they constitute real work, and such work demands a man's whole energy." (*The Magical Ritual of the Sanctum Regnum* by Eliphas Levi, Introduction by R.A. Gilbert. Ibis Press, Berwick, ME. 2004, p.2–3)

And again:

> "Magical ceremonies may be regarded as a sort of gymnastic exercise of the will power, and for this reason all the great teachers of the world have recommended them as proper and efficacious... The more one does, the more one can do in the future... Those who watch, those who fast, those who pray, those who refrain

from pleasure, those who place body at the command of mind, can bring all the powers of nature into subjection to their purposes." (p.43–44)

For this reason, we remind the reader of the famous quote from Dante's *Inferno*, above the gateway to hell which read, "Abandon Hope All Ye Who Enter Here", for in Old System Magic the Devil certainly is in the details.

Chapter Two

Preparations for Old System Magic
Part I

This material has been written for not just 'any' reader, as were the *Author's Response to Readers' Questions* and *The Magical Thought for the Week* columns that appeared on my website for one year and two weeks. The questions answered in the Q&A column, and the issues discussed in the magical thought column, were directed at a broad-spectrum audience. Generally speaking, the readers of those columns showed themselves to belong to one or more of the following groups:

1. Those who were completely disgusted with the New Age and its lack of results.

2. Those interested in Old System Magic but who did not know where to turn.
3. Those who were trying to decide if the ways of the Fathers of the Grimoires were for them.
4. Young people who were/are trying to find or establish a sound, lasting philosophical or spiritual basis for their lives, after having realized the lies and double standards of dialectical materialism in general, and of the 'American Dream' in particular.

Owing to this diverse audience, the answers given were either brief or very simple, while the rituals and magical practices discussed were presented only in a very general template-form manner. Not any more. For the overwhelming number of you who have taken up the practice of Old System Magic have distinguished yourselves as being separate, progressive individuals who have turned their backs on the absurdities of the New Age, and don't care what those "Masters" and magical order "Officers" think. You have seen enough of their personal failures and have grown tired of their lame excuses as to why their 'magic' failed, and why they still remain in squalor and poverty while "...living lives of quiet desperation..." You are reading this now because you have had enough and want—demand—'something' which works. That is, teachings that will give you what you desire most of all: control over your own personal lives, and success in your daily, worldly endeavors. Period. No lies, no explanations, and most of all, no 'reasons' (veiled excuses) as to why you can't work at a Magic that produces *results*.[1]

---

[1] Eliphas Levi wrote in *The History of Magic*: "Magic, therefore, combines in a single science that which is most certain in philosophy which is eternal and infallible in religion. It reconciles perfectly and incontestably those two terms so opposed on the first view—faith and reason, science and belief, authority and liberty. **It furnishes the human mind with an instrument of philosophical and religious certainty as exact as mathematics, and even accounting for the infallibility of mathematics themselves** [emphasis added]... There is an incontestable truth; there is an infallible method of knowing truth; while those who attain this knowledge and adopt it as a rule of life, can endow their life with a sovereign power

For as much as I can convey to you through the written word, I will. I will give you all that I can through the use of this rather limited medium of expression. In short, I will do my best to enable you to fulfill those two desires I spoke of above. But *you* will have to work. No 'talk,' no speculation, no comparison of this ritual or that rite to the empty 'wonders' and theory of the Golden Dawn, the Argentum Astrum, or any of the myriad number of Orders, Temples, groups, or organizations.[1] You are here to *work*. To carry out to the best of your ability what I teach herein. And if you do; if you dedicate yourself to the Magic of the Old System. We demand one and only one thing from ourselves in this pursuit of Magic: work. And that work produces results. It can be no other way. For in Old System Magic, we summon up, call down, or otherwise employ secret, occult forces that are governed by Law; as perfect and exact as are the Laws of the physical universe in which we live and move daily. And that is what you will get: results if you work.

I also ask that you understand something that is of critical importance to your personal growth and worldly success: I will write here as I speak to my private students in the Oral Tradition. You know how pointed I am: directness in life is always best, and always will be. Hence my liberal use of it. Conversely, if there is something you do not understand in these writings, research the subject for yourself. *Seek to know and understand that which is*

---

which can make them masters of all inferior things, all wondering spirits, or, in other words, the arbiters and kings of the world."

[1] In addition to being a personal student of Dr. Israel Regardie, Dr. Lisiewski was, like many students of the esotericism, also a member of the Argentum Astrum, an order devoted exclusively to magical training, an initiate of the Golden Dawn, a member of the Rosicrucian Order (AMORC), and several other organizations. What became apparent, even as it was clearly visible during the earliest days of the Hermetic Order of the Golden Dawn and Israel Regardie's rational for publishing the Golden Dawn manuscripts in his possession, was that many of the leaders of occult and mystical organizations are, in fact, esoteric theorists and not practitioners. For additional information see: *The Golden Dawn Scrapbook: The Rise and Fall of a Magical Order* by R.A. Gilbert, Samuel Weiser, Inc., York Beach, ME. 1997; and "An Interview with Jean Dubuis" by Mark Stavish, M.A., originally published in *The Stone: The Journal of the Philosophers of Nature*, available at www.hermeticinstitute.org.

unclear to you through your own physical and mental efforts first! Go to libraries if you must to avail yourself of the needed grimoires and support material. Do your best to make clear that which, for you, is unclear at any given moment.

It is intended to sharpen your mind and refine your questions, so your queries will be pregnant with content thereby providing you with the means of realizing the answer you seek. Clear questions create space for clear answers.

Preparations for Old System Magic
Introductory—and Necessary—Remarks

"Preparations for Old System Magic? Me? I already prepared myself with umpteen years of Golden Dawn practice, or Yoga practice, or Wicca rites, not to mention this study and that discipline. Now there's more? Is he kidding?"

Nothing, and I mean nothing of what you have done in the past—ritually speaking—will be of any use to you here. Not in this Work. Not in Old System Magic. And if you think that all of that "visualization" and "astral projection" you engaged in; all of those Tarot spreads you cast and sets of cards you personally fashioned for yourself; all of that "scrying in Spirit Vision" and psychometry work you did; all of that crystal gazing and 'pendulum' swinging you busied yourself with throughout the years; all of those Lesser Banishing Rituals of the Pentagram and Banishing Rituals of the Hexagram you performed so religiously two or three times a day for months or years; all of those Middle Pillar Rituals you performed throughout the past ten years, and all of those paper 'talismans' you made and 'charged' by this New Age technique or that New Age expediency; all of those 'Evocations' you did in your miniature circle taped off with masking tape on the floor of your apartment or basement, and all of that gift shop Indian-compounded incense you burned for a spirit you never saw and the results you never got: if you think any or all of that has prepared you for this ancient Art and Science, guess again. Because if they prepared you in any way for your entrance and Work in Old System Magic, you would not be sitting where you are now reading this which should be making no small number of you angry enough to spit bullets, and irritating the hell out of an equal number, if not more, of you. But before you go off into some self-justifying, self-aggrandizing episode in an attempt to make yourself feel all those years of struggle and practice were worth at least 'something,' ask yourself: "WHERE ARE THE RESULTS?" Ask honestly, "Did I get—even ONCE—all or everything I wanted? And if I did (or didn't), what price from the Slingshot Effect did I receive from those actions as well?" Ask yourself also, "Besides feeling warm and cozy inside from all my reading and practicing, what do I have to show for it? I mean really? If not in those material objects I desired, then what do I have to show for all that work in terms of my at least being a better, more spiritual human being as a result of them?"[1]

You and I both know the answers to these so very uncomfortable questions: all of those practices have brought you nothing. That is, nothing of any consequence upon which you can hang your hat. If you did get this or that every so often, you can't be sure it was the Effect that followed from your magical Cause: not unless it manifested so clearly, completely, and quickly after the rite. And you know it didn't. For if those activities did work and were repeatable, then surely, you would be happy, content, have what you desire, and be so well-balanced in so many ways, that people would seek you out simply to bask in the glow of your personality—and I'm not being facetious here. But they don't, do they? So it's time to enter a deep period of Self-Analysis, and by this I mean a period of deep self-scrutinization; a period of examination that follows directly upon a period of ruthless self-honesty such as you (may) have never known before. It's time to till the soil. Time to turn over the psychological dirt covering the

---

[1] As stated earlier, traditionally, magic is about making change in the material world, spiritual unfoldment however was the domain of religion and mystical pursuits, be they orthodox and sanctioned by the church, or heterodoxical and personal. For an explanation and listing of the difference between Objective and Subjective phenomena and aspects of magic see: *Between the Gates: Lucid Dreaming, Astral Projection, and the Body of Light in Western Esotericism* by Mark Stavish. Weiser Books, Newburyport, M.A., 2008.

gold beneath, and start removing and doing what you must if you are to have the life you desire. It's as simple as that.[1]

Oh, and before I forget any of you "Theoretical Magicians" who have read, and read, and re-read 'all the great books of Magic of the twentieth century'; all of the great writings of William Butler to Franz Bardon and Aleister Crowley to John Dee; all who have discussed these matters with your fellow magicians, and Order Heads and other occult leaders, I have a surprise for you: you're in the same boat as your hardworking, practicing colleagues. Forget all of those books and their dialogues, for you have not translated them into practice: that special action which brings about Experiential Knowledge, and which leads to a state of Apprehension whereby that knowledge is made a part of your living being, and upon which you draw—through your Subjective Synthesis[2]—to produce—through the Magic—the ends you want.[3]

The Steps of Preparation Proper

What follows below are those highly recommended steps I suggest the sincere aspirant take to prepare him or herself for

---

[1] Dr. Lisiewski suggests *Psychosynthesis* and *Act of Will* by Roberto Assangioli as an effective method of self-analysis that works well with the magical paradigm. *What We May Be* by Piero Ferrucci, a student of Assangioli, is a highly readable presentation of the principals and practices of Psychosynthesis. To this end, it would not be imprudent to mention that the masters of traditions spanning East and West have advocated the process of self-reflection as the key to self-mastery. As it is written above the portal of the Temple to Apollo at Delphi in ancient Greece, "Gnothi Seton" (Know Thyself!)

[2] Subjective Synthesis is the term used by Dr. Lisiewski to designate the subconscious and personal understanding a magician has of the material they are working with so that they are fluent in its use. All successes, failures, and partial successes are a result of our Subjective Synthesis. For more information see: *Ceremonial Magic and the Power of Evocation* by Dr. Joseph Lisiewski, and the section on "Subconscious Synthesis" in *Kabbalah for Health and Wellness* by Mark Stavish.

[3] The assumption here is that if you had gotten the results you had wanted from earlier magical practices you would not be reading this book as you would not be in need of the information it contains.

entrance into Old System Magic. That is, before even thinking about beginning any basic ritual work, you should follow through with what is given here. Some of it is physical, most mental. All has a powerful effect on your newly-forming (or reforming) Subjective Synthesis. And since Magic works from the inside out and not the outside in, you will find your efforts here will start you moving forward in discovering—and becoming—who you already are. What to do then, to implement these suggestions?

Set yourself to a six month schedule of the following (while many of these steps seem easy, you will find they are not. It will take you at least six months to complete all of them, while continuing others for the remainder of your life):

1. Discard—literally get rid of—all those New Age books, and break completely with all of those 'magical' associations and memberships that have availed you nothing, but which have consumed your life and time. You do not need to 'hope' and 'yearn' for anything. You are preparing for RESULTS. It's time to grow up magically. As you will find, your Subjective Synthesis does not work by dividing itself. "A house divided amongst itself cannot stand." You cannot serve two masters: the New Age and the Old System. "Choose ye this day, which master ye shall serve." Sell your books to your contemporaries who are still trapped in that current miasma you'll make a veritable fortune which you can use to purchase the books you need, which in turn will help finance the materials of Art that will be required. None of it is cheap. So best 'off with the old and on with the new.'[1]

---

[1] This point cannot be stressed enough. One of the main selling points used by esoteric orders today is their collective psychic strength or *egregore* as it is often called. While beneficial to students in the beginning, it can become parasitic at some point, thereby taking more than it gives. Jean Dubuis spoke often about this problem in modern orders and strongly encouraged that individuals free themselves from these kinds of psychic influences. One of the few ways to guarantee one's break with an egregore is to burn all of one's membership credentials, lessons, paraphernalia, and tools. Even those who kept some of their old items, but who ritually destroyed and discarded their magical tools have attested to the tremendous amount of energy that is immediately released from them.

Know that this more than symbolic break with your past failures and the nonsensical diatribe that brought them about will cause repercussions in your life. When my personal students in the oral tradition carried out this absolutely necessary exercise, they endured much. One spent two weeks in a hospital (nothing physically was found to be wrong with him); another went to the very brink of divorce (all matters ended on a happy note when the crisis of this action passed); another had ecstatic visions combined with terrifying apparitions during the most basic of magical routines that I set him to (all balanced out beautifully for him); while yet another underwent such psychic stimulation that his cognitive faculties increased to the point where he could not handle the energy input he received (this was brought under control quite easily). There are many other such examples. The bottom line however is all that is important: after passing through the psychological shock created by breaking with that which was false, each one's magical growth and Spiritual Unfoldment skyrocketed so safely and sanely, that they are light years ahead of others who posture themselves as 'masters' of this or that. As I have said so many times: something for nothing does not exist in this universe. And this condition has special applicability when it comes to Magic.

2. Begin to acquire those books I recommended in my books, *Ceremonial Magic and the Power of Evocation*; *Kabbalistic Cycles and the Mastery of Life*; and *Kabbalistic Handbook for the Practicing Magician*.

3. Discard all of the confusing (and even contradictory) Qabalah you learned from your various books. You can study *The Mystical Qabalah* by Dion Fortune all you want, and pour through *The Ladder of Lights* till your eyes turn blood red, and you will receive nothing more than a fragmented, hodge-podge of ideas and correspondences that are usable as references at best; much as is also the case for Regardie's classic, *A Garden of Pomegranates*. You and I both know this to be true. People praise these books from the roof tops, and 'name drop' them to their 'fellow magicians.' Yet I am still waiting to meet anyone who can honestly espouse the themes and theories in any cogent manner that these books profess to give. They are, in fact, eclectically

unbalanced presentations mixed with so much extrapolated New Age conjecture—itself based on the ramblings of Mathers and his crowd—as to be unbelievable. It was not you who could not make anything out of them: it was the material itself and its lack of intelligible presentation that is at fault.[1]

Instead, I recommend you begin to really learn Kabbala; but only the essentials that will produce two conditions within you: first, this new learning will give you one aspect (only) of a firm philosophical-theological basis from which to operate in daily life, and second, it will provide you with only those elements of Kabbalistic thought that are *absolute necessities* when working in Old System Magic. And believe it or not, those necessities are very few and far in between. For the grimoires do not—and I repeat do not—operate on the "Qabalah" as preached by the New Age. Instead, the grimoires operate on a Subjective Synthesis that is capable of channeling the forces being conjured, and directing them through your being and body into the world of form. In this way, you will truly begin to use the processes of:

Studying—>Learning—>Understanding—>Comprehending—> Practicing (experiential knowledge)—>Apprehending

that you must, so your Subjective Synthesis can be properly built and polished. Then—and *only then*—will your magic, Old System Magic, work for you.

To accomplish this, you need only the Kabbalah as I have given in *Kabbalistic Cycles and the Mastery of Life*, or as presented in *Kabbalistic Handbook for the Practicing Magician*. While the presentations in both books are very similar, the latter book is to be preferred for obtaining a more rounded view of the Kabbalistic knowledge you need—and that, for a long, long time. Later, those of you who wish to explore the Kabbalah further and for your own private reasons, would do well indeed to extend your stud-

---

[1] I have often been asked by people working both traditional and modern variants of the Golden Dawn system how it is that Hebrew God Names could call up Egyptian or Nordic deities, given the historical animosity between their cultures. If one believes in the power of egregores as living things, than Egyptian and Hebrew are clearly like adding oil, or maybe even fire, to water.

ies to the writings of Waite, Levi, and Reuchlin, particularly Reuchlin's, *De Arte Cabalistica* ("On the Art of the Kabbalah").

There is something else. There is one and only one current book on Kabbalah that I also recommend most heartily. Its author, Mark Stavish, is almost as 'Old System Magic" as I am. He has written a book, *Kabbalah for Health and Wellness*, that will afford those of you seeking to apply the Kabbalah in a more immediate, practical way to fulfill that desire. Between my hard-core approach and Mark's more temperate approach, I think you will benefit handsomely if you buy his book and use it as you feel you should.

4. Prepare or acquire your Magical Chamber.[1] Instructions for its proper construction can be found later in this book. This is the repository of your Spirit. And as such, it must be a fitting exterior-world receptacle for that which is utterly Divine and Holy within you.

5. Set aside two, 30-minute periods of prayer a day. Conduct these periods in your Magical Chamber if at all possible. Get down on your knees—you are approaching the Lord of Creation Who is also within you, and show—not preach—your respect for that Divinity which is… "nearer than your hand and closer than your breath…" The Psalms lend themselves to such a purpose particularly well. Or if you choose, use prayers from the grimoires; anything which elicits a deep and profound sense of devotion from you. For through the prayers contained in these grammars, you will come to feel those aspects of God that flow through the grimoiric system of knowledge and practice. This will, of course, only purify, sanctify, and strengthen your magical work all the more. As an example, the prayers given below may be found helpful. I have used them for decades; and always, the proper emotional and spiritual responses were immediately perceived within my Interior Realm, and the ends I sought were manifested in my Exterior World (these prayers are to be an ongoing part of your *daily* regimen and continue for the rest of your life. You *do not* do Banishing Pentagrams and Banishing

---

[1] See "The Magical Chamber" in the "Practice of Magic" section of this book.

Hexagrams, instead you pray daily, and come to touch the Face of God within you.

Prayers Attributed to Dr. John Dee

John Dee's Daily Oration for Wisdom from The First Book of the Mysteries

Before my other extemporaneous prayers and more ardent ejaculations to God: This one was the most usual.

My Morning and Evening Oration: for Wisdom.

In the Name of God the Father, of God the Son, and of God the Holy Spirit. Amen.
Almighty, Everlasting, True and Living God stretch forth, now, to my help:
Lord of Lords, King of Kings, Jehovah Lord of Hosts, hasten to my assistance.
Glory to God, Father, Son, and Holy Spirit: As it was in the beginning, and is now, and will be always, even unto the Age of Ages: Amen.
Teach me to properly sense, and to rightly discern, (O Father of all things,) For I desire your Wisdom, because it is all that is: Give your word to my established practice,(O Father of all things,) and fix your wisdom in my heart.

O Lord Jesus Christ (who art the true wisdom, of your eternal, and Omnipotent Father) Most humbly I entreat your Divine Majesty, that you might think myself worthy, in respect of my general piety, to promptly send forth your Wise and tested Philosophical assistance, to that fulfillment of understanding and perfection, that will be of the greatest value towards the enlarging of my praising and glorification to you. And when no one is subject to Death, and at last there is Life in the Earth, to which office is it that I will have been fitted: In particular to whom, according to your eternal foresight, will your beneficent eminence have assigned me: Moreover, truly and most humbly it is my most burning and most steadfast quest to your Divine Majesty, that you would think worthy to send forth from heaven to me, your good Spiritual Ministers and Angels, Namely Michael, Gabriel, Raphael, and even Uriel: and (in accordance with your Heavenly favor) as often so ever as any other of your true and faithful Angels, who might completely and perfectly inform and furnish me, in the true and accurate, knowledge and understanding of your Secret Mysteries and Mighty Works (Concerning the properties of all of your Creatures and the best use of those natures) and of the unavoidable necessity for the Decree of our Deaths; to the praising, honoring, and glorification of your name; and to confirm to me, and of others (through me) of your many faithful encouragements: and to the disorder and ruin of your enemies. Amen.

Let the Will of Jehovah Zebaoth be done: Let the Will of Adonai be done, let the will of Elohim be done, O Blessed and Most Beneficent Almighty Trinity, yield to me (John Dee) this request, for such a method, whereby to most appease you. Amen.

Since the year 1579 in general by this mode;

It has been most pleasing to me to pour forth prayers to God; Either in the Latin language or in the English (moreover since around the year 1579 by a particularly strange and different method: sometimes for Raphael; occasionally for Michael) Let God, his own mercy, be glorious in me. Amen.

Prayer of John Dee

O Almighty, Eternal, the True and Living God: O King of Glory: O Lord of Hosts: O thou, the Creator of Heaven, and Earth, and of all things visible and invisible: Now, (even now, at length,) Among others thy manifold mercies used, toward me, thy simple servant John Dee, I most humbly beseech thee, in this my present petition to have mercy upon me, to have pity upon me, to have Compassion upon me: Who, faithfully and sincerely, of long time, have sought among men, in Earth: And also by prayer, (full often and pitifully,) have made suit unto thy Divine Majesty for the obtaining of some convenient portion of True Knowledge and understanding of thy laws and Ordinances, established in the Natures and properties of thy Creatures: by which Knowledge,

Thy Divine Wisdom, Power and Goodness, (on thy Creatures bestowed, and to them imparted.) being to me made manifest, might abundantly instruct, furnish, and allure me, (for the same,) incessantly to pronounce thy praises, to rend unto thee, most hearty thanks, to advance thy true honor, and to Win unto thy Name, some of thy due Majestical Glory, among all people, and forever.

(Of course, where Dee's name appears in the above prayers, insert your own and mean what you are saying during the recitations. *Do not miss these periods of prayer under any circumstance!* Use no candles, incense, etc. The Magical Chamber or room must be bare and hollow. It must contain only you, a chair (if necessary) and a small table.[1])

Some Words of Caution and Encouragement

For those of you who insist that they have severed themselves from the religion of their birth and cannot enter into communion with the Christ within them in any way, so be it. But I remind you: before you were able to reason; before you could accept or reject at the level of your current consciousness any concepts and ideas whatsoever, a constellation of such were placed into your unconscious mind.[2] They reside there still, regardless of how much you fume and fuss. That is why I recommend you to "…light a small candle to the God of your youth at least once a year…" By appeasing that area of the unconscious, you will be able to work freely and effectively. Otherwise, you will receive more interference than you may be able to handle. The choice is yours. I know of what I speak, for I was one such as you long ago and that for decades—until I learned. Be guided accordingly.

---

[1] For a mystical interpretation of the Magical Chamber, see my comments on "The Chamber of Reflection" used in Freemasonry, in *Freemasonry: The History, Rituals and Symbols of the Secret Society* (Llewellyn).

[2] We might rephrase this to be not an unconscious mind, but rather, aspects of the mind that operate below the threshold of immediate consciousness until they are brought forth through memory, creative action, spontaneous realization, or associative stimulation.

For those whose Catholic or Protestant background is not an issue, availing yourself of the prayers given above will be found to be an enormous asset as you travel your personal Path in Old System Magic.

6. In addition to the above, set aside one, 30-minute period every other day for introspection. That is, establish a session of self-analysis which is marked by a ruthless self-honesty. Consider carefully all of the work you have done in Magic thus far using those New Age (or other current, contemporary approaches such as Santeria, etc.) 'techniques,' and ask yourself: "What have they gotten me? I mean, really, how better off am I now for having spent all those months (or years) doing this ritual or that rite; this ceremony or that astral projection? What have I to show for it? Am I better off materially? Socially? Personally? And most important, Spiritually? And if so, then how? And how can I measure this supposed 'spiritual development?' Do I still fly off the handle at things that bothered me before I 'developed' spiritually? And if I do, then where is the 'development?'

Don't rationalize with yourself: therein lies great danger. With sufficient mental effort and honesty, you can either directly trace a given *effect* to a *magical cause*, or you cannot. If you can, fine. If you can't: if there is even a whisper of a doubt as to the connection between a perceived (or imagined) Effect and its attributable Cause, disregard the Effect as having been brought about by your magical work. You will be surprised how this seemingly simple exercise will clear away the self-illusion and self-delusion so many of us have been living with for so long. In (self) honesty will be your strength.

I strongly suggest that those of you who are intent in following the way of Old System Magic take the next six months to follow through with this "Seven-Point Preparatory Protocol for Old System Magic". Do not even think of performing the simple—yet extremely powerful—ritual technique that will be given herein until you have done so. You are not ready for it—period. You must eliminate much from yourself: all of that which has been preventing you from becoming who you already are and the steps necessary to effect this process begin with the following:

7. There is something else. Something so important, that it may be the single-most vital requirement needed for Magic to work properly. And ironically, it can be the hardest discipline for many people to implement. While this admonition has appeared across time in many books and manuscripts, my first introduction to it impressed me so much, that I would like to pass this same admonition on to you. Perhaps by your considering its original phraseology, it will make the very same marked—and necessary—impression upon you that it did upon me, and guide you unerringly in your magical efforts. The following is quoted from Book II, Part I, Cabalistic Magic, Chapter I, of the *Magus: A Complete System of Occult Philosophy*, synthesized by Francis Barrett in 1801, from the *Three Books of Occult Philosophy* and the *Fourth Book of Occult Philosophy* (spelling has been modernized):

> "Therefore, all we solicit is, that those who perceive those secrets should keep them together as secrets, and not expose or babble them to the unworthy; but reveal them only to faithful, discrete, and chosen friends. And we would caution you in this beginning, that every magical experiment flies from the public, seeking to be hid, is strengthened and confirmed by silence, but is destroyed by publication; never does any complete effect follow after; likewise all the virtue of thy works will suffer detriment when poured into weak, prating, and incredulous minds; therefore, if thou would be a magician, and gain fruit from this art, to be secret, and to manifest to none, either thy work, or place, or time, nor thy desire or will, except it be to a master, or partner, or companion, who should likewise be faithful, discrete, silent, and dignified by nature and education; seeing that even the prating of a companion, his unbelief, doubting, questioning, and lastly, unworthiness, hinders and disturbs the effect in every operation."

Clearly, the astute reader will see herein not only the warning I gave in my own book on ceremonial magic regarding the Slingshot Effect and the counsel to work alone, but further on the inadvisability of trusting anyone so ever when it comes to this Work.[1] Companions cannot be trusted—none of them. Over

---

[1] Individual mileage on this may vary. However, the more people involved, the more unconscious forces that must be assimilated into the Operation, thereby providing an opportunity for error or backlash.

thirty–seven years ago I made the error of trusting such a one, only to have him turn on me years later, such that our forty-two year friendship ended, essentially over the very magical matters and experiments in Evocation to Physical Manifestation that he assisted me in carrying out all those years ago. Years later I found out he not only doubted the Operations would succeed, but that he was approaching them as one would an idle curiosity. Such attitudes contributed enormously to the disastrous results (suffered by me, the Operator) of the first Operation, and the near-disastrous results of the second Operation. Add to this his literal "prating"—exactly as Barrett coins—coupled with an overwhelming attitude of self-righteousness and contrived self-importance in 'doing God's work,' and I finally realized that he could not reconcile what he experienced in those experiments in particular (and in Old System Magic in general) with his chosen religious vocational 'calling.' It took me decades to realize that what he knew from his experience in those two Evocations to Physical Manifestation clashed head on with his comfortable ego-driven sense of religiosity, making it absolutely necessary for him to (eventually) end our friendship in order to self-justify his own comfortable, personally convenient, untested religious 'beliefs'—not a set of religious tenets that issued from a faith based upon his own inner religious experience. If he were to read this today I am certain he would disagree violently, and armor himself all the more with his maniacal sense of self-righteousness, religious orthodoxy and dogma in order to 'prove' his 'holy and ecclesiastical position.' No matter. "Not by their words, but by their deeds, shall ye know them." The results speak for themselves, as is always the case.

Let this hard-learned example of mine be a light to you in those dark places of Old System Magic in which you must walk. You will be the better for it, as you will find out for yourself if you heed these words of caution.

Therefore *be warned—trust no one in this Work*! Rely solely upon God and your own Self—otherwise, you truly can, "Abandon all hope, all ye who enter here." That is, put no trust whatsoever into any alliance which presents itself to you in any guise, let alone that which disguises itself as the truest of friendships. The admonition, "**To Know, to Will, to Dare, to Keep Silent**"[1] must be held to if you are to do your Work and not only survive, but grow as well.[2]

8. Beyond the seven points cited above, there are no other preparatory requirements for you to concern yourself with, as my experience has taught me. You do not have to starve yourself, switch to eating brown rice, sit in some excruciating yoga position, dance around naked, shave your head, have your fingers drip with rings and other assorted baubles, wear pentagram necklaces, stare at people with bulging eyes, walk around in black capes while wearing two pounds of pancake makeup on your face, or put earrings through your ears or bones through your nose. All of that is nonsense. Of course, you must obey the strict requirements set down in any of the grimoires you will be working with; but then, that is a future matter and need not concern you now. No, now is the time for you to begin your entrance—or is it, "descent"—into Old System Magic. And of course to do that, all you must do is work.

Ritual Techniques of Old System Magic

The following ritual technique I have termed, *The Daily Aspersion Ritual*. In its brief form, it was dealt with on my website in the column, the *Magical Thought for the Week*. Many of those who read this technique tried it and found it to be extremely effective. In turn, they sensed that there was more to it, wrote to me, and asked me if I could be more specific and give additional detail that would make the rite even more effective in their daily lives.

Now, however, with the skilled, intelligent group I am now addressing, I can spell out in no uncertain terms just how to perfect this ritual. For by doing so, you will find that it not only offers you an ever increasing level of protection from those evils that truly do roam this world, but that in addition, it will attract

---

[1] The qualities of the magus and whose saying is attributed to Zoroaster.
[2] Magical workings involving two or more people require the unusually hard to find state of a high degree of harmony and agreement between the participants. Each will act as a link in a very real magical chain with the chain being only as strong as its weakest link.

increased opportunity of all types to you: material, social, and mental, while balancing your emotional nature in a way you have never experienced previously.

Additionally—and perhaps most importantly of all—it will enable the unfolding of your spiritual nature in a balanced and harmonious manner and to such an extent, that you will truly 'feel' yourself becoming more and more spiritualized for the first time. That is, your unfolding spiritual nature will become a vivifying reality to you.

As you continue these daily aspersions, the concept of "spiritual growth" will be replaced by that of "Spiritual Unfoldment," and you will know just what that means by your realization of it. For it will result in a growth of consciousness that will enable you not only to call down or summon up power, but to direct it safely, effectively, and flawlessly through your newly forming subjective synthesis. It is important that you adopt a highly discriminating and analytical attitude in these matters: an attitude that careful comparison will indeed help to foster within you.

A Simple Magical Aspersion for Protection and the Attraction of Opportunity

If you would believe the current trends of the times, your daily regimen of magical activity would probably begin with the Lesser Banishing Ritual of the Pentagram (LBRP) followed by the Banishing Ritual of the Hexagram (BRH), not to mention all of those 'necessary' signs and gestures that are 'indispensable' in getting you started for the day, or ending your day on a 'proper' magical note. Then too, after years of faithful execution of these required rites, you might be wondering why you are in the same place you were when you began. Or indeed, at a worse place in life than the day you started. All too often, such are the complaints made by those who have accepted the "Magical Currents" of the day. These sincere workers in magic found that these so called "Currents" and rites just do not work. So what to do?

The following is an Old System of Magic derivation and application that is simplicity itself—but one that works very well. It has not only been used by myself successfully throughout the decades, but by my current students in the Oral Tradition as well. Additionally, my friend and colleague in these matters, Mr.

Mark Stavish, has also been recommending it to his own students: and they have been reporting rather interesting and positive results by using it, to say the least. These highly educated, intelligent and hard working people have attested to it as being indispensable in their daily lives. For this simple ritual not only provides a maximum of protection in all daily activities, but attracts to the practitioner no small amount of opportunity—both spiritual and worldly. It does this, because unlike the LBRP and the BRH which—as their own adherents admit—diminishes throughout the day and night, the effects of this ritual act build up and actually intensify over time. Day after day, week after week, month after month, its effects continue to build, bringing more and more of those desirable things in life; while neutralizing or removing those negativities and evils that can beset the magical practitioner.

Throughout the following ritual act, do not concern yourself with any visualizations, gestures, or the like. Instead, *focus on your movements*, i.e., *on the physical actions themselves*, and *recall to mind your purposes*: to invoke protection and to bring forth those opportunities of the Spirit and of the material world which you desire. Nothing more. Simply be conscious—but fully conscious—of your actions and intentions

Magical Rite for Protection and the Attraction of Opportunity

Obtain a new, earthen vessel never used for any other purpose (thus assuring its efficacy).[1] Be sure the vessel is unglazed. It is best to do this on a day and hour ruled by Venus. Likewise during this time, obtain a new container of ordinary table salt, and a new bottle of Extra Virgin Olive Oil.

On a day and hour ruled by Jupiter, obtain a new container of mountain spring drinking water. That is, water that has only been filtered and irradiated by ultraviolet light.

Enter your Magical Chamber, stand at the center of the room, face East, and add some of the water to your earthen vessel. After this, place a small quantity of salt from the container into

---

[1] See that article on Efficacy in the "Theory of Magic" section of this book.

your right hand, and slowly pour the salt into the water. Do not stir the salt/water mixture.

Now, take one step forward with your right foot, and bring your left foot up to meet it at your new position. Place your right hand into the water, withdraw it, and begin sprinkling in the East as you recite the following:

"Thou shalt purge me with hyssop O Lord, and I shall be clean. Thou shalt wash me, and I shall be whiter than snow." (From Psalm 51)

Recite this blessing only *once* as you move from the East, through the South, through the West, the North, and return to the East. That is, you repeat the prayer and the sprinkling slowly, *focusing on the words and your mechanical actions.*

Return to the center of the room, and face East once more. Take a drop of Olive Oil from its container, and place it on the tip of the index finger of your right hand. If you are a Christian or come from this tradition, mark a Cross on your forehead (Up to down, and from right to left) while focusing on your intentions of protection and opportunity. If you are from any other religious tradition, simply touch the Olive Oil to the center of your forehead. This ends the rite.

As you will find, this Old System Magic rite—as with all Old System Magic—is most certainly built upon principles. But it is not my intention to go into them here. Nevertheless, what is given here will be of inestimable value to those who follow it—daily.

One final note. This ritual action is to be performed twice a day, **every day,** the second performance to be done no sooner than 8 hours from the first, and no later than 12 hours.

Enjoy your newfound protection and opportunities.

The full Daily Aspersion Ritual (also referred to as the Magical Rite for Protection and the Attraction of Opportunity) now follows. As mentioned, it is the exact, expanded form of that which I teach to my personal students. Nevertheless, it is quite effective. If you follow the instructions given, I think you will be more than a little surprised at the results you receive—and even more delighted with that which it brings to you.

The Full, Expanded Magical Rite for Protection and the Attraction of Opportunity

Obtain a new, earthen vessel never used for any other purpose (thus assuring its efficacy). Be sure the vessel is unglazed. It is best to do this on a day and hour ruled by Venus. You may also want to consult my book, *Kabbalistic Cycles and the Mastery of Life*, as it gives further explanations on the correct use of the Cycles. Likewise during this time, obtain a new container of ordinary table salt[1], and a new bottle of Extra Virgin Olive Oil.

On a day and hour ruled by Jupiter, obtain a new container of mountain spring drinking water. That is, water that has only been filtered and irradiated by ultraviolet light.

Enter your Magical Chamber, stand at the center of the room, face East, and add some of the water to your earthen vessel. After this, place a small quantity of salt from the container into your right hand, and slowly pour the salt into the water. Do not stir the salt/water mixture. Place your right index finger into the salt water, and trace a cross on your forehead. Trace the vertical arm first, from top to bottom. Then, trace the horizontal arm from right to left. While tracing the cross, recite,

"In nominee Patris, et Filii, et Spiritus Sancti. Amen."

NOTE: Use the salt water for tracing the cross for 4–6 weeks. This establishes a 'baseline' for the ritual in your Subjective Synthesis. That is, it allows your subconscious mind to become used to the rite, and enables it to channel ever-increasing amounts of spiritual energy through you and into your daily life. After the initial 4–6 week period, continue tracing the cross, but do so with the olive oil only. That is, do not use the salt water anymore for the cross. Thus, once you finish your 4–6 week training period, simply trace the cross using the olive only from that point onward.

---

[1] The salt should be iodine free, as such, sea salt obtained through the evaporation process maybe substituted. Salt that was obtained through evaporation was highly prized by the ancients for purification purposes.

Now, take *one step* forward with your right foot, and bring your left foot up to meet it at your new position. Place your right hand into the water, withdraw it, and begin sprinkling in the East as you recite the following:

"Thou shalt purge me with hyssop O Lord, and I shall be clean. Thou shalt wash me, and I shall be whiter than snow." (From Psalm 51)

Recite this blessing only once as you move from the East, through the South, through the West, the North, and return to the East. That is, you repeat the prayer while sprinkling slowly, *focusing on the words and your mechanical actions.*[1]

Return to the center of the room, and face East once more. Take a drop of salt water from its container with the index finger of your right hand once again. While tracing a Cross on your forehead as before, focus on your intentions of protection and opportunity. This ends the rite. (Of course, after the initial 4–6 week period, you will change this part of the rite too, by replacing the salt water with the olive oil.)

As you will find, this Old System Magic rite—as with all Old System Magic—is most certainly built upon principles that will be explored throughout this text. What is given here will be of inestimable value to those who follow it—daily.

ONE FINAL NOTE: This ritual action is to be performed twice a day, ***every day***, the second performance to be done no sooner than 8 hours from the first, and no later than 12 hours. Should you encounter some extraordinary conditions in daily life; situations that have been thrust upon you by others, seeming to have come out of nowhere, or should you feel as if some unknown evil or negative condition has entered your life, *do the ritual three times a day and continue as such until the evil or negative condition has been*

---

[1] The Chaldean Oracles state, "Let the very priest among the foremost, guiding the works of fire, sprinkle [them] with the coagulated waves of the deep-echoing sea." Salt and sea water were common tools for purification, and this fragment shows that the Chaldean system was similar to the Greco-Roman religion of the day. See: *Hekate Soteria: A Study of Hekate's Role in the Chaldean Oracles and Related Literature* by Sarah Iles Johnston, American Classical Studies 21, Scholars Press, Atlanta, GA.

removed. Such events are likely to happen when you begin working in Old System Magic, simply because you are attracting the attention of 'things that go bump in the night.' Make no mistake about it. These evils (or intelligent, invisible malignancies) will be initially attracted to your actions to free yourself from the ignorant slumber that keeps you bound to materiality out of fear and ignorance.[1] This rite will protect you from them like a lamp that draws the moth, but destroys it as well.

Enjoy your newfound protection and opportunities.

Studies in the Grimoires
The Fourth Book of Occult Philosophy
Part I of II
Concerning the Three Books and The Fourth Book

All of us have heard it: *The Three Books of Occult Philosophy*, written by Henry Cornelius Agrippa are the most important; the most necessary; the most vital books on Western Magic ever written! No one can live without them! No one can do their magic successfully without understanding these books in their entirety, and using them as constant companions in their research into that great cathedral of 'modern magic,' the Western Magic of the Golden Dawn, etc., etc., etc.!'

Well, ladies and gentlemen, I am here to tell you that this rote fabrication is just that: a fabrication of New Age dilettantes. If the truth be known, there are very, very few contemporary practitioners of magic that are capable of understanding a single page of that tome. They use it as a magical 'name dropping technique' to impress others of their lodges, groups, and Orders, as well as their 'adepts' and 'masters,' but that is about it. In reality, neither they nor their 'superiors' have the faintest idea of what the books contain. Why? Because besides the specific reasons I cite below, such individuals are not interested in true magic, but in the quick-fix which of course, does not exist. Nevertheless, we must look to specifics in order to understand why we use them in a rather different way.

---

[1] "The gods do not like it that man should have knowledge." — Vedas

As to the actual authorship of the *Three Books,* I have covered this point in my first book, *Ceremonial Magic and the Power of Evocation,* so it would be pointless to rehash it here. However, due to the enormous number of circular arguments in the *Three Books,* their unbelievably bad rhetoric (which is poor even for its 16th century Latin edition and equally so for their 17th century English translation) their stilted logic combined with dense ramblings that confuse a specific point under investigation beyond all recognition, it is my position that these three books are simply not needed as postured, since they do not initially aid the Operator in any *practical* way whatsoever. That is, there can be a vast difference between *desirability* and *applicability;* and in this instance, that difference is astronomical.

In addition, their format of presentation compounds the usability issue even further, introducing no end of doubt into those conclusions that the assiduous researcher will eventually come to after he or she has labored to unravel the mass of confusion as best they can. This, due to the *Three Books'* absolute lack of *interior logic* which must be *assumed,* if sense is to be made of the material given in them such that the *inferred* information can be applied in practice. Such an assumption can be disastrous in and of itself, for a myriad of reasons.

But—and this is the key point—that which is said to have been synopsized from them—the *Fourth Book of Occult Philosophy*—is the most valuable single reference work we have when working Old System Magic.

In the 1985 Heptangle Books edition of the *Fourth Book,* the publisher writes:

> "Viewed as a manual, one would expect to find and does find much summarization from the other three books. Some would criticize the work for the repetition it does contain, and on this basis affirm that no author would so liberally reproduce himself; and on that basis the work is condemned as a technically superior forgery. It is, however, inherent in the nature of a manual to be a summation and a repetition of the text to which it is a hand-book. If there is a complaint concerning repetition and lack of originality, it is due to a lack of understanding of the work."

Of course, "...lack of understanding of the work" refers to the one condemning the *Fourth Book* for its supposed "...lack of originality..."

What we have in the *Fourth Book* then, is a direct, clear, succinct abridgement of those qualities, conditions, and properties—not only of the mental state the magician must achieve—but of the materials of his Art and Science that are needed for Old System Magic to work. This is the *Fourth Book's* virtue. This is why it is to be studied with a religious zeal, after the would-be magician of Old System Magic has diligently completed his or her "Preparations for Old System Magic" (Chapters Two and Three). That is, in addition to one's ongoing daily prayers and sundry other tasks, the *Fourth Book* is to be studied and restudied until not only are its admonitions and counsels comprehended by the magician's subconscious state of Subjective Synthesis, but that the peculiar magical feelings underlying the material are powerfully felt; experienced as a strange sensation in the consciousness of the reader: this, as a consequence of the material having been apprehended by the Subjective Synthesis of the magician.

I refer to this "feeling-phenomenon" as a "change-of-brain state": one in which the magician perceives the outer world as a magical realm wherein all possibility exists. In other words, he or she literally sees the world as a place of magical existence; one in which even a drop of dew on a leaf in the early morning hours, will send the magician into a state of ecstasy or rapture. This is the 14th century *change-of-brain state*. *This is the state in which all Old System Magic must be performed, if it is to be successful.* I am aware that you, the reader, have not previously heard of this. I am also aware that I have not mentioned it in any of my other writings. I purposely chose not to go into this matter until now, since it is something I teach only to my private students in the Oral Tradition; something which all of them have found to be a very real and true experience, and one that enables their magic to work.[1]

---

[1] This is also known as the "Magical World View" and is not well discussed in practical literature in the various Western schools. A fine description of it, however, is found in the writings of Tulku Urgyen Rinpoche, when he writes in his book *Vajra Speech: Pith Instructions for the Dzogchen Yogi*, "The worldly experiences of phenomena is called impure perception.

While I cannot instruct you further in this change-of-brain state through the written word, yet it may be that you being aware of it as a conscious construct will in some way help you along your own Path in Old System Magic.

As to the *Three Books* themselves? They are to be used after—and only after—Comprehension and Apprehension of the material of section I in the Fourth Book has been achieved, as counseled above. That section, "Of Occult Philosophy, or of Magical Ceremonies", is the section of the *Fourth Book* being referred to here. When this material has become part of your subconscious state of Subjective Synthesis, and you then turn your attention to the *Three Books* proper; then and only then will you find your eye of understanding has been opened. Then and only then will you glean in the *Three Books*, wonders and knowledge such as you could not have seen, let alone understood, before. This is how to use the *Three Books of Occult Philosophy*. This is how to have them open their treasure vault to you; not in the happenstance way you have been advised by those who live in ignorance and call it bliss.

When indeed you are ready for them, I strongly recommend the presentation of the *Three Books* as given by Donald Tyson. He has been careful not to change the original material, but to add his edits and annotations in a clearly marked way so as not to destroy, or in any other way alter, the original material. This is the mark of a true scholar.

Concerning the *Fourth Book* proper. Personally, I use the original 1654 edition along with the 1985 Heptangle printing. However, since Stephen Skinner has produced his masterful 2005 version of this book, I have added it as well to my list of research copies when delving further into its mysteries. I strongly recommend that readers use it as instructed herein.

Impure perception is the confused perceptions of sentient beings. For someone who only has pure perceptions, a house will be experienced as a celestial palace. In the celestial palace, there is no experience of earth, water, fire and wind. Everything is rainbow light, major and minor bindus [marks of enlightenment]. How amazing that would be!"

The Fourth Book of Occult Philosophy

Stephen Skinner's production of the complete *Fourth Book of Occult Philosophy* is the finest version I have seen outside of the 1654 original edition (a copy of which I am fortunate to have in my own library). Word for word—whether in Latin or English—his impeccable scholarship and magical accuracy shine through. The book's annotations—clearly indicated by copious footnotes; its structural rearrangement of the six works it contains; and its placement of the Latin verses in the conjurations of the *Heptameron*, set this text apart as one of the most important texts of Renaissance Magic extant.

Skinner's book is judiciously divided into two parts, making it easier to see and understand the flow of the material. This alone is a great improvement over the original 1654 edition in which the six volumes were randomly scattered throughout the book. The six works contained in the two parts, and which make the *Fourth Book* complete, as I have noted, are:

Part I — Magic

1. Of Occult Philosophy, or Of Magical Ceremonies: The Fourth Book
2. Heptameron or, Magical Elements (what my own book, *Ceremonial Magic and the Power of Evocation* is based upon)
3. Isagoge: An Introductory Discourse on the Nature of Such Spirits
4. Arbatel of Magick: Of the Magick of the Ancients

Part II — Geomancy

5. Of Geomancy
6. Of Astrological Geomancy

His Bibliography is also interesting, and most of the works cited there—his own included—certainly belong in the library of every serious Practitioner of Old System Magic.

In one of my own books I commented upon the current day change of spelling of the word, "magic" to "magick." Notice that in Book 4, the Arbatel, we find the addition of the letter "k" to the word. Meaning that at least as far back as 1654, the word had a dual spelling. While the New Age claims this as their own invention, clearly, it is not. Crowley is credited with having 'devised' the word so to speak, in order to distinguish his version of "true magick" from the "magic" practiced by 'ignorant, superstitious fools'—such as the geniuses who gave us *The Fourth Book of Occult Philosophy*? Clearly, he popularized the contemporary spelling and used it in devising his own system of Magic. But from what it has come to mean today in the New Age community, I for one am absolutely ecstatic in numbering myself among that group of ignorant, superstitious fools who hold to Old System Magic exclusively.

As Skinner also points out in the *Fourth Book*—and as I have indicated in my own books—the serious magician should also purchase a copy of Joseph Peterson's, *The Lesser Key of Solomon*. As with Skinner's books, Peterson's labour is also an example of impeccable scholarship; an erudite production that requires detailed study and careful understanding if for no other reason than—it works!

Concerning the Suffumigations and Fire of the Magical Art
Part I of III

Usages of Terms, Herbals, and Some General Considerations

"Why do you advocate using the term, "Suffumigation," instead of the more familiar terms, 'Incense' or 'Perfumes,' when referring to odiferous materials that are employed in various magical rituals, rites, and ceremonies? Indeed, are the terms not interchangeable? Don't they really mean the same thing?" I have been asked this question many times.

These are all valid questions, and ones that deserve a concise answer. If for no other reason than to enable your Subjective Synthesis to understand precisely how these burning masses and their odors enable or at the very least enrich the materialization of magical efforts. So let us begin.

In the grimoires, one typically finds the terms, "Perfumes" or "Suffumigations" or even, "Suffmigations." For instance. In the *Heptameron* we find, "The Benediction of the Perfumes" in one place while the phrase, "The Fire which is to be used for the *suffumigations* is to be in a new vessel of earth or iron; and let it be..." In the *Grimorium Verum*, mention is made "of the Perfumes" and "The Orison of the Aromatic Perfumes." The *Grand Grimoire* refers to the herbs and woods used in the Rite as either a "...wood or incense..." while the *Goetia* simply refers to such materials as "Fumes," "Perfumes," "Stinking Fumes" or "Sweet Perfumes." In the *Clavicula Salomonis* the terms used are "Perfumes...Spices...and Fumigations."

It certainly seems that the terms for these materials are interchangeable, and I am nitpicking over unnecessary detail. Let's see if this self-leveled accusation is correct or not.

If you study the use of odorous materials in Old System Magic, you will find two obvious things:

1. The material itself—be it a herb, wood, oil, or even the Fire used in the rite—is a static thing in and of itself until...
2. The two are combined, at which point the union produces a fume...or *suffumigation*.

That is, the 'virtues' or magical properties of the herb, wood, or oil are not 'released' until they are activated by a convenient Fire built at the site of the Operation. It takes but little analysis to realize that the Fathers of the Grimoires employed the terms perfumes, fumes, incense, suffumigations, etc., in an interchangeable way when writing, yes. But not in terms of their use. That is, they saw the use of herb, wood, oil, and Fire as a *Cause-Effect relationship: one that was vital in producing the result the ritual or rite was designed to produce.* They did not interpret these "suffumigations' as moderns do today: as some convenient odor meant as a "stage prop" to 'get them in the mood,' or to generate a cloud as a "vehicle" for an evoked spirit to manifest into! There is a fundamental difference in understanding and establishing a Cause-Effect relationship in any matter, and using some ill-understood or misunderstood contrivance to add 'mystery' to those already sacred magical mysteries with which Old System Magic is concerned!

Thus, in order to keep my own Subjective Synthesis clear on this matter, I always think and use the word, suffumigation to mean that herb/wood/oil and Fire combination meant to establish a particular Cause-Effect relationship that is congruous to the nature of the magical operation, and therefore to the manifestation of the intention for which I an carrying out that operation. In short, I am keeping my magical script, 'literate.' But just what does this suffumigation produce that enables the rite to go off smoothly, and what are the mechanics behind it that helps to support the successful conclusion in any magical operation?

Of itself, the odor of any herb, oil and wood produces a change-of-state in the ambient atmosphere of the site of the Operation. That is, there is a change in the physical atmosphere that is induced by the odor of the substance being used. In the same way, the Fire produces more than simple heat: it produces its own change-of-state in the ambient atmosphere of the Operation as well. However, neither one—in or of itself—is either capable of, or conducive to, producing that ideal third change-of-state required for the manifestation of the spirit (if one is summoned for this purpose) and for the intention of the Operation to be made manifest (over some interval of time).

To put it another way, the odor of the suffumigation produces one—let us call it—frequency, while the burning Fire produces another frequency in the atmosphere of the Site of Operation. Neither has the ability to support the Operation and its intention, until the suffumigation and Fire are combined, i.e., until the suffumigation is added to the Fire. When that is effected, a third frequency—completely different from either that of the suffumigation itself or the Fire itself—is thus created. And that third frequency is what enables both the manifestation of the spirit (if called for) and the intention of the Operation to successfully manifest in the world of form. *Thus, the herb/wood/oil suffumigation constitute a CAUSE, and the Fire, another Cause. But when the two are combined, an EFFECT is produced: the effect necessary to support and sustain the entire rite itself.*

Of course, the other parts of the ritual, rite, or ceremonial action must also be carried out correctly so success can be attained. *But without the correct Suffumigation and Fire combination, it has been my experience that no magical rite—no matter how flawlessly carried out—will succeed without this vital Suffumigation and Fire combination.* We are not dealing with magical "props" or "neat smells" that get us "into the mood" and "...like ya' know, feelin' groovy, man, so I can do my magic thing." Never. We are dealing with components of a solemn rite; components that are necessary for the intended effects to manifest in the world of form; components that are very similar in form and purpose to the numbers of a combination lock that—when dialed in the correct sequence—open that lock for us, so we can obtain that which we desire. You would do well to consider this argument and its line of reasoning in further building and polishing your subconscious state of Subjective Synthesis.

There are a few Herbals I recommend. All are immediately available, and will provide you with the research base you will need for determining the correct Suffumigations to use in your own Old System Magical Work. Do not be deceived: remember Step 1 mentioned earlier in "Preparations for Old System Magic". Scrap them all! They will get you into no end of trouble, and have you wondering where you went wrong as you are licking your wounds from that botched magical operation. Recall my analysis above as to the mechanics behind the use of the Suffumigation and Fire combination, and you just might agree with the reasoning presented there.

Realize that save for Culpeper's book[1] cited below, the others do not list immediate planetary or zodiacal attributions of the plants. However, they give you the much needed information so that you can determine the herbs, woods, or oils that are essential to your own magical efforts. Don't fret: the faculty for making such personal determinations will come to you quicker than you may now suspect. While you may temporarily default to certain New Age herbals as an excuse until you "get your feet wet" I do not advise this. There is no time like the present for anything, and never an ideal time to break a habit or dependency. Meaning, it is in your own best interest to learn the details of making such herbal, wood, and oil assignments now. The herbals you should obtain are:

1. *The Herb Book* by John Lust

---

[1] For a detailed discussion of the role of astrology and astrological symbolism and theory in Medieval and Renaissance herbalism and medicine, see: *Culpeper's Medicine: A Practice of Western Holistic Medicine* by Graeme Tobyn. Element Books, Rockport, MA 1997.

2. *Culpeper's Color Herbal*, edited by David Potterton
3. *A Modern Herbal* by Mrs. M. Grieve In Two Volumes

In reality, these are all the herb books you will ever need. Remember also that most of the grimoires will have their own recommendations for the suffumigations. For example, in the *Heptameron*, for *Operations on the Lord's Day*, you will that find "Red Sanders" (Red Sandlewood) is called for.

Chapter Three

Preparations for Old System Magic
Part II

In the previous chapter, I recommended that the sincere aspirant to Old System Magic 'religiously' perform the following acts, a brief recapitulation of which are listed below. That is, before even thinking about beginning any basic ritual work the aspirant should follow through with what is given here. As counseled, some of these actions are physical: most however, are mental. I also cautioned that all given below has a powerful effect on one's newly forming (or reforming) Subjective Synthesis. Since magic works from the inside out and not the outside in, your efforts here will start you moving forward in discovering—and becoming—who you already are.

Further, it was strongly recommended that the would-be magician of Old System Magic set him or herself to a *six* month period during which the following steps should be executed as six months is the very least period of time in which the following actions could be accomplished. Indeed—and what it is so important to remember here—is that while some of these actions can be completed within the six month timeframe, others will continue to be worked on for the remainder of your life.

There is also more and in truth, what I am about to write will be for some the most difficult of all to accomplish—that is, at least it will be for those who are as yet so wrapped up in previous studies that they cannot extricate themselves from it by doing what must be done next.

For to move into the realm of Old System Magic—where the power lies; where wonders and signs such as you would not believe at this moment become a matter of course; where the fulfillment of your most earnest desires and deepest yearnings change from a fantastic dream to a hard and fast reality—you must deface, destroy, and consign to fire, all of your former magical impedimenta. That is correct. Whether they be the weapons of the Golden Dawn or any of its multitudinous variations; whether they be of some amalgam between the Golden Dawn and Old System Magic or any of the latter's variants; whether they be of Wicca or one of its offshoots; or belonging to some other way; all must be utterly destroyed in order to free you to move into that darkly splendid realm of Old System Magic proper.

"What! Give up what I have labored so hard and long to create? Something that looks so beautiful and pristine, and which contains so much holy power? Something which is so much a part of me, I couldn't think of handling them improperly, much less 'desecrating' them by doing what you suggest! Are you mad?" you ask.

As always, ask yourself those four most powerful words that I consider to be the foundation of all success. Those four words that stop self-illusion dead in its tracks, and kill self-delusion with one swift, clean stroke. The four words that constitute the most fundamental question in all activities; the four words that I insist be applied to all areas of life, and most importantly, that *must* be applied to *anything* of an Occult nature—and most of all to Magic. These four words are:

"Where Are The Results?"

Your weapons may indeed be beautiful and pristine: but that does not create or lend efficacy to them. If your artistic nature seeks outlet, direct it into some other artful pursuit. But not here. It has and will do you no good in this vein whatsoever—and you (already) know it. If they contain so much "holy power" then, **Where Are The Results**? Why haven't you been able to make use of that power in order to obtain the very real-world results you and I know all of your 'Magical Work' is all about?

How about those unpaid bills that are staring you in the face this month? And the unpaid ones from last month, and maybe the month before that? Afraid to answer the phone because it might be another bill collector? Or what about that item you truly need, or perhaps that bead or bauble you're just dying to buy but which you "...can't afford yet..." even though you have been invoking the Earth Element for weeks or months now with you weapons of 'holy power' in order to improve your financial position, thereby enabling you to obtain your cherished ends? So, where is this 'holy power' anyway? In the weapons, or in your belief that they contain some 'magical power' because they are inscribed with Hebrew letters and strange sigils and signs, and maybe even those "barbarous words of evocation" you were told contain all the power you need to make your life a heaven on earth? Well, are you living such a sanctified, full, and happy life now, that they promised you, after having done all those rituals for all those years, with all those pristine and beautiful weapons filled with all that 'holy power?' Of course you're not. That is why you are reading this book right now.

No, Old System Magic is not easy, but it's easier than continuing in failure and living in lack, always wondering when the next financial or other assault by the world will be made upon you; that assault that could undo you or your life for years to come, if not forever. For the truth is, those weapons you worked so hard to make have not done the job that you were promised. But then it wasn't your fault after all. You did your best in making them—and both you and I know that. You worked hard at your ritual work—and again, both you and I know it. And yet, you have very little that you can call your own as a *result* of all of this, and virtually nothing of which you can *prove* was due to all of that work—or even part of it. But these modern Elemental and other weapons did do something; something that immediately causes you to jump to their defense, and in spite of the lack of results in which you find yourself, you still 'feel' you must yet continue to use them, doing your daily ritual work with them. Ritual work that now makes you numb at the thought of their daily performance, again and again, as both you and I know. Granted, in some instances, they may have done 'something' *for* you; something you perceive on a subjective level. But more importantly, they have done something *to* you. Something much, much more important and powerful.

And what they did *to* you far, far outweighs what they did for you. And that is, these devices have formed 'links' with the deepest levels of your psychic nature; links that continually draw psychic energy from your very being, robbing you of clear thinking, balanced emotions, and deep concentration, second to none. Those who have managed to fight through such an energy drain over years or decades report they have done so only through consistent effort: an effort that was exerted over those long periods of time. And even here, these same people report that when the links were broken through the act of destroying these 'magical' impedimenta, the effect of their restored psychic force was so dramatic, it was as if a dense fog had lifted from their minds, with corresponding physical sensations that made them feel light and 'free.' Thus, the energy that was being drained from their subconscious nature ceased, providing them with an enormously powerful energy-source from which they could now draw; an energy that could be directed and devoted to other things in their lives, not the least of which was the preparation of the impedimenta needed for working Old System Magic—after they first prepared themselves.

The following letter illustrates this better than any other example I know. It was received it from one such individual who dared to do as I suggested. He destroyed his Golden Dawn weapons by defacing, destroying, and consigning them to the flames of a physical fire—a fire that is in every way symbolic of their energy being returned to the Fire of Spirit.[1] In turn, this released energy coursed back into his Inner Nature, and reawakened even more of itself within his own psyche, allowing him to make phenomenal strides in the various activities in which he is engaged. His letter follows—

Dear Dr. Lisiewski,

I am writing to share with you some of my experiences regarding the advice you have given in the premier issue of *Howlings from the Pit*. For several years my Golden Dawn tools have been sitting in a wooden chest beneath my altar, wrapped in colored silk cloths, rarely used. I learned a great deal about myself, and magic, in the process of making them. In particular, that making the tools is the magical act and not their consecration. This is anticlimactic at best. Second, after making them, that it is the preparation or journey that is important—it defines how we experience the end goal. In this case, preparation for a ritual is more important than how well we perform the ritual, in fact, our performance is an expression of how well we have prepared, as are our results.

Destroying my Golden Dawn tools was a modest price to pay, as I did enjoy making them and they reminded me of many good times with friends and co-workers on the journey. To destroy them was to move on and this was clear. So, on a Tuesday, the day of Mars, I took an ice pick and in a clean stroke defaced each tool after saying a short prayer—audibly—thanking the tool for all that I learned from it, and that with this stroke its energy was released and our connection broken. The lotus wand was snapped in two, the sword hammered and bent, the blade of my dagger bent as well, the cup wrapped in its silk and smashed, and all was consigned to water and fire to eliminate any residual etheric link.

---

[1] Please re-read what has been said in previous notations about the psychic entity often called, an egregore. According to tradition, the link between an egregore and the physical world can only really be weakened, or broken through the use of fire. Fire both purifies the physical object by freeing the energy it contains, thereby returning it to the invisible, or in simpler terms, taking energy that is discrete and returning it to the general pool of psychic energy, as well as destroying the vehicle that was used to keep it anchored to the physical world. Smoke and incense do this in part, but only on a subtle level. Once the energy has a concrete link, the link itself must often be destroyed.

When the first tool, the lotus wand, was snapped, a tremendous amount of energy was released and I felt freed. This was a genuine visceral feeling. This point must be emphasized.

By the end of the destruction of these tools, my sensory and mental clarity dramatically increased, my connection to the material and my sense of the spiritual (Kether is in Malkuth, and Malkuth is in Kether) enhanced, and above all—there was a tremendous opening up in my solar plexus.

This opening was like a tunnel of energy moving out from me and somehow, like a wormhole as there was only the end points and no sense of the line of connection itself, a link to my pituitary (in the lower back of the head).

When I was able to perform my nightly meditation, I lit my candles, sat, and as I relaxed, a distinct sphere of energy formed around me at a distance of approximately nine feet. This occurred on its own, and came through my solar plexus. What normally would have been initiated by myself, simply manifested on its own.

You may share all or part of this with your students, simply keep my identity anonymous.

Sincerely,

A student

Such is the virtue in destroying connections between one's self and ritualistic devices of an eclectically imbalanced magical system that simply does not work, and does not produce the results in the student's life as it has claimed it would for nearly one hundred twenty years.[1] If you still doubt this, visit any of the

---

[1] Dr. Lisiewski is specifically referring to the methods of the Hermetic Order of the Golden Dawn, but also to those systems that draw from it directly or indirectly. Possibly the finest description of what had occurred to the magical texts of the papyri, as well as the medieval grimoires, and even alchemical texts, during the British Occult Revival of the late 19th and early 20th Centuries can be found in Dr. Stephen Edred Flowers' book, *Hermetic Magic*: "The magical papyri were discovered in Egypt in the early part of the 19th century and transported to various western European libraries and museums. But these seminal magical texts made little or no impact on the practice of magic in the occult revival. The traditions they represented had undergone such transformation through the centuries that the original essence could hardly be recognized as being

so-called magical blogs, or various internet posts and read their posts: a plethora of hate, personal attacks on each other and even on those who refuse to waste their time becoming a part of their particular brand of insanity, posturing, innuendo, lying, trying to out do each other, the list goes on. Then ask yourself. "Is this the 'spiritual development' promised by their system of magic?"

Once this "Act of Release" is completed and the weapons are destroyed, and the admonitions given in Part 1 are executed over a (at least) six month period of time, the desirous student is then most ready to enter into those forbidden halls of Old System Magic. And then the real work begins—as do the desired results.

Those who are sincere about entering into Old System Magic will do what is required of them. Those who refuse to see what is required and why will continue on as they are. However, both groups have to ask that damning four-word, "Where Are The Results?" And then act accordingly.

Ritual Techniques of Old System Magic
Introductory Remarks

What is about to follow is a very unusual and useful magical experiment that will test the newcomer to Old System Magic; and test him or her to no end. Either traces of this magical/mystical technique—or full instructions—have appeared throughout the centuries in such diverse writings as the Rosicrucian Order, one or two 12th century grimoires, in 3rd century B.C.E. Graeco and Graeco-Egyptian Hermetic texts, as well as in some early Gnostic texts, and those dealing with Roman Catholic Mysticism. While all of them are interesting and do contain some useful information, I have developed the following ritual-technique using an *Experimental Magic*[1] approach; one that I developed throughout

---

truly 'Hermetic'. So much elegant Victorian refinement and civilization had turned the vital and vibrant tradition of the papyri into the long-winded mutterings of a few old gentlemen." (p.13).

[1] Experimental Magic is like any other experiment—it has a distinct set of theories, possible outcomes, methods, and seeks to discover something not readily known. In the case of occultism, we often seek to find the missing pieces to specific operations or rituals. In this case, those things added to the

the past four-plus decades of working in Magic. It is based upon a ritual given in 'The Minor and Miscellaneous Processes' found in *The Book of Ceremonial Magic*, by A.E. Waite. It was this book that first came into my possession in a strange way in March of 1963. Little did I know at the time, but it would be this classic that would propel a very dear friend of mine and me into Magic. This ritual-technique is an adaptation of the rite termed, "To Compose the Magic Mirror of Solomon", and which appears in the text cited. It was found to be the most effective and efficient means in creating the psychic entity that follows me to this day, and which performs some 'special duties' for me from time to time. For the entity I am speaking of is the "Magical Watcher"—a being that possesses a separate and distinct life and consciousness of its own, while yet remaining connected forever to the mental fabric of the magician, since it is generated by his mind through a relatively simple magico-mystical ritual.

As is the case with much of Old System Magic—and as was exemplified by the Simple Magical Aspersion for Protection and the Attraction of Opportunity—the items required to perform this rite are rather simple in nature and relatively easy to obtain. Independently, they do not amount to much. Collectively, however, when put to use through an eclectically-balanced ritualistic structure,[1] they produce effects that most people can only dream about. It is always the same with Old System Magic:

---

existing ritual, to ' fill in the blanks' as it were, must be carefully chosen and supplement the existing material. Laboratory alchemists are very familiar with this process as they often work from incomplete texts, or texts were inference and suggestion give the keys, but clarity and direct explanation are absent. For better or worse, this forces the practitioner to become awakened to the inner voice of their intuition.

[1] Magic, regardless of its historical origins, works primarily on the notion of sympathy, or "like attracting like." To understand why it is important to keep ritual integrity and continuity, consider the following: "The *symbola* [symbols] that Hekate revealed to men worked by means of sympathy; they where the hylic emblems of the celestial powers the theurgist sought to reach. The closely related iynges, which sprang from and depended on Hekate, helped the theurgist "attune" himself sympathetically to the celestial realm; the sounds and movements they gave forth represented the cosmic harmony or music of the spheres." (p.143)

simple in essence, easy-to-rigorous in practice, full results in terms of effect.

All items to be used are to be 'virgin.' That is, they must not have been used for any other previous purpose whatsoever. Thus, they must be newly purchased. In this instance, the items used are not to be exorcised or consecrated in any fashion either, owing to the mystical overtones of the experiment. Indeed, any consecration that does occur will come about as an automatic result of the individual's searching for and purchasing these items, all the while holding in consciousness the use to which they will be put. The following are the items needed for this work.

- Saffron suffumigation ("incense") in cone form (as you will see, the cone form provides for a controlled rate of diffusion of the smoke that is crucial in the experiment. Stick, oil, and cube forms do not provide this property. I used India brand cones decades ago, and had overwhelming success with them.
- Wisteria suffumigation ("incense") also in cone form, and for the same reason as above.[1]
- Two glass plates or trays (such as an "ash tray") approximately 4 inches square.
- Two candlestick holders, light blue in color, shaped like a sphere sitting upon a square base. They are to be ceramic, no other material being acceptable. The sphere—into which the candles are placed—should measure approximately 4 inches in diameter (the square base supports the sphere-candle assembly, of course.)

NOTE: Geometry and material compositions are important in these matters, as it is in all of Old System Magic. One has only to

---

[1] The influence of proper odors during rituals cannot be stressed enough. Not only do they have a slight purifying effect on the psychic body, as previously mentioned, but they also attune it to a particular psychic frequency. The 'body of air' is a common term for what we now refer to as the psychic, or astral body and its corresponding senses. In addition, odors strike directly at the oldest area of the brain, and draw forth a host of unconscious forces to the surface. It is no surprise that the much valued resin frankincense, used in a host or occult, mystic, and religious rites is a proven mood elevator; or that high quality perfumes act as aphrodisiacs.

study the construction of various Circles of Art, such as those in the *Heptameron* and the *Clavicula Salomonis*, or the admonitions given in the *Third and Fourth Book of Occult Philosophy*, to understand the significance of lines, angles, areas, and surfaces, and materials from which the various weapons and supporting impedimenta of Old System Magic are produced.

- Two candles, red in color throughout, each 12 inches in length, minimum.

NOTE: in all of your Old System Magic work, please make sure that the colored candles you will be using are a solid color throughout. In fact, as you will find out as you work Old System Magic, you will need only two colors unless otherwise specified: red and white.

- A Mirror "Portal." This is a special mirror, in that we are once again concerned with its geometry. This mirror must be shaped like a portal. That is, it has two straight parallel sides, a straight bottom, and an arc at its top. I am certain you have seen many of these in the literature. It is very straightforward. The height of the mirror should be no less than 12″ and no greater than 14″ with a width 8″–10″ but no more.
- A large sturdy table, preferably made of wood. It must not shake or wobble whatsoever. A size of 48″ × 48″ is ideal.
- A plain white robe that girds at the waist. Note that it too must never have been used for any other purpose. That is, it must be virgin in all respects. In this instance the robe should be made of cotton, a plant which has aerial characteristics. This, as opposed to a standard linen robe which possesses earthy attributes.[1]

---

[1] The robes mentioned in many of the grimoires are made of linen. Modern cotton, and cotton polyester blend are used extensively by contemporary Protestant and Catholic churches, and are easily found at local church supply stores. The standard ' choir ' robe works well for this operation.

WARNING!

This ritual can be performed *after* completing Parts 1 and 2 of "Preparations for Old System Magic". If performed before these essentials are completed, I assure you, your efforts in creating the Magical Watcher will fail. You must have the maximum psychic force at your disposal when working in Old System Magic, since Old System Magic itself is, in the main, a psychic endeavor, and not a spiritual one as I have stated so many times. That is, the correct usage of the psychic faculties eventually allows the spiritual unfoldment of your interior nature, such as occurs during a properly executed Evocation to Physical Manifestation. Therefore, your entrance into Old System Magic must be completed prior to working in it. Remember also, you cannot mix systems by using some of Old System Magic and some of that which is promulgated today. To do so is to use a New Age mentality, and that is not what we are about! We are here for results. And that is exactly what you will get if you follow my teachings.

The Operation should be performed on a Wednesday during a Mercury or Jupiter hour, or on a Thursday during a Mercury or Jupiter hour, or on a Sunday during a Sun hour. See *Kabbalistic Cycles and the Mastery of Life* for details concerning these Cycles. The Moon must be waxing to full but she must not be combust. Additionally, she must be in either an Air or Fire Zodiacal Sign.

The Technique Proper

Recommendation—The prayers and conjurations to follow in the body of this technique proper should be ***memorized*** by the magician prior to attempting the Grand Experiment. It does no good—in this instance—to break one's concentration and focus in the midst of this particular Work.

This Operation, as with all others possessing a magical structure or nature, is to take place in your Magical Chamber. Of course, the chamber should be bare, except for the altar in the center of the room. The wooden table is to be placed against the wall which is geographically located on the west side of the room—no other direction will do—the wall serving as a back rest for the Mirror.

The room must be dark, except for the candles that will eventually be lit. There must also be great silence and quiet during this Operation. Above all, make certain you are not disturbed. Dawn the vestment. Seat yourself in front of the table. Place the mirror in your lap, and with your right index finger, stroke the mirror across its upper rim (from the top of the arc) down the right side, across the bottom, up the left side and back across the upper rim. Continue to do this (being careful not to cut yourself on the sharp edge of the mirror near the rim.) until you feel a 'pull' from the mirror's surface. The sensation will be unmistakable. It will feel as though the mirror is actually stopping you from stroking it further. At this time, cease stroking the mirror's surface. Hold it up in front of you, gaze at your countenance in it, and let your mind be exalted toward your highest concept of God and say:

> O Eternal! O King Eternal! God ineffable! Thou who hast created all things for love of men, and by a secret judgment for the health of man, do Thou deign to look upon me (state your full name here) Thy most unworthy servant, and upon this my intention. Vouchsafe to send unto me Thine Angel Anael, even upon this mirror, who doth order, command and ordain his companions and Thy subjects, whom Thou has made, O Thou Almighty Lord, Who hast been, Who art, Who shall remain eternally, that in Thy Name they may judge and act justly, instructing me in all that I shall require of them.

After doing so, place the mirror upright such that it leans securely against the wall itself.

Situate a red candle into each of the candlestick holders. Now, place one candlestick-candle assembly off to the left side of the mirror and another off to the right side of the mirror. Place them in such a way that when they are lit you will not be able to see the flame in the mirror, but yet their soft glow will still illuminate the mirror's surface, but barely. In front of each candlestick-candle assembly place a glass (ash) tray. Following this, place a single wisteria incense cone in the glass tray to the right of the mirror, and a single cone of saffron incense in the glass tray to the left of the mirror.

Light the candle on the left first, and then the one on the right. Take the saffron cone, light it, and when it begins to smoke, place it back in its glass tray. Next, do the same for the wisteria cone. Situate the glass trays with their suffumigations in such a way that they cannot be seen in the mirror, but that their smoke gently swirls across your reflection in the mirror. As the suffumigation continues to swirl, look into the mirror and say:

> In this, by this, and with this, which I pour out before Thy face, O God, my God, Who art blessed, Three and One, and in the most sublime exaltation, Who sittest above the Cherubim and above the Seraphim, Who wilt judge the world by Fire, hear Thou me! [Repeat this prayer three times.]

Take up the mirror in your hands, breathe upon the surface of the mirror three times and say:

> Come, Anael,[1] come, and may it be thy good pleasure to be with me by thy will, in the Name (make the Sign of the Cross over the mirror with your right hand) of the Father most mighty, in the Name (make the Sign of the Cross over the mirror with your right hand) of the Son most wise, in the Name of the Holy Spirit most living! Come, Anael, in the Name of the terrible Jehovah! Come, Anael, by the virtue of the immortal Elohim! Come, Anael, by the right arm of the almighty METATRON! Do thou come unto me (state your full name here, *over the mirror*) and so command thy subjects that in love, joy and peace, they may make manifest unto my eyes the things which are hidden from me. So be it. Amen.

While still holding the mirror in your hands, lift your eyes to heaven and say:

> O Lord Almighty, Who doest cause all things to move according to Thy good pleasure, hear Thou my prayer, and may my desire be agreeable unto Thee! Lord, O Lord, if Thou wilt, condescend to look upon this mirror and bless it, that so Anael, one of Thy

---

[1] It would do the operator well to consider this operation in light of the method used by Cagliostro to invoke the angel Anael in his Egyptian Rite. The magical system of Cagliostro was essentially that of Martinez Pasqualez's *Elu Cohen*, or Elect Priests, which was essentially that of the medieval grimoires. Despite difference in external appearances, they were internally and functionally identical. See: *The Masonic Magician: The Life and Death of Count Cagliostro and his Egyptian Rite* by Philippa Faulks and Robert L.D. Cooper, Watkins Publishing, London.

servants, may pause thereon with his companions, to satisfy me (here state your full name), Thy poor and humble servant, O God, blessed and exalted above all the heavenly Spirits, Who livest and reignest for ever and ever. Amen.

Now make the Sign of the Cross upon yourself and upon the surface of the mirror, being certain to trace the Cross on the mirror from top to bottom, and then from left to right.

Place the mirror against the wall, allow the indirect glow of the candle flames to barely illuminate its surface, and the swirling smoke of the suffumigations to move across the mirror's surface. Stare into the mirror, through the smoke, and say:

> Come Anael, come, according to thy good pleasure, and bring unto me he who will watch over me and mine and all that I assign him to according to the Office of his nature and my commands, both he and I always respecting the Law of the God, Lord of Hosts, and Father of All Creation! Come Anael, and bring him unto me! Bring unto me he who will fulfill my demands according to my expressed will!

Now sit silently and continue to stare at your own reflection in the dimly lit mirror surface, and through the swirling smoke of the suffumigations. Do not strain. Simply stare at your own image. Shortly, it will begin to change. Strange, terrifying features will come over your image, and as they begin to fade in and out, prepare yourself for what is to follow.

As your image continues to change, you will suddenly become aware of either a hissing or rustling sound behind you. DO NOT BREAK YOUR FOCUS OR LOOK BEHIND YOU! Continue to stare. The sounds behind you will cease after a while, only to give way to something else. Something that will utterly terrify you at first.[1] For suddenly—you will feel a strong grip on

---

[1] This terror and desire to turn around cannot be stressed enough as it is the result of a subjective experience materializing into a physical one. I performed a simple operation similar to this involving a bowl of water and an invocation of the Babylonian god of water Ea over twenty-five years ago and remember it like it was yesterday. The tangible presence and shock that accompanies it as it becomes present for the first time cannot be put into words.

your left shoulder. It will be difficult, but DO NOT JUMP UP OR LOOK BEHIND YOU! Remain seated and continue to stare at your reflection in the mirror, despite your terror. It is then that you will see, in the mirror, your Watcher standing behind you. The terror will be overwhelming, but you must hold your ground. The hand will remain there for either seconds or minutes, but it will be there. Say nothing. When the hand's grip is removed, continue staring into the mirror. At this point the Watcher may either be visible or invisible, but it matters little, for he has appeared to you and is now and forevermore with you. Now say,

> I welcome you, who have been brought to me by the Grace of Our Father, the God of All Things, and of Heaven and of Earth and of all that is in them, who hast seen fit to grant unto me the Great Angel, Anael, by whose power and authority thou hast been made real unto me! Enter now into my life, you who I now name (devise a secret name for your Magical Watcher: one only you will know. It is not be revealed to anyone, ever.) From this day forth, by the Ineffable Power of God, and by the power of His Great Angel, Anael, thou shalt serve me in those things which I find useful and necessary unto myself. I welcome thee, oh thou Watcher, who now bares the name I have given. (say his name again)

Look away from the mirror now and toward heaven and say,

> I thank thee, Anael, because thou hast appeared and hast satisfied my demands. Do thou therefore depart in peace.

Return your gaze to the mirror and say,

> Hear thou me (state the name you have given your Watcher) and be attentive unto my demands. I (state your full name) am he from who thou hast sprung through the Power of God the Father, and through the intercession and strength of the Great Angel, Anael! Listen to me, and be ever attentive to my spoken or mental words! I charge thee to do all I say, and quickly, that lies in thy Office, and which is permitted me and thee by God, and to stay with me for the course of my life upon this earth! I charge thee to follow me wherever my travels take me, to protect me from all harm, whether physical, psychic, or spiritual, or whatever kind soever, and to protect those others whom I charge thee to protect as well, and to protect all those material possessions of mine which I have and which I will have, at any time, and in whatever form, and to

secure all for me as of this instant. Do thou attend unto me, and be ready and willing to carry out my commands when they are given. It is so.

Extinguish the candles, exit the Magical Chamber without looking back at the mirror or around the Chamber, and allow the suffumigations to burn out completely. That is, the suffumigations will still be burning as you leave the Chamber.

Return to the Chamber the next day. Have with you a large, heavy cloth bag such as a burlap bag, and a new hammer which has never been used for any other purpose. Take the mirror, ceramic candlestick holders, and glass trays, place them securely into the bag, seal the bad tightly so as to prevent cutting yourself, place the bag with its contents on a hard surface such as the floor, and with the new hammer, smash the bag repeatedly, thus destroying the mirror, candlestick holders, and the trays. Finally, dig a hole in the East and bury the bag and its contents. The rite is finished.

At first, you will have a very distinct, subjective awareness of your Watcher. In fact, you will not be able to get your new creation out of your mind: this is as it should be. But as with all things, you will find that your conscious awareness of it will decrease over time. This too is as it should be. Mine has been with me for over forty years, yet I am rarely aware of it. That is, until I need it. Then, its reality for me is as great as the night on which I created it, all those decades ago. You will find this to be true for yourself as well.

When you need your Watcher to do something for you, do not fear that its 'leaving' to accomplish its task will leave you unprotected. These beings are as angels or the Fallen in that they are a conscious, intelligent energy. And as such, they are not limited by space or time. In fact, as with any of the physical forces, they have existed, exist, and will exist across all space and time simultaneously.[1] Therefore, while it is off tending to things, you will also find that it is still very much with you, protecting you and yours, and your property. Remember also to treat this

---

[1] For additional insights into a similar phenomenon from the Nyingma Tibetan Buddhist perspective, see: *The Protectors: A Teaching Given by His Eminence Shenpen Sawa Rinpoche* in Los Angeles, CA, 1988.

being with respect. It was created from and through you by an act of God through the intercession of the great Angel, Anael, and deserves the same respect and consideration you expect from others. Do not err in this.

Studies in the Grimoires
The Fourth Book of Occult Philosophy
Part II of II
Concerning the Three Books and The Fourth Book
Some Further Comments

Previously I discussed the *Three Books of Occult Philosophy*, their actual authorship of which I mentioned was covered in my first book, *Ceremonial Magic and the Power of Evocation,* and flat out stated that—in my opinion—the *Three Books* cannot be easily utilized by the aspiring magician. The reasons cited were the enormous number of circular arguments in the *Three Books*, their unbelievably bad rhetoric (poor, even for its 16th century Latin edition and equally so for their 17th century English translation) and the stilted logic, combined with dense ramblings; all of which confuse a specific point under investigation enormously. As a consequence, I concluded that *these three books are simply not needed as claimed, since they do not initially aid the Operator in any practical way whatsoever.*

Further, I mentioned that their format of presentation significantly compounds the usability issue even further, introducing no end of doubt into those conclusions the assiduous researcher will eventually come to after he or she has labored to unravel the mass of confusion as best they can. This, owing to the *Three Books'* absolute lack of *interior logic* which must be *assumed*, if any sense is to be made of the material given in them such that they can eventually be applied in practice.[1]

---

[1] It is my impression that the *Three Books of Occult Philosophy* is a giant encyclopedia, or notebook, of various occult ideas of the period rather than a practical manual of magic. The practical applications have, as Dr. Lisiewski and Stephen Skinner pointed out, been distilled into the material of the *Fourth Book* whose authorship is in question, but both Lisiewski and Skinner believe to be that of Agrippa.

I then went on to say that the *Fourth Book of Occult Philosophy*, which is actually a synopsized form of the *Three Books,* is the most valuable single reference work available for those of us who work with Old System Magic.

It was further pointed out that in the 1985 Heptangle Books edition of the *Four Books*, the publisher writes:

> "Viewed as a manual, one would expect to find and does find much summarization from the other three books. Some would criticize the work for the repetition it does contain, and on this basis affirm that no author would so liberally reproduce himself; and on that basis the work is condemned as a technically superior forgery. It is, however, inherent in the nature of a manual to be a summation and a repetition of the text to which it is a hand-book. If there is a complaint concerning repetition and lack of originality, it is due to a lack of understanding of the work."

which sets the record straight as the *Fourth Book* actually being a 'User's Manual' for Old System Magic.

In the conclusion, it was stated that the *Fourth Book* is actually a direct, clear, succinct abridgement of those qualities, conditions, and properties—not only of the mental state the magician must achieve—but of the materials of this Art and Science needed for Old System Magic to work. This then, I postulated, is the virtue of the *Fourth Book*. Hence the reason offered for it being studied with a religious zeal, after the would-be magician of Old System Magic has diligently completed his or her "Preparations for Old System Magic" as outlined earlier. That is, in addition to one's ongoing daily prayers and sundry other tasks, the *Fourth Book* is to be studied and restudied until not only are its admonitions and counsels comprehended by the magician's subconscious state of Subjective Synthesis, *but that the peculiar magical feelings underlying the material are powerfully felt; experienced as a strange sensation in the consciousness of the aspirant: this, as a consequence of the material having been Apprehended by the Subjective Synthesis of the magician.*

I further made plain that what I refer to as a 'feeling-phenomenon' is a "change-of-brain state": one in which the magician perceives the outer world as a magical realm wherein all possibility exists. In other words, he or she literally sees the world as a place of magical existence; one in which even a drop of dew on a leaf in the early morning hours, will send the magician into a state of ecstasy or rapture.[1]

This is the 14th century change-of-brain state. This is the state in which all Old System Magic must be performed, if it is to be successful.

And finally, I strongly recommend that when the aspirant to Old System Magic is ready to study the *Three Books,* that is, after he or she has Comprehended and Apprehended the material of Section I of the *Fourth Book,* which is, "Of Occult Philosophy, or of Magical Ceremonies", then and only then should one proceed on to Donald Tyson's magnificent tomb of the *Three Books of Occult Philosophy.*

So where does the above brief review take us to next? It takes us to that quintessence for which all magicians of Old System Magic seek: to the ceremonial act of Evocation to Physical Manifestation which is represented by the *Fourth Book's* second section—*The Heptameron, or Magical Elements of Peter de Abano.*[2]

In my first book, *Ceremonial Magic and the Power of Evocation,* I gave extensive commentaries for nearly every paragraph of the original *Heptameron,* regardless of how brief many of those original paragraphs were, with the intent of providing an example of a flawless presentation of the ceremonial act of Evocation to Physical Manifestation. I sought to present as much as I could between the covers of a single book of the exact knowledge and conditions necessary; not only to successfully work this magnificent grimoire, but to provide a template-like process by which almost any grimoire could be successfully worked. From the hundreds of letters I receive each week from readers of *Ceremonial Magic and the Power of Evocation,* approximately 98% tell me they understand the text completely, and thank me profusely for

---

[1] For an examination of the similarities and differences between Medieval and Renaissance Magic, and a discussion of the 'Magical Worldview' see: *Drawing Down the Life of Heaven: An Introduction to Renaissance Magic* by Mark Stavish at: www.hermeticinstitute.org.

[2] The *Heptameron* appears to have been a favorite working text among 18th Century magicians and some of their later successors. Several modern Martinist groups use it as part of their work after having completed the degree of Unknown Superior.

having written it. Of those individuals, over 50% have already employed the instructions I gave for working the *Heptameron*, and have informed me they have either experienced success in Evocation to Physical Manifestation for the first time, or have experienced such "...incredible success in what occurred during the ceremony, and in the results I received from it..."

Experimental Old System Magic
The Blasting Rod — Its Purpose and Use
Part I of III

"Blasting Rod? What is that?" you ask. "I've heard about wands such as the Fire Wand and the Lotus Wand of the Golden Dawn, but what is this thing?" To adequately answer this question for yourself you will need to make reference to *The Book of Black Magic and of Pacts*, by Arthur Edward Waite. From here, we will begin our discussion by giving the sum and substance of that which Waite has expounded upon concerning the Blasting Rod.

There are many editions of this book available, mostly cheap paperback and even hardcover editions whose depiction of the seals, characters of the Theban and Crossing the River magical alphabets, pictorial illustrations and the like are anything but clear; not to mention 'editorializing' the text which has rendered it an atrocious, and in some instances, inaccurate restatement of that which Waite actually wrote.

The print quality of this book is exceptionally good, rendering all characters, sigils, artistic depictions of images, as well as the text itself, very readable and understandable. Clearly, their reprint has been made from an original copy of *The Book of Black Magic and of Pacts*.

When you obtain the book, I suggest you study the material both before and after the section on the Blasting Rod, such that you understand where this weapon fits in with the other materials of "The Initial Rites and Ceremonies" chapter in which the information on the Blasting Rod is given. Also be certain to re-read in the book the section on the Rod that I quote here. In this way, you will not only acquire a knowledge of the Rod and its use, but you will be prepared to enter into the deeper discussions that will be presented here in Parts II and III regarding this all important magical weapon. What follows next, are Waite's comments on the Blasting Rod. (p.155)

Concerning the Rod and Staff of the Art

The great mystery of practical magic is supposed to be centered in the Magic Rod, and Eliphas Levi, who claims to have reconstructed the primitive ceremonial, but seems to rather have over-edited his materials, supplies a highly sensational account of its powers and an elaborate method of its preparation. For him it is the sign of the transmission of the magical priesthood, which has never ceased since the darksome origin of transcendent science. The operator is overwhelmed with precautions concerning the secrecy which must be maintained in regard to it, and dejected by the difficulties of its consecration. In view of such imputed importance it is curious that De Abano and pseudo-Agrippa omit all mention of this tremendous instrument, and the 'Key of Solomon' dismiss it in a few lines of easy instruction. It would appear, however, that a staff and rod are both necessary, especially in Goetic operations, though their distinctive provinces are in no case described. According to the Book of 'True Black Magic,' the staff should be of cane, and the wand or rod of hazel, both virgin—that is, having no branches or offshoots.[1]

They must be cut and trimmed on the day and in the hour of the Sun, while the following characters must be inscribed upon the staff, but on the day and in the hour of Mercury:[2]—

—Magical Characters are inserted here
as you will see in the book—

Note: Such characters are from the Theban, Celestial Writing, and Crossing the River (sometimes called, "Passing the River.") There are also magical characters from the alphabets called, "Malachim" and "Transitus Fluvii." Of particular interest are the last two mentioned, along with the alphabet termed the "Celestial

---

[1] The definition of virgin wood differs in the *Key of Solomon* which says: In all cases the wood should be virgin—that is, of one year's growth only.

[2] According to the *Key of Solomon,* both staff and rod should be cut on the day and in the hour of Mercury at sunrise, which limits the operation to the few days of the middle of winter, when the sun rises about eight o'clock.

Writing." These three are alphabets that were really derived from the Hebrew during Medieval times.

"If engraved with the sacred instrument, it will be so much the better.[1]

"In either case, let the following words be recited when the writing is finished:

> 'O ADONAY most Holy and most powerful vouchsafe to consecrate and bless this Staff and this Rod, so that they may possess the required virtue, O most Holy ADONAY, to whom be honour and glory for ever and ever. Amen.'

"Lastly, the two instruments should be asperged, fumigated, and put away in the silken cloth.

"The *Grimorium Verum* directs the operator to make two wands of wood which has never borne fruit. The first should be cut at a single stroke from an elder-tree on the day and in the hour of Mercury. The second should be of hazel, free from bud, and cut in the hour of the Sun.[2]

"The magic characters which should be engraved upon each have been omitted by the printer, but they are supplied in the modern Italian versions. They are, for the first, the seal or character of Frimost, and that of Klippoth for the second (see Chap. III., Sec. 2). The prayer of consecration offers no variation of importance from that of 'True Black Magic,' and does not need to be reproduced. Aspersion and fumigation are prescribed, as in the previous case.

"The 'Grand Grimoire' devotes an entire chapter to the true composition of the Mysterious Wand otherwise the Destroying or Blasting Rod. It mentions no other instrument, and ascribes to it all power in diabolical evocations. It would seem to have supplied Eliphas Levi with the first hint of his still more potent Verendum, to which, however, an allegorical significance may perhaps be attributed. On the eve of the great enterprise, says this Ritual, you must go in search of a wand or rod of wild hazel which has never borne fruit; its length should be nineteen and a half inches. When you have met with a wand of the required form, touch it not otherwise than with your eyes; let it stay till the next morning,

---

[1] This is presumably done with the burin or graver.
[2] This variation seems to reconcile the "Book of True Black Magic" with the "Key of Solomon," and is probably the true reading.

which is the day of operation; then must you cut it absolutely at the moment when the sun rises; strip it of its leaves and lesser branches, if any there be, using the knife of the sacrifice stained with the blood of the victim. (See Chapter VI., Sec. I.) Begin cutting it when the sun is first rising over this hemisphere, and pronounce the following words: —I beseech Thee, O Grand ADONAY, ELOIM, ARIEL, and JEHOVAM, to infuse into this Rod the whole strength of Samson, the righteous wrath of EMANUEL, and the thunders of mighty *Sariatnatmik*, who will avenge the crimes of men at the Day of Judgment! Amen.

"Having pronounced these sublime and terrific words, and still keeping your eyes towards the region of the rising sun, you may finish cutting your rod, and may then carry it to your abode. You must next go in search of a piece of ordinary wood, fashion the two ends like those of the genuine rod and take it to an ironsmith, who shall weld the steel blade of the sacrificial knife into two pointed caps, and affix them to the said ends. This done, you may again return home, and there, with your own hands, affix the steel caps to the joints of the genuine rod. Subsequently, you must obtain a piece of loadstone and magnetise the steel ends, pronouncing the following words: —By the grand ADONAY, ELOIM, ARIEL, and JEHOVAM. I bid thee join with and attract all substances which I desire, by the power of the sublime ADONAY, ELOIM, ARIEL, and JEHOVAM. I command thee, by the opposition of fire and water to separate all substances as they were separated on the day of the world's creation. Amen.

"Finally, you must rejoice in the honour and glory of the sublime Adonay, being convinced that you are in possession of a most priceless Treasure of the Light."

Another method of preparing a Magic Rod ordains that it shall be a branch of the hazel-tree put forth during the year of operation. It must be cut during the first Wednesday after the new moon, between 11 P.M. and midnight. The knife must be new and the branch severed by a downward stroke. The rod must then be blessed; at the stouter end must be written the word AGLA (sign of the Cross), in the centre ON (sign of the Cross), and towards the point TETRAGRAMMATON (sign of the Cross). Lastly, say over it: *Conjure to cito mihi obedire*—I conjure thee to obey me forthwith.

This then, is what we know of the Rod of Power, or the "Blasting Rod" as it is also referred to in the literature. I have investigated the sources that Waite cites in this section of *The Book of Black Magic and of Pacts*, and while his descriptions are concise, they lack nothing which would either prevent the Operator from making the Rod, or lead one astray in the preparation and consecration process. Hence, in Waite, we have all we need to know to produce this most valuable of all the Impedimenta of the Art. Later we will go into the mechanics of preparing this weapon, and after that, we will discuss its proper use in Ceremonial Magic. There is much hidden in what Waite gives here; and as usual, all is not obvious. It never is in Magic.

Concerning the Suffumigations and Fire of the Magical Art Part II of III

A Review of The Theory and General Considerations of Herbs in the Magical Arts and Sciences

Previously I discussed the important features of suffumigations, *i.e.*, the 'virtues' or magical properties that a given herb, wood, or oil possess, and stated that such virtues are not 'released' until they are activated by a convenient Fire built at the site of the Operation. It was also pointed out that the Fathers of the Grimoires most certainly did employ the terms perfumes, fumes, incense, suffumigations, etc., in an interchangeable way when writing; but not in terms of their use. That is, they saw the use of herb, wood, oil, and Fire as a *Cause-Effect relationship: one that was vital in producing the result the ritual or rite was designed to produce.* They did not interpret these 'suffumigations' as moderns do today: as some convenient odor meant as a stage prop to 'get them in the mood,' or to generate a cloud as a 'vehicle' into which an evoked spirit was to manifest. There is a fundamental difference in understanding and establishing a Cause-Effect relationship in any matter, as opposed to using some ill-understood or misunderstood contrivance to add 'mystery' to those already sacred magical mysteries with which Old System Magic is concerned!

I further mentioned that in order to keep my own Subjective Synthesis clear on this matter, I always think and use the word, "Suffumigation" to mean *that herb/wood/oil and Fire combination* meant to establish a particular Cause-Effect relationship that is congruous to the nature of the magical operation, and therefore to the manifestation of the intention for which I am carrying out that operation. In short, I am keeping my magical script 'literate,' thereby suggesting that the reader do the same. Then the question was posed, "Just what does this Suffumigation produce that enables the rite to go off smoothly, and what are the mechanics behind it that help support the successful conclusion in any magical operation?"

The explanation was given that of itself, the odor of any herb, oil or wood produces a change-of-state in the ambient atmosphere at the site of Operation. That is, a change in the physical atmosphere; one that is induced by the odor of the substance being used. In the same way, the Fire produces more than simple heat. It produces its own change-of-state in the ambient atmosphere at the site of the Operation as well. However, neither one—in or of itself—is either capable of, or conducive to, producing that ideal third change-of-state required for the manifestation of the spirit (if the Operation is for this purpose) or for the intention of the Operation to be made manifest (over some interval of time).

The above explanation was elaborated upon by stating that the odor of the Suffumigation produces a single frequency, while the burning Fire produces another frequency in the atmosphere of the Site of Operation. Yet neither has the ability to support the Operation and its intention, until the Suffumigation and Fire are combined by the addition of the Suffumigation to the Fire. When this happens, a third frequency is produced—one that is completely different from either that produced by the Suffumigation itself or the Fire itself. Further, it was stated that it is this third frequency that enables both the manifestation of the spirit (if called for) and the intention of the Operation to successfully manifest in the world of form. *Thus, the herb/wood/oil suffumigation constitute a CAUSE, and the Fire, another Cause. But when the two are combined, an EFFECT is produced: the effect necessary to support and sustain the entire rite itself.* And while the other parts of the ritual, rite, or ceremonial action must also be carried out correctly for success to be attained, *without the correct Suffumigation and Fire combination, it has been my experience that no magical rite—no matter how flawlessly carried out—will succeed unless this vital Suffumigation and Fire combination is seamlessly interwoven into the Operation.*

I further cautioned the reader to eliminate from his or her thinking that we are dealing with some type of magical 'prop' or 'neat smell' that is supposed to get us 'into the mood,' but rather, remember that we are dealing with components of a solemn rite; components that are necessary for the intended effects to manifest in the world of form; components that are very similar in form and purpose to the numbers of a combination lock that—when dialed in the correct sequence—open that lock for us, so we can obtain that which we desire. You would do well to consider this argument and its line of reasoning in further building and polishing your subconscious state of Subjective Synthesis.

The Preparation of the Fire

In Old System Magic we use what the Fathers of the Grimoires used and in doing so we are not 'mimicking' the old magicians when we do such things. We are dialing those same numbers in the combination lock—the ritual, rite, or ceremony that they used—in order to produce the same effect they produced. We are communicating with our well-built, polished subconscious state of Subjective Synthesis, allowing the energy-geometry of the force of the ceremonial rite to flow through us while retaining its exact geometrical shape, and through us, into the rite, and out into the world of form to produce what we want, by having it initiate the 14th century brain changes that will allow the Operation to succeed to the extent that it was designed to succeed. This is why we do what we do, and why we pay attention to the mechanics behind the 'why' of what we do. And to do this, we must do some simple analysis that will reveal things that normally would escape us.

The early magicians did not have the convenience of purchasing instant lighting charcoal and often used woods of various types as called for in the Operations. For instance: in the *Grand Grimoire*, the "Karcist" (magician, or Operator) as he is termed in that text, is instructed to use "White Wood"—which is actually Willow—while in the *Heptameron*, all we are told is that "...The fire which is to be used for suffumigation, is to be in a new vessel of earth or iron..." with no mention being made of the wood to be used. (In fact, when not specified by a grimoire, the wood of choice is always the "White Wood" or Willow, of the *Grand Grimoire*. I have found it works flawlessly every time.) Yet in the *Greater Key of Solomon,* all we are told is, "…light the fuel in the earthen pots…" These grammars are not speaking of the Suffumigations proper here, but rather, the heated platform upon which the Suffumigations are cast—what we consider to be the charcoal or the "Base Fire," as I term it.

So what do we do when it comes to practical work? We use the specific wood as the Base Fire if the grimoire being worked from specifies it. If it does not, then we use Willow, or—since all burned wood is reduced to charcoal, and it is this which actually provides the highest temperatures for the Suffumigations to continue burning throughout the rite—we can use readily available charcoal if we treat it in the following manner. I have found this not only to be consistent with the interior logic of every grimoire, but, importantly, I have found that it works.

You see, it is not enough to assume we can do this or that; that we can use this or that. We must be able to analyze and understand the *fundamental principles* upon which a given phenomenon rests, in order to know not only why we are doing what we are doing, but to understand why a particular thing is required, and how it is to be implemented in practice. THIS is the task of the Old System Magician—his or her task is the same as that of the scientist; for Magic is not simple an 'Art'—it is also a 'Science.' And THIS analytical process of the mind IS the 'Science' part of the 'Art and Science' we have been told for so long that Magic is. As to preparing the charcoal as the Fire of the Art:

Purchase briquettes as are used for picnics, but they must not be the 'Quick Lite' variety. They must not contain any naphtha or petroleum products that give them the 'Quick Lite' characteristic. Take the briquettes needed for the Operation, and with a hammer and chisel, split them along their edge such that their open face is flat, while their outside conical-shaped bottom remains intact. Split as many as you need, and then place all into a container containing 'antique oil lamp' oil until they either float in, or are submerged in the oil. In this way, they will absorb the oil through the rough, porous flat side, and burn consistently and evenly throughout the rite.

NOTE: the oil that is used in these lamps is a vegetable-based oil that does not contain any petroleum products. It is much like the olive oil that was used in ancient Egypt to fuel the 'magical lights' for Egyptian ceremonies and rituals. Once again, it is not easy to obtain, but it can be had.

When lit on their edges at the appropriate time in the ceremonial act, they will provide the magician with that proper 'Third Frequency' which is so important to the rite itself. That is, we want the 'Fire-Cause' discussed above to be the correct one. One that resonates with the ceremonial act proper, as it was conducted centuries ago by the Fathers of the Grimoires. Thus we too can produce that 'Third Frequency' which allows for the materialization of what we are after.

Chapter Four

Efficacy: Its Mechanics and Role in Old System Magic

As a natural consequence of all of this work, many questions are often generated, the most common one being that of Efficacy and its role in this action or that magical process. More precisely, "How is it that the difficulty encountered in obtaining whatever implement was being searched for in order to carry out one of the basic rites presented, will increase the power of those rites and influence their success?" Of course, if the theory behind something is not clearly understood, it cannot be successfully applied in practice, and in Old System Magic, Efficacy is the foundation upon which the entire ritual structure is constructed. In the end it is essential that you have a deep understanding of the concepts behind the very real force that lies behind or within Efficacy, so that you will be able to use it consciously, purposely, and for the attainment of your own ends.

In Old System Magic, there is simply no place whatsoever for 'convenience' and whose absolute necessity is one of the strictest requirements of this form of magic as *Old System Magic is based strictly in efficacy.* That is, the harder something is to acquire; the more difficult it is to prepare the Place of Working, the Impedimenta, the Operator himself or a combination of any of these, the more efficacy—and hence power—that is welded into the process of the specific rite or ceremonial act itself. Thus, the more efficacy contained within the process, the more power is projected by both the Operator and implement into the magical work itself. Let's use the Acquiring the Magical Sword for working with a given grimoire as an example. Remember, the same magical impedimenta cannot be used for working different grimoires. Each grimoire will be found to have its own requirements, all of which must be strictly adhered to. In my own practice throughout the years—I would travel to where these things were sold, regardless of the distance, and purchase the weapon during the day and hour required, personally: all as one, single, action. *Therein lies the power: not in ease or convenience.* Read this well and remember it.

The underlying idea here is that there is a price to be paid in order to insure that the magic we do brings about the success we so fervently desire. For in point of fact, the idea of something for nothing simply does not exist in the universe—at any level; much less in the strange realms in which we work. *The price we pay then is the mark of our physical, mental, emotional, and psychic commitments we make to the goal we so desperately seek to realize.* How often have you heard of a case, or been asked by someone for help, "Listen! I'll do anything! Anything to learn magic (or alchemy, or divination, *etc., etc., etc.*). Just tell me what to do and how to do it, that's all I ask! And I swear to you, I'll turn Heaven and Hell upside down if I have to in order to do as you say!"

But you have only to ask a few questions to realize that the person who has come to you asking for your time, knowledge, and experience, places more emphasis on their monthly cable TV fee, martial arts instruction, or a visit to the tattoo parlor or body piercing salon than in actually learning the occult arts. They are not willing to do whatever it takes, only to mouth with empty words that they will do whatever it takes. Their time, energy, and material resources are channeled exclusively into the good times they can't remember the next day, and into more technological nonsense: those beads and baubles that not only drain their wallets, but defocus them from the Interior Realm in which magic and mysticism are truly done. You quickly come to find that all they are concerned with is justifying the price they paid for their new electronic device so they can stay 'in touch' with their friends, and 'keep current' on the affairs of a society that is contrary to their magical and spiritual pursuits.[1]

In effect, their underlying unwillingness to do whatever it takes to succeed is their unconscious rejection of the Principle of Efficacy.[2] Yes, it manifests in the ways stated in the above quotation. But always this deep, fundamental rejection is the causal agent behind the effect that manifests as one's refusal to work. That is, to do real work, regardless of the cost in time, effort, energy, or money.

Why should we be so concerned with this causal force? Why did the Fathers of the Grimoires insist on an absolute adherence to its dictates? Why should we expend every effort to comply with the injunctions laid down by this 'old fashioned' principle? The answer is quite simple yet the mechanics behind it may surprise you.

The noun 'efficacy' literally means "The power to produce an effect." That is, efficacy—in and of itself—is a power or force which, when directed in some way through the will, mind, and emotions of the Operator (Magician) is projected in order to

---

[1] "Sometimes I thing that the greatest achievement of modern culture is its brilliant selling of samsara (cyclic existence) and its barren distractions. Modern society seems to me to be a celebration of all the things that lead away from truth, make truth hard to live for, and discourage people from even believing that it exists... This modern samsara feeds off an anxiety and depression that it fosters and trains us all in, and carefully nurtures with a consumer machine that needs to keep us greedy to keep going... Obsessed, then, with false hopes, dreams, and ambitions, which promise happiness but lead only to misery, we are like people crawling through an endless desert, dying of thirst. And all that this samsara holds out to us to drink is a cup of salt water, designed to make us even thirstier." — *The Tibetan Book of Living and Dying* by Sogyal Rinpoche, p.20–21.

[2] The Law of Cause and Result, or Karma, is easily seen here in the old adage, "You get out of it, what you put into it." Without the necessary emotional commitment on the part of the Operator, there can be no effective magic regardless of what system is followed.

produce a predetermined effect. Without this power, nothing can be accomplished; for the *energy of motivation and manifestation*—so important in the production of the desired effect—is missing. This most basic of all magical principles was second nature to the magicians of the Dark Ages, the Medieval and Renaissance eras, and was as much a part of their ritual acts or ceremonial actions as was the construction and consecration of their Circles of Art. This is why many of the grimoires do not belabor the point or go into it beyond only the briefest of mentions. It was understood to be the foundation upon which the entire magical rite was based.

But why is this so? What is the nature of this energy? In the seemingly endless search for "a black rooster that never trod hen," or in the effort to obtain a ring of pure gold with certain inscriptions upon it, what is this energy which is transferred to the rite such that success is more probable with it, and utterly impossible without it? The energy that is imparted is so great and of such magnitude, that all other natural phenomena must kneel before it. *For it is the energy of the Hidden Self: the energy of the magician's Spiritual Source, operating through his five psychic faculties—which is then projected through and by the magician using his will, mind, and emotional natures—that manifests in and through the rite to produce the desired effect.*[1] And this projection is brought about by the magician involving his total self in acquiring just those 'rare' and hard-to-find materials, altered states of consciousness, or correct use of the Names of Power, that are required by the ritual acts or ceremonial actions.

---

[1] For Jakob Boehme "Imagination" is the divine tool in man, the power of creation, whereby self-realization and divine integration can take place. The "Fall" as mentioned in Genesis is caused by turning our imagination—creative power of desire and action, to make the invisible visible—away from God and towards ourselves alone. The passion to achieve or possess something, to make it material, pulls forth from our subconscious images that create a feedback loop that further fuels our inner passion. It is this passion to achieve, accomplish or possess that is the real power behind any images that they may stimulate or stimulate it in return. This is what causes us to move forward on our magical quest, for when we think of the 'wand' needed for the rite, it is this inner passion that drives us on and both grows stronger with each step on the path towards the performance of the rite, and is satiated by each accomplishment.

For it is through the intense thought; the self-disciplined searches; the step-by-step, daily, weekly, or monthly one-pointed conscious focus of the magician's will, mind and emotions on the rite and its requirements, that those channels needed for the force to flow from his Spiritual Source through his psychic faculties and out into the ritual, are established.[1]

This is why so many today fail in their modern day magical practices, and in their daily, mundane lives. Instead of using the Rod made of Hazel or Oak, they use a dowel stick purchased from their local hardware store. Instead of devoting an extra four hours after the workday to that report the boss wants done in a certain way, they grudgingly give an hour to it by simply highlighting what is expedient. Then such people wonder why their magic fails, or why one of their co-workers gets the raise, promotion, or both, and always, it's the book's fault or their 'bad luck.' No. It's their lack of Efficacy, their refusal to apply their entire *conscious—and therefore unconscious*—selves to the task at hand.

It would do all of us no end of good when facing some seemingly daunting tasks to stand back, take a deep breath, and decide which way we will proceed: give the efficacy to the act that is required if we want it to succeed, or pull back and do what is expedient and easy. For if we do the latter, we had better prepare for something else too: inevitable failure. But then, you just might be surprised how many people 'demand' success from life in all things—and most especially, magic—because they have been taught to give the least and expect the most. To be certain, that is the "American way." After all, it is their "right." But it is not our way: the way of the magician who adheres to Old System Magic, or the way of the true mystic.

Efficacy is the basis upon which all lasting efforts are built in mundane as well as spiritual activities. It is a force—pure and simple. An irresistible force that can and will cut through or disintegrate any immovable object or impossible condition, regardless of how immovable that obstacle may be, or how

---

[1] To use a metaphor, each operation is a "quest" in which the magician takes on the role of a "knight" in search of the "grail" of his heart's desire—the purpose of the ritual. By overcoming the difficulties involved in preparing, he affirms to himself and all the forces of the cosmos that this is indeed what he wants to accomplish

impossible that condition may seem. So get used to it. There is simply no other way to make your magic work—or any other way for a man or woman of honor to live their life.[1]

Concentration and Meditation as Applied to Old System Magic

We have all heard of the importance of Concentration and Meditation in magic. Heaven knows, there are a plethora of New Age hype books out there giving this technique and that instruction, promising that if we 'turn inwards' and 'still the mind' we will enter into that state of 'no mind' in which all thoughts will cease; one in which we will either become 'one with the universe,' or 'attain the faculty of concentration,' the method of attainment which is either confused, ill-defined, or just another exercise in "visualization". Few if any of these so-called exercises in meditation lead to concentration. That is, if the books being studied even differentiate between the two states. In fact, of the several I have just reviewed in an effort to see if anything of value has been added to what is already out there, I found several fairly recently published works in which the terms are used interchangeably. In other cases, the 'exercises' given for the development of concentration are the ones that are supposedly used to induce the meditative state, and this by the author's own definition.

What we need is a clear understanding of what meditation is, and how—while in that state—we can induce a concentration so great that we elevate the ideal we are seeking to express in the world of matter to the realm of the Divine Consciousness Itself.

And by doing so, to aid its materialization (realization) in the material world. This, to me, is what meditation is all about. It is

---

[1] If one is a failure in their mundane life then it is guaranteed that that they will be a failure in their occult life as well, in that both draw upon the same basic human abilities for their operations and outcomes, they simply focus them in different directions. To paraphrase Goethe again, "Neither God nor the Devil wants a lazy man." It is critical to read the biographies of spiritual 'heroes' or conquerors and to note the struggles they overcame. Even Jesus was tempted and suffered, and temptation would be meaningless if he could not have possibly given into it.

both a process and a sub-process that possesses the following properties:

Meditation — a sequential stage of mental actions by which one's conscious awareness (eventually) reaches a state of inner reflection in which the Self—the "I"—*naturally* occupies the full awareness of the individual as its starting point in the process. Through further mental manipulations, this awareness of the "I" gradually leads to a state of

Contemplation — a state in which the consciousness of the Self expands to such an awareness of the Inner Realm, that the External World ceases to exist for that consciousness involved in this meditative act.

This condition (eventually) leads to a conscious connection with the Divine Intelligence that exists within and through all existence, and which Itself is all existence. At this point, all awareness of a sense of self vanishes as a separate entity, since to yet remain aware of itself would introduce separation into the unity that has occurred through the connection.

Concentration — There are two 'phases' of this interior act. The first is that which enables focus such that Meditation can be entered into. The second phase is that which occurs after Contemplation, in which an emotionally-charged Image of that which is desired is then brought into the focus of the (now) Contemplative mind; a mind which is yet only aware of its connection to, and (even) unity with the Divine Intelligence.

Realization — The mental act of elevating the emotionally-charged image to the level of the Divine Consciousness itself through the connection made with the Divine, and which occurs through Contemplation.

This process of Meditation, Contemplation, Concentration, and Realization then, constitutes an action I term, "Interiorization": a mode or condition of being in which a state of readiness, characterized by those definite qualities we term, Meditation, Contemplation, Concentration and Realization, exists within the individual.

Thus, Meditation and Concentration are not separate states: they are different phases of the same process; a process by which we access the Divine Mind in an effort to transform a desire (a potential state) into a manifestation (a kinetic state), thereby producing Realization of some desired External World or Interior Realm desire, goal, or end.

I also use another phrase to encompass this process of Interiorization (which includes the [sub] processes of Meditation, Contemplation, Concentration, and Realization) and which the reader may very well benefit from enormously if he or she so chooses, which is *Entering the Silence*.

I wish I could say I invented this beautiful expression, "Entering the Silence," and the simple, yet precise techniques by which one effects 'entry' into the magnificent world within, but I did not. Through years of study and practice however, I have learned to use the techniques and to structure the information in a more formal way as given above. But the credit for the fundamental insights and techniques must be given to another author who wrote long ago, and who has been all but forgotten.

That author is Helen Rhodes Wallace. For in her incredible book, *How to Enter the Silence*, 1920.[1] Wallace thoroughly discusses the states of meditation and contemplation. Although she gives a different order of the processes, her fundamental position is correct and extremely valuable in understanding the Meditation–Contemplation–Concentration–Realization components of the Interiorization process. That is, by carefully reading her book and using the more structured approach I have given this process, the reader will be able to attain to a profound understanding of those powers of the Interior Realm that can be successfully applied to the furtherance of their lives: either through the daily periods of prayer between their ritual performances and ceremonial acts, or through additional 'static' periods when entering the silence, which can be used as a "New Thought" technique to manifest that which is desired. That is how potent her work is.

---

[1] *A Handbook of Mystical Theology* by G.B. Scaramelli (1687–1752), Introduction by Allan Armstrong (2005) is indispensable for those seeking to understand the mystical attitude and its accompanying phenomena from the perspective of the late Renaissance. Scaramelli was a Jesuit priest and wrote extensively on the effects of contemplation and inner preparation for the Mystical Marriage.

Wallace makes several things clear at the outset of her work; matters that set her book apart from all the others, and which invite the reader to journey with her into their own Inner Realm. She writes,

> In order to enter the Silence it is necessary to anchor human intelligence to a higher degree of consciousness. This Silence is not an inert passive state nor psychism nor trance. It is a lucid work of the highest spiritual activity. The experience clarifies perception, intensifies effort, creates efficiency and establishes prosperity. The guarantee of arrival is practice. 'Do the thing and you shall have the power.'[1]

But she does not leave us hanging with generalizations that make for warm and fuzzy feelings. Rather, she emphasizes the pragmatics of this state called Meditation when she states:

> There is an act of the mind, natural to the earnest and the wise, impossible only to the sensual and to the fool, healthful to all who are sincere, which has small place in modern usage and which few can distinguish from vacuity. Those who knew what it was, called it meditation. It is not reading, in which we apprehend the thoughts of others. It is not study, in which we strive to master the known and prevail over it till it lies in order beneath our feet. It is not reasoning, in which we seek to push forward the empire of our positive conception. It is not deliberation, which reckons up the forces which surround our individual lot and projects accordingly the expedient on the right. It is not self-scrutiny, which by itself is only shrewdness. Its view is not personal and particular, but universal and immense. It brings not an intense self-consciousness and spiritual egotism, but almost a renunciation of individuality. It gives us no matter for criticism and doubt, but everything for wonder and love. It furnishes immediate perception of things divine, eye to eye with the saints, spirit to spirit with God, peace to peace with heaven.
>
> In thus being alone with the truth of things and passing from shows and shadows into communion with the Everlasting One, there is nothing at all impossible and out of reach.
>
> Let any man go into the Silence; strip himself of all pretense and selfishness and sensuality and sluggishness of soul; lift off thought

---

[1] "Dare to do, and you shall have the power to do." — Ninth Degree Monograph, Rosicrucian Order (AMORC).

after thought, passion after passion, till he reaches the inmost depths of all, and it will be strange if he does not feel the Eternal Presence close upon his soul—if he does not say, 'Oh Lord, art Thou ever near as this and have I not known Thee?'

The Methods of Use of Concentration and Meditation in Old System Magic

Given all of this, how does the Practitioner of Old System Magic use this meditative process to manifest that which he will in the External World, by creating it first in the Interior Realm: the only place where creation truly can occur? For in creating that which he desires in the Interior Realm, he will find that through the processes of either Magic—ritual performances or ceremonial acts—or through pure Mysticism—the strict use of the process discussed here—he will project that creation outward into the world of form—into Malkuth, or the External World.

There are two related methods by which the process of Concentration and Meditation as discussed here and in Wallace's book can be successfully used in Magic. The first way I term the "Magical Dynamic Method." The second, the "Magical Static Method."

The Magical Dynamic Method

In the Magical Dynamic Method, the magician performs the *Simple Magical Aspersion for Protection and the Attraction of Opportunity*. However, in this instance, only olive oil (it must be pure, Spanish Olive Oil obtained from the first cold pressing) is used to anoint the forehead. The salt and water are only used for the aspersion as usual.

Make certain you begin the Rite—that is, perform it for the first time—only on a Monday, during a Mercury Hour, the Moon waxing to full, with Mercury being in direct motion (not retrograde). In this way, the magician will invoke the energy of Path 30, Resh, which connects Hod and Yesod, and which takes the XIX Card of the Major Arcana of the Tarot, The Sun, giving happiness and contentment as that which will flow from your work. Note too that the forces of Hod and therefore Mercury, the planet ruling Magic, as well as Yesod and thus the Moon which rules the unconscious, will all be added to your work in a balanced way. Of course, you must be in your Magical Chamber to carry out that which is to follow.

After the Aspersion is performed, return to the center of your Circle, kneel down, and recite the Prayers of Dr. John Dee as also given earlier. Once completed, seat yourself on a wooden—not metal—chair[1] and begin the process of Concentration and Meditation as laid down in Wallace's book. (Of course, the information given herein regarding the process of Meditation will serve to guide you even deeper into the process, so be certain to review it prior to using Wallace's techniques.)

In brief, after the connection has been made to the Divine Intelligence, the student elevates the Image of his completed desire to the level of the Divine Intelligence which he is experiencing at the moment. There will be a distinct perception of it being received by the Divine Intelligence Itself. At that point, the student terminates the period immediately, thereby releasing the energized Image to the Divine Mind. Thus, the process and Rite ends in an instant. There is to be no 'backing out' of the meditative state slowly. It must end instantly for release to be complete and absolute. There will be a period of disorientation to follow, but it will pass in an hour or so.

The Rite is to be performed twice a day for a period of 30 days. During these sessions, you will elevate the desire which is greatest in you to the level of the Divine Intelligence Itself, such that any ritual performance or ceremonial action you intend to execute in order to bring that desire into your world will be enhanced by your practice of the Meditation Process. Such will then bring forth the fruit you seek that much sooner, more completely, and with as little Slingshot Effect as possible. Pay special attention to inner promptings that occur both during and after using this method. For bursts of inspiration and illumination will most certainly occur. They make take the form of deep insights into the ritual you are preparing to perform for manifesting your desire, or these inspirations may direct you into

---

[1] The presence of metal not specifically called for in a ritual is discouraged as it acts like a magnet and pulls energy away from the Operator, and in this case, more importantly, the object being consecrated. Also, metal chairs would have been rare, if not unheard of, during the period in which the principals of Old System Magic were codified in the grimoires.

different ritual performances than the one you were originally planning in order to manifest that which is of importance to you. Yet again, you may experience extremely lucid dreams: ones in which you are instructed in the exact way to proceed, by a beautiful being clothed in a silver-white robe. There are an infinite number of possibilities as to how you will be led.

The Magical Static Method

This method is simplicity itself. In fact, it incorporates no small number of "New Thought" principles which are interlaced throughout Wallace's book, and which the student will use—no doubt unknowingly, at first—to bring about the materialization of their desire.

In this method, the student merely uses the process as given in Wallace's book along with the ideas of the process as discussed here. That is, two separate 30–45 minute periods are set aside each day for a span of 45–60 days. As before, not ONE day or ONE period is to be missed. In using this method, the student does not even have to enter his Magical Chamber since there are no aspersions or prayers involved. (Please note: as in the Dynamic Method, the first performance of this method is to be done when the Moon is waxing to full, with Mercury direct, on a Monday, during the hour of Mercury, and for the same reasons as discussed above.)

After the connection has been made to the Divine Intelligence, the student does as is done in the Magical Dynamic Method: he elevates the Image—not "visualization"—of his completed desire to the level of the Divine Intelligence which he is experiencing at the moment. He then terminates the meditative process immediately, as given in the Magical Dynamic Method, and proceeds about his normal business.

In point of fact, Wallace's book most certainly can be used by those who wish to enter into Higher Mysticism. For it gives that most fundamental process of all by which the Images of desire can be transferred to the Mind of God Itself through which the desires are materialized in the life of the Mystic. In a way, what we have here is a transition point from Magic to Mysticism. Yet this process can be used by both the Magician and Mystic. Hence its greater virtue.

I assure those of you who are ready to work at this, that you have been given a technique, process and methods which can—and will—literally turn your lives around, regardless of the method you choose to do this work.

Experimental Old System Magic
The Blasting Rod — Its Purpose and Use
Part II of III

In the section "The Blasting Rod — Its Purpose and Use Part I of III" in Chapter Three, I gave the text from A.E. Waite's (in)famous book, *The Book of Black Magic and of Pacts,* in which Waite not only discusses the Blasting Rod proper, but in which he explores different requirements for this magical weapon as set down by different grimoires. The fact that Waite provides different instructions from several grimoires supports my position: that systems of magic can never be mixed. Thus, a different set of such weapons are to be prepared according to the grimoire being worked from by the Magician at any given time. However, Waite confuses the issue by his writing style and his syntactical arrangement, so that we are left wondering, "Is there a Blasting Rod that I can use for those grimoires in which no such Rod of Power is mentioned, *e.g.*, the *Goetia*?" Or *The Secret Grimoire of Turiel* or *The Sword of Moses*? And the answer to that very valid question is, YES.

What we are going to do now, is make a *Commentary* which will reveal HOW that 'general purpose' Blasting Rod can be made, while all the while REMEMBERING that if a particular grimoire calls for a different process in making (another) Rod of Power, then THAT specific one must be made if one intends to work from that grimoire, *e.g.*, as given in the *Clavicula Salomonis*.

Let us proceed then to an investigation of these footnotes and *Commentaries* and see how all of this can be brought together to produce the 'general Blasting Rod.' For along with the Knife with the Black Handle as given in the *Clavicula Salomonis*, the Blasting Rod is the most feared of magical weapons among demons. The Sword of Art pales in comparison to these latter two magical weapons, for reasons we shall now see.

What follows is what I have found to be true, experimentally, for both myself and those to whom I have taught this procedure to over the past several decades. In all cases those individuals who followed the instructions that are to follow, experienced enormous success in the Evocations to Physical Manifestation as have I, and all with the most minimal of the Slingshot Effect.

According to *The Book of Black Magic and of Pacts*, the staff should be of cane, and the wand or rod of hazel, both virgin—that is, having no branches or offshoots.[1]

Commentary 1 — The tree from which the Rod will be cut must be "virgin." That is, it must not have been used for any other purpose, which of course would have to be the case since the branch (Rod) is a part of the living tree from which it will eventually be cut. However, when the tree is found, it can only be 'touched' with the eyes. Under no circumstances must the Operator touch the tree after he has finally discovered it. The tree must be of wild growth, not cultivated by man, i.e., not one purchased from a gardening store and then replanted by the Magician for the purpose of obtaining the Rod from it. The process of finding such a wild tree will take months. In my own case, it took one year of frequent searching through the mountains and deep forests of Pennsylvania to find it. And when I did, I accidentally touched it. The tree had to be abandoned, and my search begun all over again. It took another six months to find another so that branch that would become the Rod could be procured. Let this be a lesson to the wise.

> They must be cut and trimmed on the day and in the hour of the Sun, while the following characters must be inscribed upon the staff, but on the day and in the hour of Mercury:[2]—
>
> —Magical Characters are inserted here
> as you will see in the book—

---

[1] The definition of virgin wood differs in the *Key of Solomon* which says: In all cases the wood should be virgin—that is, of one year's growth only.
[2] According to the *Key of Solomon* both staff and rod should be cut on the day and in the hour of Mercury at sunrise, which limits the operation to the few days of the middle of winter, when the sun rises about eight o' clock

[Note: Such characters are from the Theban, Celestial Writing, and Crossing the River (sometimes called, "Passing the River.") There are also magical characters from the alphabets called, "Malachim" and "Transitus Fluvii." Of particular interest are the last two mentioned, along with the alphabet termed the "Celestial Writing." These three are alphabets that were really derived from the Hebrew during Medieval times.]

Commentary 2 — While the Magical Characters given are correct, the instructions as to the day and hour in which the branch is to be cut from the wild tree are not. The branch is to be cut on a Wednesday, during the hour ruled by Mercury, i.e., during the first hour of the day as the sun appears over the horizon, as stated in the *Key of Solomon*.

> If engraved with the sacred instrument, it will be so much the better.[1]

Commentary 3 — No. The Magical Weapon which is to be used to inscribe the Magical Characters upon the Blasting Rod is the Knife with the Black Handle, the instructions for making such are also given in the *Clavicula Salomonis*. The bruin or graver is to be used for inscribing the seals as given in the *Key of Solomon*, which are to be in the metal of the planet to which they are ascribed. Note: today it has become 'fashionable' to use the seals as given in the *Clavicula Salomonis* as 'designs' for talismans. This is one of the most grievous errors that has ever been perpetuated! The seals in the Key are for Evoking to Physical Manifestation those particular demons so discussed in the Key itself.

> In either case, let the following words be recited when the writing is finished:
>
> 'O ADONAY most Holy and most powerful vouchsafe to consecrate and bless this Staff and this Rod, so that they may possess the required virtue, O most Holy ADONAY, to whom be honour and glory for ever and ever. Amen.
>
> Lastly, the two instruments should be asperged, fumigated, and put away in the silken cloth.

---

[1] Presumably, with the burin or graver.

The *Grimorium Verum* directs the operator to make two wands of wood which has never borne fruit. The first should be cut at a single stroke from an elder-tree on the day and in the hour of Mercury. The second should be of hazel, free from bud, and cut in the hour of the Sun.[1]

Commentary 4 — Yes, the words given are those that are to be said over the Rod after the inscribing is done. Further, the instrument is to be asperged and suffumigated ("fumigated") as directed, and placed away in a silken cloth as described. Why silk? Because silk is the product of a worm; a living creature that produces its spinnings in the air, thus giving silk the attribution of the Element, Air. Thus, the entire nature of the Rod of Power is one of the Air and Mercury, as is the case for the time when it is to be cut from the wild tree.

> The magic characters which should be engraved upon each have been omitted by the printer, but they are supplied in the modern Italian versions. They are, for the first, the seal or character of Frimost, and that of Klippoth for the second (see Chap. III., Sec. 2). The prayer of consecration offers no variation of importance from that of "True Black Magic," and does not need to be reproduced. Aspersion and fumigation are prescribed, as in the previous case.
> The "Grand Grimoire" devotes an entire chapter to the true composition of the Mysterious Wand, otherwise the Destroying or Blasting Rod. It mentions no other instrument, and ascribes to it all power in diabolical evocations. It would seem to have supplied Eliphas Levi with the first hint of his still more potent Verendum, to which, however, an allegorical significance may perhaps be attributed. On the eve of the great enterprise, says this Ritual, you must go in search of a wand or rod of wild hazel which has never borne fruit; its length should be nineteen and a half inches. When you have met with a wand of the required form, touch it not otherwise than with your eyes; let it stay till the next morning, which is the day of operation; then must you cut it absolutely at the moment when the sun rises; strip it of its leaves and lesser branches, if any there be, using the knife of the sacrifice stained with the blood of the victim. (See Chapter VI., Sec. I.)

---

[1] This variation seems to reconcile *The Book of Black Magic and of Pacts* with the *Key of Solomon* and is probably the true reading.

Begin cutting it when the sun is first rising over this hemisphere, and pronounce the following words: —

> I beseech Thee, O Grand ADONAY, ELOIM, ARIEL, and JEHOVAM, to infuse into this Rod the whole strength of Samson, the righteous wrath of EMANUEL, and the thunders of mighty Sariatnatmik, who will avenge the crimes of men at the Day of Judgment! Amen.

Having pronounced these sublime and terrific words, and still keeping your eyes towards the region of the rising sun, you may finish cutting your rod, and may then carry it to your abode. You must next go in search of a piece of ordinary wood, fashion the two ends like those of the genuine rod and take it to an ironsmith, who shall weld the steel blade of the sacrificial knife into two pointed caps, and affix them to the said ends. This done, you may again return home, and there, with your own hands, affix the steel caps to the joints of the genuine rod. Subsequently, you must obtain a piece of loadstone and magnetise the steel ends, pronouncing the following words: —

> By the grand ADONAY, ELOIM, ARIEL, and JEHOVAM. I bid thee join with and attract all substances which I desire, by the power of the sublime ADONAY, ELOIM, ARIEL, and JEHOVAM. I command thee, by the opposition of fire and water to separate all substances as they were separated on the day of the world's creation. Amen.

Finally, you must rejoice in the honour and glory of the sublime Adonay, being convinced that you are in possession of a most priceless Treasure of the Light.[1]

Commentary 5 — The Grand Grimoire is most certainly correct in some of its instructions. That is, the Rod must have a length of 19 ½ inches, and must not be 'touched' other than with the eyes.

---

[1] Another method of preparing a Magic Rod ordains that it shall be a branch of the hazel-tree put forth during the year of operation. It must be cut during the first Wednesday after the new moon, between 11 P.M. and midnight. The knife must be new and the branch severed by a downward stroke. The rod must then be blessed; at the stouter end must be written the word AGLA (sign of the Cross), in the centre ON (sign of the Cross), and towards the point TETRAGRAMMATON (sign of the Cross). Lastly, say over it: *Conjure to cito mihi obedire* (I conjure thee to obey me forthwith).

But there is more to the instructions than are given in this grammar that I will explain in detail in the "Synthesis" that is to follow.

There is also the condition laid down by this grimoire which cannot be met. And that condition is finding a hazel tree from which the Rod will be produced, so that it is discovered on the eve of the Operation. Only if one lives in an area where hazel trees are so plentiful that it would be almost impossible not to find one on the eve of the Operation, can such a condition be met. Hence my stomping around mountains and forests for one year to find that which I needed, only to be followed by an additional six month search, for the reason stated.

In the footnote we find a more liberal interpretation, i.e., that the branch which will compose the Rod can be of the growth of the entire year during which the Operation is to be conducted. This allows for more time in finding the tree, as well as giving a branch of more manageable size with which to work. Its instructions as to when it is to be cut are, however, disputable as we shall see in the "Synthesis" to follow. As to the Divine Names, they too (as are the Magical Characters as stated in Commentary 2) are to be inscribed upon the Rod. As in the case of the Magical Characters, the Divine Names are also to be inscribed with The Knife with the Black Handle as given in Commentary 3.

These then, are the various 'blended' compositions from which the Blasting Rod is to be produced. While Waite most certainly did give all that is needed by referencing and concisely stating the different and varying conditions set down in making the Rod according to different grimoires, his statements are yet too concise and 'undifferentiated.' They lack 'integration' or "Synthesis" that makes them of value to the Operator. The instructions are there, and technically speaking they lack nothing which would prevent the Operator from making the Rod. Additionally, there is nothing in his 'reporting' of the Rod that would lead one astray in the preparation and consecration process, provided the Operator has enough 'field experience' and knowledge in reading and understanding the grimoires. Hence, in Waite, we have all we need to know to produce this most valuable of all of the Impedimenta of the Art.

But yet, we must look deeper. For the contradictory instructions presented in the grimoires Waite cites need clarification. A clarification he did not make, no doubt due to him not attempting to produce this Rod of Power himself. Now we will provide the last piece in the puzzle and see just HOW the Rod is actually made.

The Synthesis

What do I mean by "Synthesis," and just what gives me the basis or the "right" for employing such a construct to further explain and clarify once and for all the proper method by which the Blasting Rod is obtained, inscribed, consecrated, and used?

I have always based my work—from religious to scientific; from magical to mystical—upon the concept of the Dialectic, created by the famous German Philosopher, Hegel. Essentially, the Dialectic is a fancy word used to describe the way something develops, or "evolves." It can be anything from an idea or concept, to a pattern or personal project, it makes no difference. For the dialectic is not based upon the linear process of evolution or development that occurs in incremental steps or in a straight line such as is expounded by biology. Rather, dialectical evolution or development proceeds through a series of triangles. In this view, when true evolution (or development) occurs, it begins at a specific point called the "Thesis." And as I pointed out, this can be anything, even a theological system of belief, a scientific theory, a psychological process, or anything else one can imagine. As this evolutionary process continues, the original starting point—the Thesis—turns into something entirely different: its opposite, much like the differences in the instructions for the Blasting Rod, where we are given one set of instructions in one grimoire, and another set of instructions in another grimoire; or worse yet, when we are given contrary instructions in one grammar, *e.g.*, the Rod must be cut at sunrise, while another tells us it must be cut at 11 PM or Midnight: an opposite. This opposite, according to Hegel, is called the "Antithesis."

But it is in the next step in this process of 'triangular evolution' that things really get interesting. For in this next step, the Thesis and Antithesis combine into a third state: one completely different from the Thesis and Antithesis, and yet which contains elements of both the original Thesis and its opposite, the Antithesis. This third step Hegel termed, the Synthesis. (The process goes on so that the Synthesis actually becomes Thesis 2 of a new triangle, and gives rise to Antithesis 2, the process ending in Synthesis 2, which becomes Thesis 3 and so on.)

For our purposes though, it is sufficient to know that throughout the decades I applied this model of the Dialectic to all of my Science, Magic and Mysticism, including the method by which the Blasting Rod could be properly made and used. Based upon this Dialectic, the disparate and contradictory instructions and requirements as set down by the different grammars were brought together through another concept that to me was the only way such a Synthesis could be achieved in order to form the final Synthesis as to HOW the Rod should be made. And that other 'concept' was EXPERIMENTATION. In short, by using Hegel's ideas, and then experimenting with them over the decades, I was able to 'discover' that Synthesis which contained elements of the different, conflicting grimoires, such that they gave rise to the final method by which the Blasting Rod was to be properly produced. From all of this, the reportings of Waite were merged into the final result that is now presented below for the reader. Up to this point I never explained the 'method to my madness' behind the Experimental Magic I did throughout a forty-one year period and of which I have mentioned so many times in my writings. And frankly, I never intended to—unless there was sufficient reason for doing so. Ironically it was through this particular subject that this explanation was finally called for, and so I give it for what it might be worth to the reader.

Synthesis — The Production and Consecration of the Blasting Rod

A Hazel tree of one or two to four years growth is located growing in the wild. (Hazel trees will grow for three to four years before bearing fruit. However, at least I have found that finding such a tree over two years old is well nigh impossible.) If the tree is one year old, the diameter of the largest, straightest—which must be a concern—branch will be approximately 5/16″–3/8″. A two year growth tree will generally produce a straight branch of 1/2″–5/8″ in diameter. Is it possible to find such a tree of two year's growth that never bore fruit before? Absolutely. The larger diameter branch makes it much, much easier to inscribe the Characters and Divine Names, and so the Magician may very well want to consider not settling for less than an 'older' tree. It is not easy to find to be certain. But then, that is what Efficacy and the force behind it is all about in Magic.

On a Wednesday, during the first hour of the day—a Mercury hour—as the sun rises the Operator is to prepare to cut the branch from the tree. When the sun is exactly halfway on the horizon, the branch is to be cut with one, single, strong downward blow. He must not grasp the branch prior to cutting it. He must so strike it that it is cleanly severed from the tree, and caught as it falls with his other hand. While cutting it the Operator says:

> I beseech Thee, O Grand ADONAY, ELOIM, ARIEL, and JEHOVAM, to infuse into this Rod the whole strength of Samson, the righteous wrath of EMANUEL, and the thunders of mighty Sariatnatmik, who will avenge the crimes of men at the Day of Judgment! Amen.

And what particular knife must be used to cut the branch? *The Knife with the Black Handle*, as given in the *Clavicula Salomonis*. Thus, it must be prepared before the branch that will become the Blasting Rod can be obtained. This knife is to be made according to writ, and in no way are there to be substitutions or changes made in either its construction, preparation, or consecration. The exact procedure as laid down in the *Key of Solomon* is to be followed without question.

The branch is to be removed from the site and taken to the Magician's Magical Chamber where it is to be stripped of leaves and its outer bark, and cut to an exact length of 19 ½ inches, all by using the Knife with the Black Handle. These tasks are to be performed during another Mercury hour on that same day.

During yet another Mercury hour on that same day, the Magical Characters referred to in Commentary 2 are to be inscribed in the middle of the Rod, all Characters and Names of God being inscribed on the Rod with the Knife with the Black Handle.

The following words are to be recited over the Rod after the Characters are inscribed:

> 'O ADONAY most Holy and most powerful vouchsafe to consecrate and bless this Staff and this Rod, so that they may possess the required

virtue, O most Holy ADONAY, to whom be honour and glory for ever and ever. Amen.

After the Characters are inscribed, at the stouter end—the end the Operator will be holding when he is using the Rod to command a spirit—the word, AGLA is to be inscribed, a small cross placed before and after it. In the middle of the Rod—immediately BELOW the Magical Characters—the word, ON must be inscribed, a small cross placed before and after it, as before. Finally, toward the point—that end of the Rod that will directed toward the spirit—the word, TETRAGRAMMATON must be inscribed, a small cross placed before and after it as well. At this point you are to hold your arms out at your sides as if making a gesture of 'welcoming,' and say in a powerful voice, in Latin:

Conjure to cito mihi obedire! (I conjure thee to obey me forthwith!)

Following this, "You must next go in search of a piece of ordinary wood (which is the exact diameter of the ends of your branch) and fashion the two ends like those of the genuine Rod, and take it to an ironsmith, who shall weld the steel blade of the sacrificial knife into two pointed caps, and affix them to the said ends."

However, since the Knife with the Black Handle was used to sever the branch, you most certainly do not want it destroyed by having it 'welded into steel caps' for the end of the Rod. Instead, the Operator obtains thin gauge sheet steel (not "sheet metal") and using a wooden cone-form (obtainable at a craft or hobby shop) cuts two small squares from the steel sheet and wraps them from the edge of one corner toward the edge of the opposite corner thus forming a 'cap' like covering. After doing this, the Magician smites the caps, each with three blows, hard, using the cutting edge of the Knife with the Black Handle. While he is doing this, he is to image in his mind the terror and agony that any spirit at which the Rod is directed will suffer; and if the spirit shall still refuse, the image should include that spirit being dragged down into the Pit of Hell, tormented for all time, never to be released from the torment and agony.

"This done, you may again return home, and there, with your own hands, affix the steel caps to the joints of the genuine rod."

In other words, after you have accomplished the above, you are to affix the pointed caps to the ends of the Rod yourself.

"Subsequently, you must obtain a piece of loadstone and magnetize the steel ends, pronouncing the following words (a strong magnet must be used here). The end that will (eventually) be pointed toward a spirit must be magnetized with the South end of the magnet, thus making its magnetic polarity 'positive,' *i.e.*, magnetized such that it (effectively) becomes a North Magnetic Pole. The cap that will be held in the Operator's hand must be magnetized with the North Pole of the magnet, making its magnetic polarity 'negative,' *i.e.*, magnetized such that it (effectively) becomes a South Magnetic Pole. While stroking the caps you are to say:

> *By the grand ADONAY, ELOIM, ARIEL, and JEHOVAM. I bid thee join with and attract all substances which I desire, by the power of the sublime ADONAY, ELOIM, ARIEL, and JEHOVAM. I command thee, by the opposition of fire and water to separate all substances as they were separated on the day of the world's creation. Amen.*

The Blasting Rod is now finished. It is not to be either asperged or suffumigated whatsoever. Instead, a 24" × 6" piece of pure, white, virgin linen is to be asperged with Holy Water obtained from a Catholic church. The aspersion is to be done so that the water is cast upon the linen in the Sign of the Cross. It must then be suffumigated using a suffumigation composed of cedar, myrrh, and musk, in equal proportions. The linen must be left alone to allow the water of aspersion to become completely dry. After this, the Blasting Rod is to be wrapped in the linen and put away for future use. The Rod of Power is now finished.

This weapon can be used in operating any grimoire in which no mention is made of a wand or Rod, or one in which mention is made but in which no instructions for composing it are given. The Operator will find that if this weapon is used during Evocation to Physical Manifestation, the most spectacular and amazing results will be achieved.

Experimental Old System Magic
The Blasting Rod — Its Purpose and Use
Part III of III

In the first two parts of this topic, we covered the details of the Blasting Rod: what it is, how to obtain the tree limb that will serve as the Rod, how to prepare the Rod, and how to consecrate it. In this final part, we will discuss the ways in which the Rod is used in actual practice.

After having followed the instructions from Parts I and II, you now have the finished Blasting Rod. Further, you made no error by either asperging or suffumigated it whatsoever. Rather, using a 24″ × 6″ piece of pure, white, virgin linen, you asperged that linen with Holy Water obtained from a Catholic church, and asperged it in such a way that the water cast upon the linen was done by making the Sign of the Cross over it (the linen). After completing this, you suffumigated the linen using a suffumigation composed of cedar, myrrh, and musk, in equal proportions. As a last step in the process, you left the linen alone to allow the water of aspersion to dry completely. Finally, you have the True Grimoric Blasting Rod, which you wrapped in the linen after the linen was dry, and now you have the Rod safely put away for future use. Your Rod of Power is now finished.

As you know you were instructed as follows: this weapon can be used in operating any grimoire in which no mention is made of a wand or Rod, or one in which mention is made but in which no instructions for composing or using it are given. You were also counseled that you will find when this weapon is used during Evocation to Physical Manifestation, the most spectacular and amazing results will be achieved.

The final question becomes: exactly how do you use it when working with it, and in what types or rites, ritual, or ceremonial actions can it be used?

The Blasting Rod cannot be used for any other magical practice other than Evocation to Physical Manifestation: for that—and only that—is what the grimoires are about; hence the reason for it appearing in their texts as a vital weapon necessary for success. In cases where there are no explicit instructions for its use during the Evocation to Physical Manifestation—which is the predominant situation among the different grimoires—it is not enough to have it simply lying on the Altar so as to pose some type of 'threat;' a threat that will be used against the demon if necessary. For when dealing with one of the Fallen Hierarchy you must not—cannot—'wait' until the situation reaches such a point. For by then it will be too late, and you will have lost the control which is so desperately needed in Ceremonial Magic.

Remember what I wrote in my first book, *Ceremonial Magic and the Power of Evocation*: "You must have full manifestation before you can control, and you must have complete control before you can command." And that is what the Rod does. For while the Operator is evoking, he is to hold the Rod in his right hand, the end of the Rod pointing in the general direction from which the demonic manifestation will occur. Further, since he is calling forth one of the evil ones, he is to have the end of the Rod which is fitted with the metal cap that attracts the North part of the compass needle—and thus the cap with the South Pole magnetic charge—pointed to the direction of manifestation in order to attract the demon.

The Rod also does something more, something not discussed in any grammar, but which I have found out throughout decades of practicing Experimental Magic—it aids and balances the Magician during his entrance into the state of Divine Bliss, and thus protects him during his struggle to maintain some semblance of his consciousness. The Rod provides a hold on some part of his individual "I" so that he does not dissolve into the Bliss, and either fall out of the Circle or become unconscious, and thus lay helpless and at the mercy of the demon he has summoned forth. Thus, it not only aids in forcing the demon into manifestation by attracting him to the site of Evocation to Physical Manifestation, but it protects and balances the Magician so he can endure the Bliss and yet retain that ever so tenuous beam of personal consciousness in order to complete the Ceremonial Act, and complete it successfully.

THIS is the secret of the Blasting Rod. This, and no other. THIS is why it is so important: it gives a power and control over the demon and over the Magician himself; a control that is absolutely necessary if the Magician is not only to succeed in the Ceremonial Act, but if he is to survive this most dangerous of all magical practices.

When the Magician has delivered his charge to the demon, rather than engage in the silliness of 'banishing' with pentagrams, he turns the Rod so that the end with the metal cap that attracts the SOUTH end of a compass needle is pointed toward the demon. An action that—by virtue of the cap being charged with a North pole magnetic flux—repels the demon, and forces it to relinquish its hold on this four-dimensional world of ours, and return to the depths from which it was summoned.

Now you have the full and complete knowledge of the Blasting Rod. Use it well in your work.

Concerning the Suffumigations and Fire of the Magical Art
Part III of III

A Review of The Theory and General Considerations of Herbs in the Magical Arts and Sciences

In part one of this topic I covered features of suffumigations and the theory behind them, aspects of the Subjective Synthesis in all of this, and the role of the Cause-Cause--->Effect relationship that the herbs and the Fire have to each other. In part two, I covered the way in which the Fire is to be properly prepared so that the Magician can proceed with knowledge and confidence in the proper and correct use of these ancient devices.

Now it is time to deal with the Preparation of the Suffumigation proper as we did with the Fire. As mentioned in Part II of this topic, it is not so simple and mindless as throwing some powdered herb onto a charcoal surface. There is more to it. And that 'more' will be given now so that you can operate your rituals, rites, and ceremonies successfully.

Preparation of the Suffumigation Proper

The herbs that are selected to serve as the suffumigation should be fresh if possible. Realistically, this is usually not possible for many reasons, most of which are valid. In such a case, they must be procured from an extremely reputable supplier such that they are as fresh as possible. Years ago there were many such including botanical gardens that supplied the cut and even powdered form of fresh herbs that were quick dried so as to preserve their overall qualities. While these people did not know it, the drying processes they used insured the integrity of the alchemical Salt (the body), Sulphur (the Consciousness, whose vehicle is an oil in the Herbal Kingdom of Nature) and the Mercury (the Life of the herb, whose vehicle in the Herbal Kingdom is an alcohol). Such is not the case today. From head shops to disreputable dealers in malls and on the web, there is so much deceit in obtaining quality in these things that I have come to recommend one and only one supplier of herbs:

When you obtain your herbs, always store them in airtight tins[1], or follow the instructions for "Storing Herbs" as given in *The Herb Book*, by John Lust—a book you cannot do without.

For those of you who wish to collect your own herbs from the wild, or else choose to grow your own, I strongly recommend you follow Mr. Lust's counsel as given in the section of his book entitled, "Drying Herbs." You cannot go wrong by following his directions in either storing or drying your intended "suffumigations."[2]

There is one thing about his council that you should know. Do not concern yourself with replacing your herbs after one year as suggested by Lust or others. This is most true if you are using the herbs for medicinal purposes. But when using them for suffumigations, you will find that their virtues and potency only increase, and increase greatly, with the passage of time. Why is this? Because the Mercury of the herb, trapped in an airtight vessel 'refluxes' through the container and therefore through the herb, greatly increasing its strength. You will find this to be true as you continue to practice your magical Art and Science.

Remember that for magical purposes, you can get the 'whole' form of the herb if you must, although the 'cut' form is to be

---

[1] Having the herb in direct contact with metal should be avoided. Glass jars are preferable.

[2] While extremely rare, some herbs and compounds are toxic when burned. For example, Abramelin oil is often used as a suffumigation, wherein unknowingly to the Operator, the olive oil, when burned, is harmful to the lungs. In general, if the herb irritates the skin when touched, such as poison ivy, it will irritate the mucus membranes when burned. Check it out before you burn it in large quantities in an actual evocation.

preferred. The cut form not only burns cleaner, but its potency will increase in its airtight container throughout the years, since the alchemical Mercury[1] can reflux more easily through the 'pores' (except for barks) of these smaller pieces and the interspaces between them. It is best to stay completely away from the powdered form of any herb, unless you intend to use it up completely within a few months. Why? Because powdered herbs have a tendency to 'sweat' in the airtight containers, forming lumps which begin to decay in the absence of fresh air, thus destroying the occult significance of the herb, and adding that negative condition to the rite(s) in which they are employed.

Finally, prior to using a herb in any rite, ritual, or ceremonial act, place it on a clean sheet of white paper, of virgin quality, *i.e.*, never used for any other purpose previously, and sprinkle the herb with Holy Water from a Catholic church. Sprinkle in such a way that as you cast the water upon the suffumigation you form the Sign of the Cross over it. While so asperging say,

> *I so exorcise thee, O Thou Creature of Perfume, by all of the Names and Powers of the One, Living True God, who hast created thee and me, and all things, by His living Will and Breath, and who has given and sustains the life of thee and me!*

After this, proceed with your work, using whatever additional exorcisms or consecrations the particular grammar you are working from calls for.

---

[1] This is the life force of the herb that ties the visible to the invisible. When the body decays the energy is released. Because the container is closed, it has nowhere to go, and instead is concentrated back upon its 'corps' and a minor alchemical operation is conducted. The jar becomes a de facto retort. In this case, a touch of the 'smell of death'—even that of an herb—aids in attracting the demon on some level.

You now have all you need to know of Suffumigations—their Theory, Handling, Storage, Preparation and Use, that will enable you to work unimpeded in that which you choose to do.

Chapter Five

The Theory of Magic

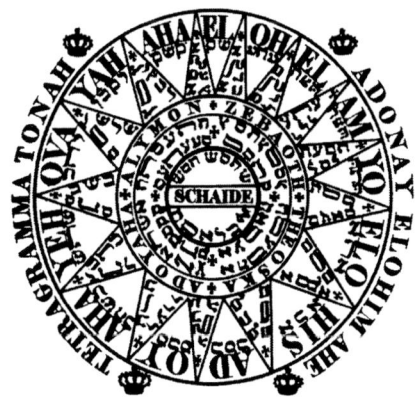

The Magical Will

There is a power within the human consciousness that has been extensively explored in magical writings. Or so it seems. I say this, because to the best of my knowledge, while the term and its use are frequently employed, the specifics of that power; that is, its nature, composition, and use, have not been clearly defined in magical or occult writings. Certainly, the field of so-called "modern psychology" has bastardized this incredible force, proclaiming it to be nothing more than a mechanistic effect, due to so many chemical and neurological processes occurring within the brain and nervous system of the individual. Yet those same 'scientific' schools of psychological thought fail to define these exact chemical compositions and interactions, while offering nothing but the most vague definitions of the neurological processes they insist are the cause behind the production of this human force.

The power (or force) to which I am referring is that of the Will. Notice I use the term "Will" instead of "Magical Will." I do this because quite frankly, this power is available for use in any human activity—not simply for its employment in some magical ritual or ceremony. However, even though we are concerned here with the Will as it applies to magical rites, it will simply be referred to as the Will throughout this paper.

We can therefore define our investigation of the Will—the Magical Will—as being a threefold phenomenon consisting of its:

1. Nature
2. Composition
3. Use (or application)

To determine and understand the nature of a thing, it is necessary to observe the effects it produces on some other thing. If we apply this to the idea of Will, we find that an equation from the physics of elementary classical Newtonian Mechanics provides a hook upon which we can hang our hat. That is:

$$W = F \bullet D \quad \text{(The Equation of Will)}$$

Here, the work, W, done on a thing (or body) is equal to a Force, F, acting on that body through a distance (or a displacement), D. The specifics of the mathematics doesn't concern us here, but the essence of the analogy does; for it brings together those features of the Will that allow us to understand its nature. Since the purpose of the Will is to bring about some exterior (external world) or interior world change (both types of change being similar to a displacement) we can conceive of the Will as being the product of an interior thought–force acting upon either some external object—or upon some internal thought, idea, or desire—that produces a state of work. That is, the exertion of this Will–force brings about a change in the initial thought, idea, desire, or physical condition of the individual. That change is a change of state in the interior condition (such as a physical cure) or in an external dilemma (such as the manifestation of some intense, personal desire.) Thus, the 'W' above not only stands for work, but for the Will, and can be seen as being the product of a though–force acting upon some desire or condition to bring about a change of state in that desire or condition. In other words, to manifest the Will of the Magician.

But the general use of the terms 'power' and 'force' are all too easy to get away with; to substitute these generalities for the real meaning of that essence which lies behind the 'Force' component of the "Equation of Will" given above. What then, can this power or force be? In physics, force is equated to energy, which is simply the ability to do work. That is, energy is defined in nonmathematical terms, as a process though which a displacement and a change of state occur, leading us right back to the concept of Work, discussed above. The same idea applies to the Will, except here we can identify F in the Equation of Will with the thought–force. Now we see that this Will, this mover of personal mountains and the initiator of one's becoming, is actually a process—not a simple event: one that is usually shrouded in secret occult jargon.

To sum up this first part of the discussion on the Will then, we see that the Will is a thought–force whose source is the energy of human consciousness, which when directed toward any external or internal condition, brings about a change of state in that condition; a change that is in line with the desired outcome of the one doing the "willing." Consequently, work is produced: work that is in keeping with the end result required by the Magician's Magical Will.

While the above discussion may seem a bit complicated at first, the reader who truly desires to intelligently use and direct his or her Will in the most dramatically effective ways possible in order to change their life conditions, will think this discussion through carefully. I have tried to word it in several different ways so that it appeals to different readers who will approach these ideas from different perspectives. For the understanding gained will be directly added to their subconscious state of subjective synthesis, thereby endowing that synthesis not only with the awesome power of understanding, but also with the power of the Will itself.

But what of the composition of the Will? Isn't the above equation enough to bring it under our dynamic conscious control through an understanding of its nature? And of our integrating this understanding into our subjective synthesis? Unfortunately, it is not. While the discussion of the *nature* of the Will is integral in placing it under one's conscious control, yet there is more to flesh out and embed into one's subconscious state of subjective synthesis if the final end—that of full conscious control of this enormous force—is to be achieved.

The Will is not composed or made up of a set of purely electrical impulses or of chemicals and their interactions, as psychologists insist. Rather, the Will is a function of a changing, conscious state of thought. We know that the Will is a process by which a thought–force acts on an object or condition to bring about a displacement and therefore a change of state of that object or situation. But this changing state of thought itself is the actual 'material' of composition' of the Will itself. Did you ever buy a movie, only to find a later "Director's Cut" version come out? You viewed the first, then the later one. While you enjoyed the first presentation, you found that the Director's Cut possessed more dialogue, action, or intense drama by the way it was edited, and that it was even better. Both contain most of the same material, but the changes in the second gave you a deeper insight and more enjoyment: a clearer 'picture' of what the movie was about. The same holds with the composition of the Will. It is in the changing images and feelings that lie behind the Will, themselves functions of the conscious states of thought, that constitute the 'stuff' of which the Will is made. It is as simple as that.

Now, what about the use or application of the Will? Put bluntly, the Will; the object or end purpose of the Will's intent, is not achieved by straining to project that intent outside of one's self into the world, or into some nebulous void 'out there.' But rather, the **use of the Will lies in what I term "Image–Emoting."** That is, **the enormous power or force of the Will is directed and guided** through the **interior processes** of using the imagination (Imaging) to build a picture of that which one desires to manifest, and to this picture (or image) add the propelling, dynamic, charging energy of the emotions (Emoting: as in, the desire to have). It is this **charged vision** which the Magician takes into the final ritual or ceremonial act. These final, physically based psychic actions of Ritual or Ceremonial Magic then, act as a *series of lenses* through which the desires and wants of the Will are not only projected into the world of form, but through which those desires and wants are magnified in intensity. Thus, it is through these final actions—that the interiorization which has taken place in the Astral, and which has taken on astral form through the action of the Will—become exteriorized in world of form known as Malkuth. For it must be remembered at all times that the **Process of Creation** begins; has its point-of-origin or First Cause, *within the mind of the Magician*. This is the **World of Causation**. It is only *manifest* in the **Word of Effects**; into this ever-changing state of Malkuthian *Actuality*. I use the term "Actuality" because what we see in the world of form; what we observe in our daily lives, are only so many shadows thrown upon this ever changing world–screen by the creations that occur within the mind: where the source of all creation truly and exclusively occurs. It is this inner world, this realm of the mind, that constitutes the only **Reality** we can ever know.

How does one go about effectively strengthening and placing the Will under full control? I recommend that the interested reader look for and study the following:

- "Imaging Versus Visualization" (below)
- In the "Questions and Answers" chapter of this book in which Concentration and Meditation are dealt with.
- Step VI in Israel Regardie's classic, *Twelve Steps to Spiritual Enlightenment*.
- Roberto Assagioli's book, *The Act of Will*.

Regardie's Step VI, while important, does not give one full *conscious* control over the Will, simply because it places only those subconscious (unconscious) elements of the Will under the aegis of the conscious mind's control. As important as this is, it is not sufficient, since the conscious mind's interaction with—and control of—the Will is not addressed. Assagioli's work, however, deals with the conscious *and* unconscious control of the Will in a very effective and complete way. Thus, by combining the knowledge given in Regardie's book with Assagioli's and my own references above, the aspirant will have all that he or she needs to effectively and fully control and direct the power of their Will.

It is also important to note that Assagioli's other book, *Psychosynthesis: A Manual of Principles and Techniques*, is an extremely valuable aid to the Magician for the psychic and spiritual exercises it gives (there is a newer version of this book currently available entitled, *Psychosynthesis: A Collection of Basic Writings*. I have no experience with this latter book, and so only recommend the manual cited above. The manual is available from used books dealers.) Assagioli was a Psychoanalyst who founded his own school of thought based upon the spiritual foundation of the individual's inner constitution, unlike the mechanistic schools of thought produced by such analysts as Freud, Horney, and Adler. As a review of that book states, 'Assagioli evolved a system of therapeutics that treats the mental, emotional, physical and spiritual components of an individual's nature, and integrates them into a whole being.' And this is exactly what his techniques do. Using it in tandem with Regardie's Twelve Steps to Spiritual Enlightenment is the best way I know of to fully explore and integrate the various *psychic and spiritual* aspects of one's own secret nature.

I trust that this short paper will be of help to many on their Paths, the final destination of which can only be the discovery of their own True Self, and that personal Truth that is theirs to claim.

"Imaging" Versus "Visualization"

Much has been made of "Visualization" or "Creative Visualization" in New Age circles. Indeed, there are entire books numbering hundreds of pages supposedly dealing with this 'arcane' function of the human psyche. In fact, this process of "Imaging" as I prefer to call it, is most readily and directly addressed and developed in the aspirant by a very simple method. If used properly (that is, 'honestly') the individual will find their ability to see—both within the mind and in their physical surroundings—that which is necessary in any given work: be it a work of magical practice or ritual, or an object or condition of daily life. Furthermore, it will also develop and hone the memory to an exceedingly high degree, as well as give the practitioner a greater sense of his or her Self. That is, the individual's self-awareness will increase sharply due to an expansion of consciousness. The method is really very simple.

Exercise 1 — Close your eyes and image any four numbers between 11 and 99, and multiply them together—in your mind—until you get the correct answer. For example. Multiply 36 × 48. As you will find, it sounds easier than it is in actual practice. Keep seeing these four numbers and the numbers they generate from the multiplication until you can see the final product clearly in your mind. Then, using a calculator or paper and pencil, multiply the numbers out and check your 'mental' result. Do this practice three times a day for as many weeks (or months) as it takes to become proficient.

Exercise 2 — After mastering Exercise 1, choose any six numbers between 111 and 999. For instance, you might select 101 × 456. Continue as before, seeing the numbers in your mind as you multiply them, one-by-one, and finally add up the rows that appear on the screen of your mind. When you are certain you have the correct answer, check your mental calculations by hand, or use a calculator. Continue this process three times a day for as many weeks (or months) until you become proficient in this practice.

Exercise 3 — You will probably notice that in the first two exercises, the numbers you 'saw' in your mind automatically present themselves in a bright, light color, or even appeared to be the color, white. This is simply because your physical eyes were trying to 'see' in the imposed darkness you created by closing them. But you were not trying to 'see in the dark,' were you? You were (and still are!) trying to *see in your mind*, and hence develop your Imaging faculty.

So how do you overcome this? Yes, you struggled mightily to master the multiplication of two numbers by two numbers, and then three numbers by three numbers, and you have succeeded. And as you mastered those two exercises, perhaps you noticed that the brightness of the colors dimmed, the better you became at the exercises. This is because your 'inner eye'—your mind's eye—became more open and began to dominate your physical eyes' attempt to 'see in the darkness.' But you are not done yet.

Your faculty of Imaging is not yet fully developed. To fully open your mind's eye, take the experiment one step further.

Return to Exercise 2, and begin multiplying any three numbers by three numbers again. But this time, *change the colors of the numbers*. You might use red at first, then change to orange, next, green, then blue, and so on. As you continue this 'coloring' process, at some point you will notice *you have become mind*. That is, you will become completely unaware of your body. The 'seeing in the dark'—which your physical eyes strived for—has completely fallen away, and you are now a only *conscious being performing the exercise*. Can you imagine how this developed faculty of Imaging will help you in your magical rituals by developing your Astral Vision? How much more self-aware and comprehending you will become in your daily life? How much more aware you will be of the streams of thought that pass through your mind? This is why I make the distinction between "Visualization" or "Creative Visualization" and what I call, "Imaging." There is a vast difference between them, both in technique and more importantly—in result.

Try these exercises if you are serious about your magical development and gaining control over your daily life.

Comprehension versus Apprehension, and Their Roles in the Magical Process of Attainment

Over the past several months, many people have written to me regarding the subject of the paper presented here. People who are *working*, and who are struggling to implement what I have written in my books and on this website. While a significant number of them have succeeded in obtaining results to their liking, others have missed the mark, becoming confused by the differences between Comprehension and Apprehension. Yet, they have continued to work, and while doing so, have written to me asking for additional concise explanations of these psychic functions. It is to these people that I owe a further explanation of the roles of Comprehension and Apprehension. For only those who *work* can gain the insights into the complexities of the process of building and polishing their subconscious state of Subjective Synthesis, so that it enables them to manifest their will in the world to the extent they wish. It is to these individuals that I dedicate this writing.

When I speak of the proper building and polishing of the subconscious state of Subjective Synthesis, it is my policy to point out the four-fold process that makes such a structuring and refinement possible. Namely,

Study—>Understanding—>Comprehension—>Apprehension

Certainly, at first glance it seems simple enough. And as far as the first two procedures are concerned, the process is simplicity itself. That is, one must first sit down and study—consciously seek to understand the subject material at hand which—after a certain period of time and with due effort—results in the individual obtaining an *intellectual familiarity* and grasp of the material: or, an 'Understanding' of the *new knowledge,* if you will. But here the simplicity of the process breaks down for some, because they cannot see the difference between 'Understanding' something and 'Comprehending' it. Usually, they mistake the attainment of deeper levels of Understanding for Comprehension, and so expect that the final part of the process, the 'Apprehension,' will occur by itself. All too often however, they find that the deeper Understanding was not the Comprehension they sought, and consequently the Apprehension never occurs—and their lack of *full* magical results stands as evidence of the correctness of their latter conclusion. So what then exactly is this thing called 'Comprehension,' and how does it lead to the final goal of 'Apprehension?'

Comprehension arises when unique insights into, and an expansion of the material studied, visits itself upon the mind. *This does **not** occur from continuous study of the material. In fact, it **never** occurs in this way. Rather, Comprehension occurs when one thinks the material through while away from the formal study of it, and while he is (usually) engaged in some non-intellectual primary—or diversionary—activity. For instance, one may be taking a peaceful walk in the mountains or in a park away from other people, and while doing so, suddenly decides to mull over the material that was formally studied. Suddenly, he begins to see the material in a new light, and gains insight into its **intrinsic meaning**. Then, he begins to make connections with other similar—or even seemingly dissimilar—material,* and so arrives at a deep, **personal** intimacy of the new knowledge previously studied and understood, and the relationship that knowledge bears to other ideas. **This is Comprehension.**

Now, Apprehension is a more difficult state to achieve, for it implies—in the sense I use this word—*the psychic assimilation of the knowledge that was formerly comprehended.* How does one attain to such a high-sounding state and what does this mean? *The Apprehension I speak of can only be obtained through the* **Practice** *of that which was formerly comprehended.* That is, when one puts into practice—into *action*, as in a ritual practice or ceremonial performance—the *knowledge* that was derived from *Study and Understanding*, and which was later **comprehended** as explained—this practice leads to an *Experiential Knowledge* which the psychic constitution of the individual recognizes as *a new dimension of existence* and one which it—sooner or later—adds to itself.

Why does the psyche react so? Because the Interior nature of the individual comes to see this newly comprehended knowledge as something 'different;' something it desires to make a part of its own constitution in an effort to *expand its own nature.* And it does this by 'owning' this new knowledge. And to own, it must make this new 'acted out' knowledge a *living part of itself.* This is why the proper building and polishing of one's subconscious state of Subjective Synthesis is such a difficult and time consuming thing to achieve; for it both presupposes and requires that the individual spends a massive amount of time in the four-fold process given in the beginning of this paper.

To be sure, without such a Subjective Synthesis, the magician can (still) most definitely make progress and manifest **something** of his will in the world of matter. But such manifestations will never be to his complete liking or satisfaction, nor will they take him to those places in life that he so desires to be. In addition, he risks no end of large-scale Slingshot Effects from the work he does; effects that are a normal and natural function of magical practices themselves. Again, why? *Because unless the psyche takes for its own this secret knowledge—by making alive through assimilation that which was comprehended—it cannot adequately adjust to, and handle the forces of, those magical practices summoned forth or called down into the magician's being. It is as simple as that.*

This is why I do my best to discourage any and all from Magic who take a flippant attitude toward it. For without a thorough knowledge of the subconscious state of Subjective Synthesis and the four-fold process that enables it; and without one putting into that process the unbelievable amount of time demanded by this process, one is not simply playing a type of 'Magical Russian Roulette:' he is playing it with all of the cylinders loaded. And this being the case, tragedy is only a simple click—or in our parlance, one poorly performed rite or ceremonial action—away. Be guided accordingly.

The Terror of Apparent Reality

We look at the world around us everyday, and react to what we see. The coldness of base matter; the rigidity of physical laws that define what we can and cannot do with that matter; the unforgiving attitudes of men and society; the tenuous nature of even our closest associations; the financial demands that press upon us from all sides; the specter of the veiled future. Is it any wonder so many of us have turned to Magic or Mysticism (or both) in an effort to change the structure of these uncertainties; to mold conditions and circumstances to our will; to find some measure of relief through such affirming activities that assure us we are not powerless, puppet-like playthings abandoned by some freak chance event of the universe that set all into motion?

This ultimate, underlying feeling of fatality of human existence is too well known by all of us: whether we be atheist, agnostic, believer, or religionist. None escape those unpredictable moments when this fatality is seen with such stark clarity that we are swept into believing that regardless of what we do, we will be pulled under by these fatalistic tides that truly do rule and govern the physical universe—and our very lives. At these times we feel it is all so pointless—this believing, struggling, striving, and working to turn those uncontrolled, ever-changing streams of limitation away from us, and somehow make ourselves lord and master of our world and our own life.

The question is, what do we really *know* of these physical and personal worlds in which we live, move, and have our being? Is there any way we can analyze them so that maybe—just maybe—all of our magical work and mystical strivings are not simply vainglorious attempts at deluding ourselves, but are actually viable methods that we can use to crown our lives with success and fulfillment? Success and fulfillment that we somehow instinctively 'feel' is our true inalienable right? I think there is. In fact, from my perspective—based upon my own life experiences 'out there' in the 'real' world, and my involvement in both Magic and Mysticism—I *know* there is. And this is what I would like to share with you here and now. Perhaps it will even give some of you new insight into your own perceptions and perspectives of this thing we call "reality" and arm you with new ways to react and interact with it.

We can *know* the following. That the world of base matter 'out there' is just that: a universe that operates according to well-defined laws. If you trip, you fall. If you stop breathing, you die. It is harder to walk up stairs than it is to walk down. All of these physical laws operating in base matter serve us well once we understand them. And while they can be modified or adapted in certain ways, in their essence, they are fixed: at least, as far as we know, based upon our everyday interaction with them. Whether new laws will be discovered that will increase our knowledge and expand our eventual use of these older laws remains to be seen. But for now, "what you see is what you get" certainly applies to the fixed behavior of these physical laws. But our problems don't generally involve struggling with these laws; at least, not so they keep us up at night, make our emotional lives pure hell during our waking hours, or turn us into mental robots, commanded to buy every new fad idiocy that crosses our television screens. No. Our problems lie in those situations and conditions that are inextricably interlinked—not with the world of matter directly—but with the world of men: the world of personal situation, apparent life-condition, and living productive, prosperous, and happy lives.

Why such a long statement of the 'obvious?' Why is it so important to differentiate between the world of base matter and those personal worlds of ours? Because all too often we allow the line dividing them to become so blurred that we forget that there are differences between them, and begin treating our personal worlds as if they too operated according to so many similar laws throughout the world of matter. Example. "If I work hard, I'll not only keep my job, but go up the company ladder." Or, "If I study hard, I'll make better grades and get into a better graduate school (or get a better job, or a position that will allow me to marry the boss's daughter, or the boss's son, or what have you)." *We have a talent for trying to take the guaranteed results of physical law and translate them into our personal world* through such 'reasoning.' In effect, *we are so sold on the apparent nature of the reality of the material world, that we feel we can mimic its laws and use them to get what we want and where we want, by clawing and scratching in the world of men.* The tragedy of this type of thinking is very well mirrored in that 1970s song, "Do You Know the Way to San Jose?" And so it goes. Year after year, decade after decade, until all that is left are those few precious, remaining years, and—the open grave. But if we are to turn this situation around, it takes more than realizing that we cannot mimic physical law and scratch and claw in the world of men. We have to look deeply into the fabric of our own personal worlds; our worlds of situation, condition, and circumstance, and see what we find there. And what we find there may very well surprise you.

When we examine our personal worlds, we see that they are composed of one singular quality upon which all other states hinge: *that of ceaseless change; of continual flux*. Nothing remains as it is: all is constantly turning into something else—whether we like it or not; whether it is what we desire or not. It is as if this thing we term "reality" is not really 'real' after all. Because if it were, then certainly there would be more permanency to it than there is; something that would mimic the permanency of physical law, but which it does not. In fact, this is correct: what we see is "apparent reality" only: that which I refer to as "***Actuality***." The very word itself—derived from the term "act"—bespeaks of a series of conditions that by definition must change until the event itself reaches culmination. And all acts take place on some type of screen or stage; one that allows the progression of events to occur, as the Causal Agent behind the act dictates.

If there is a Causal Agent underlying every human act, and if this act is the basis of all Actuality, then two conditions must apply. First, there must be some force behind the act. Second, as stated above, there must be some place for that Actuality to be played out. What could this Causal Agent be that underlies all human actions, and which gives rise to this Actuality that is then played out on some screen or stage? Of course, it is *thought* itself. The entire world of human affairs, conditions, and situations can now be seen as nothing more than a screen or stage that provides the setting for Actuality. An Actuality which is literally created by our very thoughts.

But as each act is composed of a series of movements, so too is the Causal Agent that creates this Actuality. That is, this Causal Agent does not consist of a single thought, but of *patterns of thoughts*, the individual elements of which are of like or similar kinds of thoughts. *These thoughts—whether for good or ill—are the sum and substance of Reality;* the inner Reality of the mind, not of the ever-changing forms found in the outside world of human conditions and situations. Contemplated over time, mused over, taken apart, analyzed, and considered, these patterns of thought are projected outward upon a physical and personal universe: a theater, where they take an exact form in that ever-changing Actuality which we carelessly call *reality*. In fact, there is nothing 'real' about this outer world reality at all: it is nothing more than an "Apparent Reality" or Actuality. An Actuality whose forms, conditions, and situations change as rapidly and completely as do the thoughts of the individual who is generating the Causal Agent. The terror of this apparent reality is a reaction of ignorance to something no more real than an illusionary brick wall that possesses no substance whatsoever. For if the individual learns to form, control, and project his thought by some technical device, then his Actuality will become the exact mirror image of that inner Reality: the domain of his dominant thought patterns.

But how are such thought patterns projected? Is it a matter of struggling to release some series of thoughts, or grunting and grimacing to externalize the Causal Agent on the screen of Apparent Reality so that which is desired is manifested in this ever-changing world of form? The devices used for such projection are what all of us having been doing all along: Magic and Mysticism. And in the latter case, using what I refer to as "Higher Mysticism" (New Thought) to manifest that which we will. Whether it be a mystical contemplation exercise or the fashioning of the Blasting Rod of Art, all are devices we use to project the thought patterns of our minds into the fabric of Actuality such that our will is made manifest in the world of form.

Be not deceived by the seemingly 'separate virtues' of any such device. They possess virtue, yes. But in the final analysis, even that virtue is due to the patterns of expectations and thoughts generated by the practitioner. The time comes when all such tools can and must be laid aside, and the Patterns of Creation called up by the Practitioner made manifest in the world of Actuality, due solely to the Practitioner being able to become One with both Reality and Actuality at his choosing. Continue to learn, understand, comprehend, and eventually apprehend your Magic and Mysticism. Continue to use those devices of each to achieve the projection necessary at the point you are currently at in these fields. But also remember; let that awareness be part of you, that the world you seek to change is as pliable and adaptable to your thought as a lump of clay is to your fingers. And remember too, that all of the power needed for creating all that you desire in the world of form is within you at all times, and nowhere else. The next time you undertake that mystical meditation or handle that magical weapon in some rite or ceremony, preface your work by recalling that they are tools—necessary tools for the present—but tools that your mind and hand will one day outgrow. Continue to work, but at all times, remember that all Cause lies within you, and nowhere else. You will find it easier said than done—at first.

If this paper has been difficult to read, rest assured, it was even more difficult to write. But it contains much that will enable the serious student to further build his state of Subjective Synthesis, so that he can achieve that Unity spoken of above.

Efficacy and its Role in Old System Magic

There is an underlying theme which has been all but forgotten in the practice of contemporary magic: that of efficacy. If you think about the following, chances are you just may see it for yourself:

> "Along with this is the question of 'paying the price' of success in whatever it is we do—magic, alchemy, professional or personal life choices. The price we pay is the mark of our commitment to the goal we seek to realize. How often haven't you been told by

someone who contacts you, "I'll do anything! Anything to learn magic, alchemy, etc." only to ask a few questions and realize that the person who has come to you asking for your time, knowledge, and experience places more emphasis on their monthly cable TV fee, martial arts instruction, or visit to the tattoo parlor or body piercing than in actually learning occult arts. They are not willing to do whatever it takes, only to SAY whatever it takes."

That is, underlying people's unwillingness to 'do whatever it takes' to succeed, is their *unconscious rejection of the Principle of Efficacy*. Yes, it *manifests* in the ways stated in the above quotation. But always this deep, *fundamental rejection* is the **causal agent** behind the **effect** that manifests as one's refusal to work. That is, to do *real work*, regardless of the cost in time, effort, energy, or money.

Why should we be so concerned with this causal force? Why did the Fathers of the Grimoires insist on an absolute adherence to its dictates? Why should we expend every effort to comply with the injunctions laid down by this 'old fashioned' principle? The answer is quite simple, yet the mechanics behind it may surprise you.

The noun, "efficacy," literally means "The **power** to **produce** an **effect**." That is, efficacy is—in and of itself—a 'power' or 'force' that when directed in some way produces a (predetermined) effect. Without this power (force), nothing can be accomplished; for the *energy of* **motivation and manifestation**—so important in the production of the (desired) effect—is missing. This most basic of all magical principles was second nature to the magicians of the Dark Ages, the Medieval and Renaissance eras, and was as much a part of their ritual acts or ceremonial actions as was the construction and consecration of their Circles of Art. This is why many of the grimoires do not belabor the point or go into it beyond only the briefest of mentions: it was understood to be the foundation upon which the entire magical rite was based.

But why is this so? What is the **nature** of this energy that the seemingly endless search for "a black rooster that never trod hen," or for a ring of pure gold with certain inscriptions upon it, that is transferred to the rite such that success is more probable with it, or utterly impossible without it? The energy that is imparted is so great and of such magnitude, that all other natural phenomena must kneel before it. *For it is the energy of the Hidden Self: the energy of the magician's Spiritual Source which—operating in and through the magician—manifests in the rite to produce the desired effect.* And this is brought about by the magician involving his total self in acquiring just those 'rare' and hard-to-find materials, altered states of consciousness, or correct use of the Names of Power that the ritual acts or ceremonial actions require. *For it is through the intense thought; the self-disciplined searches; the step-by-step, daily, weekly, or monthly one-pointed conscious focus of the magician's mind on the rite and its requirements, that those channels needed for the force to flow from his Spiritual Source into the ritual, are established.*

This is why so many today fail in their modern day magical practices, or indeed, in their daily, mundane lives. Instead of using a wand made of Hazel or Oak, they use a dowel stick purchased from their local hardware store. Instead of devoting an extra four hours after the (normal) workday to the report the boss wants done in a certain way, they grudgingly give one hour and simply highlight what is expedient. And then such people wonder why their magic fails, or why one of their co-workers gets that raise, promotion, or both. And always, it's the book's fault or their 'bad luck.' No. It's their lack of efficacy; their refusal to apply their entire conscious—and therefore unconscious—selves to the task at hand.

It would do all of us no end of good when facing some seemingly daunting task to stand back, take a deep breath, and decide which way we will proceed: give the efficacy to the act that it requires if we want to succeed, or pull back and do what is expedient and easy. For if we do the latter, we had better prepare for something else too: inevitable failure. But then, you just might be surprised how many people 'demand' success from life in all things because they have been taught to give the least and expect the most. That may be the "American way." After all, it is their "right." But it is *not **our*** way: the way of the magician, or the way of the mystic. Efficacy is the basis upon which all lasting efforts are built. It is a force—pure and simple. An irresistible force that can and will cut through or disintegrate any immovable object or impossible condition, regardless of how immovable that obstacle may be, or how impossible that condition may seem. So get use to it. There is simply no other way to make your magic work—or to live your life.

The Four Words of Personal Power

There are many Words of Power in Magic. From the various Divine Names of God, to the unknown words used in invocation and evocation; from the generally known names of spirits, to the derived names of others yet unknown; from the names of the mighty Archangels to names of the Angels of the NAME; from the designation of each of the Fallen, the possession and understanding of which "…giveth one control over them and their Offices…" to words given the magician by those summoned forth: Words of Power by which he can create wonders in the world of men; to the special Words given him by his own Holy Guardian Angel during the climax of the Visitation. Throughout all of Magic, we are surrounded by forms and frequencies of audible energy that have been designed to bring about the results we so earnestly seek.

But there are other "Words of Power" as well. Words that when used consciously, daily, by men and women, can enable them to rule and regulate their own lives, directly and powerfully, quite apart from the secret Words of the magical rite. At the same time—and of equal importance to their use in daily life—these "**Four Words of Power**" as I term them, will enable the astute individual to rigorously evaluate the claims made by any magical book of any era, or of any author. This alone is worth the effort to learn and use these Four Words on a continuous basis.

And just what are these Four Words of Power? They are four simple words that when strung together create a profound impression on the mind of the user. They rip away the vain hopes, empty wishes, and general mental miasma of warm and fuzzy thinking that has buried so many for so long in their own private tombs of despair and fear; of want and desire; of need and longing. These Four Words of Power are simply,

"WHERE IS THE PROOF?"

or

"WHERE (or WHAT) ARE THE RESULTS?"

Think about it. You are bombarded daily, hourly, by a continuous stream of information from others and from yourself. Whether it is your friend trying to convince you that he or she is right in this or that, or some advertisement telling you that you simply can't live without this new—and generally useless—fad product, to your own inner dialogues telling you to "do this now" and "do that later" and all "because...", and yet that blank after the "because" is never filled in. In short, most of us operate as automatons, never questioning the data that never stops impinging upon our minds and emotions, and which determines to a very large extent our actions, and therefore our lives. Let's take a few examples to examine the application of these Four Words of Power more carefully.

Let's take a look at my three books. In *Ceremonial Magic and the Power of Evocation,* I made many very direct, powerful claims as to what the Operator can expect from a properly performed Evocation to Physical Manifestation. For someone to flat out 'believe' these claims would be tantamount to their using the same 'logic' they use when buying that whiz-bang New Age book that tells them how to turn themselves invisible by going into a dark closet and thinking themselves invisible. (Don't laugh. I saw such a book 20 years ago!) This is not fair to either the individual or to the author; this blanket acceptance of what I (or any author) writes.

By asking "Where is the proof?" or "What are the results?", the individual's mental attitude toward my work (or another author's) immediately changes. Instead of their mental world being filled with fanciful images of "profit and delight" as Dr. Faustus uttered when considering his first evocation, a strong note of caution suddenly overtakes the individual's mind; a new feeling of skepticism that now tells the individual, "I'd better hold off on what I think of this. In fact, if I want to really find out if this guy is right, I'd better read this thing carefully, think it through, and decide whether or not to follow it to the letter. Not just to prove him right or wrong—if I get what I want I couldn't care less if he's right or wrong about everything—but to get what I'm after! So I'd better snap out of my cozy daydream state and treat this matter seriously if I intend to get to where I want to go!"

In *Kabbalistic Cycles and the Mastery of Life,* I laid out a system of thought which is divinatory in nature, but which can be used by anyone at any time, anyplace, in any situation, and all without others being aware the one using it is gaining the edge in the situation. Further, I stated that when the individual's subconscious state of Subjective Synthesis is properly built up and polished, the results of this system are infallible: they give the calculated results 100% or the time, and those results will always be as expected. That's some claim! So what does the intelligent individual do? He or she **TESTS** the system, and tests it ruthlessly and exactly, building and polishing their Subjective Synthesis along the way. What do you think they will find? I know what they will find, as I do with the book on Ceremonial Magic. But that is the whole point: **THEY** must find out for themselves, and always, by asking, "**Where are the results?**" or "**Where is the proof?**"

In *Kabbalistic Handbook for the Practicing Magician,* I insisted on a "Kabbalistic Analysis" being performed on each and every magical ritual, rite, and ceremony to be performed, gave examples of how such an analysis is done, and in addition, set out some rather different and unique meditative techniques and ways of entering the Sephiroth themselves by means of the Tarot and the Paths of the Holy Tree of Life. Again, some big claims on my part. But it is quite an easy matter for the individual to determine if I am worth my salt or not, and therefore benefit their life accordingly. And all by simply asking: "Where is the proof?" or "What are the results?" This is all that is necessary. Asking these questions sobers the mind, rips away any fancy delusions, and sets the mind to task. After the experimental period is completed and the data is obtained, then—and only then—can the individual determine if the system is as viable and valuable as I claim it to be, and if it has any utility in their lives.

The same Four Words of Power are easily applied to any life situation: from your boss's pat on the back for the "…good work you've been doing…" to his giving you a raise in pay because of that good work, to your friend's claim that "I'd do anything to help you! Just ask!" All can be fairly evaluated and judiciously used to your further life-advantage. It's all up to YOU—as usual.

The bottom line in using these Four Words lies simply in your using this device to clear your mind of fanciful and unrealistic expectations, and to properly, impartially, and fairly evaluate any person, claim, situation, or circumstance. All of us let far too much of our lives and the power those lives possess, disappear into mental laziness and fantastic expectations, while laying the blame for our disappointments and failures always at another place—the doorstep of another.

If you try these Four Words, I think you will be pleased with your newly discovered power. If you use them consistently, I am willing to wager you will have more personal control over your life, and experience more personal success in your daily life on all levels than you ever have before.

Chapter Six

The Practice of Magic

The Magical Chamber

In contemporary magic, the ritual and ceremonial area of operation is usually referred to as a "Temple," this tradition coming down to us from the original Holy and Hermetic Order of the Golden Dawn. To be sure, earlier sources have used this same terminology. But after the destruction of the original London-based Order of the Golden Dawn, the scattered membership popularized the term by establishing their own working magical groups here and there. But just what is this area of operation, and more importantly, why do I make a distinction between the use of the word "Temple" and "Magical Chamber?" The reasons are actually simple and are interconnected.

The performance of ritual and ceremonial work is very serious business, as any *successful* Practitioner of magic knows. Such a *performance* or *act* is not some haphazardly thrown together set of physical actions and verbal mumblings meant to produce a desired effect, although this is what the New Age has characterized it as being. The solemnity and importance of a properly performed ritual—let alone an act of High Ceremonial Magic such as Evocation to Physical Manifestation—**cannot** take place in what the popularly defined term, "Temple," has come to mean today: some hastily converted bedroom or part of a bedroom, living room, or even large utility closet. Neither can daily performances of the *seemingly* most 'simple' of ritual work—for instance, the Lesser Banishing Ritual of the Pentagram (LBRP)—take place in such a contrivance. That is, not so the work can be performed properly, and the desired results or effects obtained. For the idea of "space" is integral to the human mind. It is a concept wars have been waged over, people have struggled to claim for their own, and others have died for in order to secure. And that is what a true "Temple" or as I call it, a "Magical Chamber," really is. It is in every way connected at the deepest levels of the mind with the idea of "identity," while also being a place wherein the individual can *choose* to interact (or not) with those things that are both a part of their own nature, as well as with those things and others that are alien or not an immediate part of that nature. It becomes literally, a place or "space" that serves for deliberate meetings and exchanges; for transacting business; and as a reception area for meeting a person of rank or authority.

Over time—and through work and devotion—this place also becomes a vessel or receptacle of stored energy: whether it be the energy of daily emotion, or the energy resulting from practicing the Secret Arts and Sciences. Have you never hear a person say, "This is my home! I wouldn't sell it for anything! There is so much of me (or, "my life") in here; so much blood, sweat, and tears, that I couldn't possibly part with it!" This is because that place has become an *extension of themselves*; a receptacle of such emotional energy, that to separate one from the other would bring about the ruin of both. Hence, I use the term "**Magical Chamber**" to represent just such an area of operation, as opposed to that convenience used by 'moderns' to indicate a temporary area to 'do magic in'—what they call a "Temple."

But the complaint is immediately raised that with the prevailing economic and social conditions of the times, the 'average' practicing magician cannot afford a private house or large apartment that would allow them to establish a separate, unique room that would become their Magical Chamber. Indeed, most Practitioners complain they barely have enough room to 'live in!' If this is the case, and what I have said about "space" being integral to one's very identity is true, what then, is this saying about the individual's clear identity (perception) of 'who' and 'what' they are? How can such a basically undefined individual possibly practice the magical arts effectively? The answer is, such a one cannot; at least, not effectively. In fact, I have found this lack of clear identity to be one of the *prime reasons* many people, otherwise talented in magic, either fail to produce any magical results whatsoever, or produce those partial results that have come to define the New Age and its teachings; one of which is, 'any spare bedroom or part of one will do.' *Thus, I use the term, Magical Chamber to indicate a completely separate, enclosed, easily sealed area, that is never entered unless there is ritual or ceremonial work to do*. In this area the Impedimenta of the Art are NOT produced. There are no glaring pictures of magical or occult themes to incite the imagination. The floor is completely bare, and any windows are not only permanently blacked out, but are covered so as to remove the idea they are even present. This special space also contains only two items:

1. A properly painted "Circle Template"
2. A plain, wooden Altar with cabinet, completely undecorated

As to the "Circle Template." This is a series of concentric circles, the outer of which is nine feet in diameter, the two inner of which are a hand's breath distant from each other (I covered this matter in detail in *Ceremonial Magic and the Power of Evocation*. It is so constructed, such that the inner areas of the circles are left blank, enabling the magician to write in the appropriate names and draw the corresponding seals of the demons or beings being worked with, and according to the particular grimoire being used. During daily performances such as the LBRP, the boundary of the outer circle becomes a fixed reference point for the tracing of that ritual's pentagrams, thus insuring both the angles of the pentagrams and the circle connecting them is closed.)

The wooden Altar is that basic design taken from *The Book of the Sacred Magic of Abramelin the Mage*. It has great utility in all areas of magic, without being cumbersome and without taking up more area in the Magical Chamber than is necessary. It is placed at the exact center of the third and innermost circle, and remains there in a fixed position.

So what does the serious Practitioner of the Art and Science of Magic do? It is all a matter of priority and sincerity. Accommodations *must* be obtained that will allow the individual to perform his or her magical work in a separate room: an enclosed space that becomes the Magical Chamber, and one in which the essential guidelines given above can be fulfilled. It has never been easy for magicians throughout time to avail themselves of these prime conditions. From Henry Cornelius Agrippa to (during his early days) Dr. John Dee; from Eliphas Levy to Israel Regardie: all faced the same dilemma. Yet they—and all those who were and are serious about practicing Magic, and even more serious about obtaining *complete* results—have seen to it that these conditions were/are met.

It is not enough to justify one's current predicament by saying, "Well, that's all well and good for this writer to say! He's nothing but a purist! But I live in a *real* world, and have duties to take care of, bills to pay, and a life to live!" My answer to them is "**So do I**." But unlike the complainers and those who seek every and any excuse for the proper execution of our Art and Science, no one of good conscience—that is, one who knows what must be done—can say, "Oh well. Looks like I'd just better stay with my New Age stuff and do the best I can!" Because that "best" will never be good enough—and neither will the results.

The reigning 'wisdom' of the day which proclaims, 'It is better to do some magic then to do none at all,' is as ludicrous as is the phrase, "...a little bit pregnant." You either practice Magic or you don't; you either are pregnant, or you are not. The well-known belief, 'Well, things really aren't black or white; there are many shades of gray in between' is a catch all for failure. A timid justification for not being able to handle a situation; but rather, for allowing it to handle you. This is how Nature and its Laws work: there are never any excuses; there are no shades of gray in between. Gravity either works, or it doesn't. Electromagnetic fields either travel out into space at the speed of light (in a vacuum) or they do not. Even in that shadow world of Quantum Mechanics, the probability that an electron is either in this area or another is calculated. And even in the resulting probabilities, the results are so accurate, that such things as computers are designed by the rules governing quantum phenomena. There are 'rules' applicable to all these Laws, yes. But they are rules that allow us to use those Laws precisely, in any part of the known universe.

Look around you now, and tell yourself how delighted you are with your current position in life. Ask yourself how much you have contributed to the world, save for 'getting through' the next day, or week, or month. You are more than that. *Much, much more* indeed. For that Divine Essence within you seeks to express ITSELF and create in this world and *through you*, and either IT, you, or BOTH of you have chosen Magic as the pathway by which these expressions and creations are to come into this plane of existence. You can disappoint yourself: but please, don't disappoint the God within you. You will gain nothing if you do—and that you already know.

You do not need any books either, telling you 'how' to 'build' your "Temple." You need no New Age fad designs, pretty paintings, haunting pictures hung on the walls to make you 'feel powerful' and mysterious, or 'like a magician.' You need no music to 'get you in the mood' to do either your daily ritual work, or that High Magical Ceremonial performance which will take you to the very rim of human experience. All you need is what you already have: that Part of God within you, the Work itself, your devotion to that Work, your determination to succeed, the original grimoires—not some 'rewritten,' or 'edited' or 'expanded' New Age version of them, and—a proper Magical Chamber. When you have these things; when you weld them into a holy unity through your own efforts, then and only then will the day of your Becoming that which you already ARE become manifested in this world. And all those things; those beads and baubles you coveted throughout your life; all will be seen to be what they always were: trinkets to amuse the mind and satiate desire. The ironic part is, you will find yourself having such a wealth of them, as to truly delight the mind. And all, because you sought their opposite: your Becoming through the Great Work, and this in the privacy of your own Magical Chamber.

The Circle of Science and Art

Why do I term this device used in ritual and ceremonial magic—the Circle—as being one of both science and art? Because in fact, it is both. Or rather it should be, to the mind of the practicing magician. From the earliest grimoires of the Dark Ages to those of the Middle Ages, the Circle is found to be the principle weapon used in magical acts. It not only serves as the chief defense against demonic beings, but as a fortress from negative external influences that may operate in the area in which magical rites are performed, as well as being a unique stratagem through which the magician makes a declaration of the Divinity that is within him. It is that Holy Right by which the Operator calls Godhead down into Manhood (or conversely, summons the Divinity within from its deepest recesses in his nature) while attempting to elevate his Manhood toward Godhead.

It only requires some modest research to realize that the magicians who composed the early grimoires were anything but the ignorant, salivating, despots whose sole intent was the quick and immediate gratification of their whims, fantasies, and lustful desires. To be sure, once those grammars of magic escaped from the hands of their creators and became copied and later reprinted en masse, the latter type of individual quickly grabbed them up, and gave rise to the image of the ritual and ceremonial magician described above. But this does not preclude the fact that the creators of the grammars were educated in language, art, history, mathematics, and the science of their day, if only because they (initially) came from the priest-class of the Roman Catholic church. These men understood the geometry of the Circle, and from it, extrapolated the 'artistic' or spiritual qualities that this geometric form represented. They were aware that the Circle is the only geometrical figure whose every point lays at the same distance from a fixed point that is the center of the circle itself. They understood this idea to represent one of symmetry and harmony within Nature—both of the physical and spiritual worlds. Since a completed circle has neither a beginning nor an end, it is easy to see how they extended the esoteric meaning behind this concept to their notion of God: the Alpha and the Omega; the Beginning and the End; That which was and which is, and which is yet to be. Coupled with their knowledge of Kabbalah, they applied these basic ideas to the realms that lied below and extended above them—to the depths of Hell and to the heights of Heaven. Standing thus at the center of the Circle during a rite of Invocation or the ceremonial act of Evocation to Physical Manifestation, and armed with the declaration of the Divinity within him; with that Holy Right to command the Elements and all that is within them, the magician became aware of his role in the drama of the magical act—as that connecting agent between the Microcosm and the Macrocosm; the Divine expressed in mortal form, declaring into existence that which he wills into actuality in Malkuth, as being an act of the Will of God, Itself. Man thus becomes the pivot point or the fulcrum upon which the worlds below and the worlds above achieve balance, and the avenue through which the power of those worlds is brought into the world of physical form, adding new meaning and complexity to it.

The Circle of Science and Art, then, is not some convenient contrivance to be "visualized" in the air or on the floor at the whim of New Age 'will.' It is not some secondary tool that is meant to fill some ho-hum requirement in order to 'get on' with the 'fun of magic.' It is an instrument that channels power; both of the magician's will, and of the Will of God through him. It is a lens that focuses the dynamic, interior energy of the human psyche and the spiritual nature of the Indwelling God that resides at the center of the magician's nature. As such, the greatest care is required in its construction, consecration, and understanding, prior to its use in any magical work soever. It demands every bit of concentration and meditation so that it becomes fixed into the very foundation of the subconscious state of subjective synthesis of the Operator. And according to the grimoire being worked, the particular Circle so described must be precisely and dutifully constructed, the processes of Concentration and Meditation being applied to the specific form of the Circle being used.

Without this reverence; without this precision; without this understanding and knowledgeable use, the aspiring magician can expect to accomplish—nothing.

Evocation to Physical Manifestation: The Sites of Operation and Sundry Matters

I received the following query some time ago. It is an interesting and important question, and I trust that what light I am able to shed on this matter will be of use to anyone who is planning on conducting an Evocation to Physical Manifestation in the outdoors:

> "As circumstance would have it I will have to perform the Heptameron outside somewhere in the woods or in the desert. What is your advice in regards to items I may have to take with me that are not related to the actual grimoire but are helpful in dealing with environmental conditions? For example, portable light sources such as lanterns or flashlights, stakes to pin down the circle of art, brooms for sweeping debris, etc. Could the spirit use these items against me in a dangerous manner?
> "Is it safe to have a portable light source within the circle?
> "I am particularly concerned about the sharp stakes I am thinking of using to pin down the circle of art."

First of all, if possible, try to operate in the woods; that is, if you intend to conduct *any* Evocation to Physical Manifestation in an outdoor setting. I say this because from my experience, Spirits of *any* class eventually become more at ease in this particular environment. They become less hostile as the Evocation proceeds, thereby making them easier to control (in my opinion, this decrease in hostility is due to their preoccupation with the congestion of trees and undergrowth. In short, their sensory apparatus becomes 'overloaded' by the congestion of the deep woods, and so a large part of their chaotic nature is occupied with monitoring what is happening around them.) The more secluded the wooded area of operation the better, and for obvious reasons. In my earlier days, I would hike into the most secluded, dense, utterly inaccessible areas imaginable to insure I would not be surprised by some other human. It was very difficult carrying everything I needed, but the job had to be done and so I took the most extreme measures. In many cases, I would begin a day in advance, carry the items I needed to the site, hide them in the brush, return to my Magical Chamber, take more of what would be needed, and repeat the process. I continued this until all was at the site, and the only thing I had to do was to return to it the following day to perform the Ceremonial Magical Act.

As to other possible sites of Operation. I would sincerely discount performing any Evocation to Physical Manifestation in a desert, at a lake, or at a beach. With the population what it is today, and with the appearance of the "ATV" (All Terrain Vehicle) and the "Dirt bike," only a remote wood—and the more inaccessible the better—is the most logical choice. Yes, we work from ancient grimoires. But we must also remember the times in which we live and make those adaptations that society forces upon us: that is, if we want to work freely and secretly. Otherwise—can you imagine being in your Circle at, say, midnight, being in the middle of the Operation, and hearing from behind you, "Hey, man, what you up to?" Yes, count on it. You would attract someone with the IQ of a handball to interfere with you. And then, my dear reader, your problems will *really* begin!!

The idea of performing any Evocation to Physical Manifestation in daylight is and always has been beyond me. It *must* be remembered that in this particular Ceremonial Act we are dealing with the Fallen Angels; and the more congruous the conditions are to their natures, the more spectacular and full will be the results. Therefore, it is important to work only at night, even when a particular grimoire—as for instance, the Goetia—classifies some Spirits as being 'easier' to conjure during certain times of the day. It may be easier to summon them forth during those times, but I have found through my work in Experimental Magic that *all* are relatively easy to call forth when darkness prevails, and when all other conditions—such as operating on the bare ground or in the woods—are properly observed.

Now; as to light sources. All I can suggest is what I have found to be useful in the past. There are flashlight-type devices that have a band around them. This enables them to be placed around the head, and the angle of the light adjusted such that when you bend your head down toward the grimoire, the light falls directly on the text. I used these for reading from the grimoire I was working from, *but only after fitting the lens of the flashlight with a red filter* (the filter makes the eyes 'vision-ready' in the darkness, and keeps them adjusted to the surrounding night.)

Make certain the flashlight is equipped with fresh batteries: having batteries die out on you at a time like that will be no laughing matter!

Other lights that will be present are, of course, the candles. Regardless of the Evocation, I use four in number, one placed at each of the Quarters of the Universe. Whatever you do, please do not use those 12" taper candles so frequently found on dining room tables! I use 3" diameter, 3' high—yes, **3 *foot high*—**solid, white candles, obtainable from a good church supply store. They are expensive, but then, what you will be involved in requires that you provide the best: there must be *no* shortcuts in Evocation to Physical Manifestation. The candles are fixed onto 2' high spiked stands, which ensure that they do not topple over during the Operation. These candles function—most certainly—not as a source of light by which the Operator can read the grimoire, nor even as an "offering" to the Spirit as the New Age would have you believe. No. *They serve to produce an "Fresnel-Lens Effect" as I call it, wherein the smoke from the suffumigation blends with the rays of light from the candles. It is into this area that the magical forces of the Operation become condensed as it were, this area then acting as a lens through which the manifestation of the demon is then **projected** into some [other] area outside of the Circle, but within the confines of the Operation.* This may sound like a small and technical point, but I think it is an important one. One other note can also be added here: when lighting these candles, *never* use common sulfur-based matches. Always use the long sulfur-less matches; in fact, these should be used for *all* aspects of the Ceremony, including the lighting of the Fire. These matches are available at fine cigar stores, being used for lighting expensive cigars.

As to your concern about sharp stakes used to secure the Circle. Ideally, the Circle should be traced on the ground with the Sword of Art, or the Instrument of Art recommended by the grimoire from which you are working. In the case of the *Heptameron*, the center of the Circle is simplicity itself, containing only the words, "Alpha et Omega." The question arises: "But if I accidentally step on these words and erase them, won't I be vulnerable to attack from the demon since my Circle would be destroyed?" Absolutely not. *The fact is, once the Circle—complete with its names and figures—is drawn on to ground with the required*

Magical Weapon, it becomes 'fixed' into the Ceremonial Act and becomes a permanent part of that act **until the Ceremonial Act itself is brought to a full conclusion.** Like many before me I was so concerned about this technical point that I would lug a 12´×12´ heavyweight canvas tarp into the mountains. Finally I decided to test my idea of the Circle being fixed into the ground by the Weapon during the Operation. It worked. After that, I always drew the Circle directly on the bare ground. However, if you insist on using a 'portable' Circle, I advise purchasing tent pegs and using them to secure the Circle. I used to use rocks to secure the edges of my tarp, and never had any problem, i.e., the demon trying to remove them or hurling them at me. There will be enough physical phenomena of other kinds occurring, but this should *not* be one of them.

Concerning The Slingshot Effect: Some Additional and Important Considerations

It would not only be wonderful but indeed so very helpful, if a given book in any field of human endeavor could contain all that pertains to that realm of enquiry. Unfortunately, publication limitations, book size, design, market factors, and a myriad of other real-world necessities prohibit such complete coverage. Add this to the fact that no one writer knows all there is in any given field, then consider his own interpretation of the material and his writing style in presenting that knowledge he or she wishes to share by means of a published book, and you have a fair picture of the physical situation of things. And I am as guilty of all of the above as is any other author. In this case, the issue that arose pertains to the crucial Slingshot Effect that I discussed at great length in my first book, *Ceremonial Magic and the Power of Evocation*. While I gave all I felt could be given between the covers of a single volume, I did omit important matters. As expected, this omission came back to haunt me. But it also gave me the opportunity to address the matter further, thanks to one extremely sincere, hard working, and genuine student of magic who was preparing for his first Evocation to Physical Manifestation; and who got more during the preparatory stage than he bargained for.

His initial query follows: it is set off in italics. Please read it carefully, and follow through with my reply, thoughtfully. If you do, you just may avoid the agony he experienced, and perhaps even produce a manageable Slingshot Effect: even if you are preparing for your first experiment in this, the darkest corner of Magic.

> Dr. Lisiewski,
>
> A very strange thing has happened to me even before I have evoked to physical manifestation. I have been reading your book and am almost ready to put your theory to practice. Yet, your conditions that are suppose to occur after the rite appears to be occurring to me BEFORE the rite.
> 1. I made a purchase for $1800 that appraised for $18,000.
> 2. Some of it was taken away when I got a letter from the IRS.
> 3. A relationship with my daughter in law may have ended when I accidentally found out she was visiting bars when her husband (my stepson) was working. I just happened to be talking to a colleague of mine who, through coincidence, talked with her that evening. I showed him pictures of her to confirm. My close relationship with her is over.
> 4. My cousin whom I've not seen in 11 years called me and wants to visit with me.
> 5. I just made several thousands of dollars in the stock market
>
> Is this mere coincidence or could these "conditions" happen before practicing evocation to physical manifestation.
>
> By the way, I will be performing ceremonial magic this Friday.

This phenomenon—that of the Slingshot Effect occurring before the Evocation to Physical Manifestation is actually performed—does occur.

Fortunately (or otherwise) it is a rare occurrence; but one that is experienced *only* by those who operate with a *pure heart* and a *sincere* purpose. That is, it occurs *only* to those who are deadly serious about their practice of Magic, and whose motivations are as pure and intense as any human desire can be. These are the type of individuals in whom the process of Magic is so well understood—both naturally and completely—that they bring into the *preparatory* stage that intensity, purity, sincerity, and seriousness so integral to success in the endeavor. Further, as far as I have experienced, it occurs *only* during the individual's preparation for his or her *first* Evocation to Physical Manifestation. It does *not* occur during latter attempts, owing to the sincere individual's discovery—in one way or another—of that one simple expedient which prevents such events from reoccurring (In this case, I was so impressed with this man's genuineness, that I invited him to telephone me. We discussed the issue at length; and what I advised him to do during that conversation will be given to you here.)

Why does such a thing occur? *It is due to the interference of the Fallen themselves.* What are motives of these Fallen beings for producing such interference? They have three rationales for posing such opposition:

1. These beings *know* that such a one as he who sent me the above letter, will (eventually) succeed in his Evocations to Physical Manifestation. Why will he succeed? Because of the Fire; *that Fire of Spirit which lives within the deepest recesses of his spiritual nature and which is working its way outward through his mind, heart, and body, into his conscious life. This, as a result of his spiritual unfoldment, which is quite obviously taking place at an accelerated rate.*

    Further, this Fire of Spirit is that same Fire which manifests in the form of the Holy Guardian Angel (HGA) at the climax of the Abramelin Operation, should the individual advance that far.

    To the 'Evil" entities that will be summoned by such a one, this represents more than a "threat." Such an individual is a guaranteed menace to their world of disorder and chaos; an exalted human being who—even for such a brief time—will bring order and stability into that world.

2. Even though such beings crave for such stability and order; even though they yearn for this peace and respite from their sufferings, *their natures are so imbalanced and incomplete, that they automatically reject these very things that they crave, and pose opposition to the one who will bring them this so very short-lived respite and peace.* Such is the incomprehensible nature of these Fallen Angels and their Legions. It is hard for our contemporary minds to understand to be sure, but such is the composition and activity of *their* psycho-spiritual natures.

3. The Fire of the Spirit that is entering into the consciousness of the magician will bring about a further imbalance—on the side of "Good"—in this testing ground of Malkuth wherein the

Powers of "Good" and "Evil" are constantly at war. Not "if" but *"when"* this happens, a further imbalance is created in Malkuth: not on the side of "Evil," but on the side of "Good." This tenuous balance in Malkuth of the Eternal Struggle between the two will be upset, even if only briefly. But it will be upset (It is always so when a new Warrior of the Light emerges. This balance is likewise also upset when a new Warrior of Darkness consciously enters into his own depraved work.) The entrance of this new Warrior of Light will thus effect the Kingdom of "Evil." That is, he will introduce or accelerate—for a time—the chaos and imbalance of the individual Fallen beings themselves, thus separating them even further from the peace and stability they seek. Yet, at the same time—owing to their fluidic, disorganized nature—these malignant entities will try to thwart or destroy the vehicle—the magician's attempts—from bringing them the (eventual) respite they so desperately seek through the Evocation to Physical Manifestation.

If the above seems complicated on a first read, read it again. It is not as complicated or confused as it seems. In fact, as far as the Fallen are concerned, it is their own form of inviolable "logic." The only logic their natures *can* admit to, and the only form of justification that they know of for their damned positions.

Put yourself in the place of the Fallen for one moment: then see if this is not the only way you could survive an existence that Dante captured in *The Inferno* when he wrote of the words that appear above the entrance to Hell Mouth, "Abandon all hope, ye who enter here!"

This is their world. This is their existence. Like any creature, they must seek to make 'the best of it,' and in this way, they do. Such I have learned during my own questioning of them during my own work in Experimental Magic. Thus, the advent of such serious effects—resulting from the Slingshot Effect as the querent spoke of here—are the means used by the Fallen in attempting to dissuade him from going through with the Operation and indeed, for abandoning *all* Magic.

But what of the querent's dilemma? What is he to do now, seeing he has to shoulder the weight of the Slingshot Effect; and this, even before he entered into the actual summoning of the Operation? As I explained to him, there is only one course of action to take; only one way in which he (or anyone who experiences this phenomenon) can prevent those desirable gains derived from the Slingshot Effect from being taken from him—and which actually are manifestations of the desires he sought from the Operation—and from preventing further, more pronounced negative effects from 'suddenly' manifesting in his life. And that is, that *he must proceed with the ceremonial performance of the Evocation to Physical Manifestation itself.* This 'completes the circuit' as it were, and allows for a closure of the 'Event of the Operation' to be reached. Once this happens, the gains he made will be kept by him, no further Slingshot Effect (from this specific Operation) will occur, and he will have begun to introduce his own Fire of Spirit into the World of Malkuth, announcing to all beings—including the Fallen—that a new Warrior of Light has appeared, and is now someone to be reckoned with. The tenuous balance in the Eternal Battle between "Good" and "Evil" will begin to shift toward the side of "Good" as I have explained. But afterwards, the struggle between theses two opposing forces will continue. As it was and is, so it shall remain throughout finite existence.

But how can this person (or any of us) block or neutralize such interference—in the first place—from those beings whom we intend to summon unto us? The Key—the one so often overlooked or ignored—lies in the *Grand Grimoire* itself. *For it is in the purchasing, purification, and consecration of the "…stone called Emantile…"—the Blood Stone—that the answer lies.* This seemingly innocuous stone has the ability to either 'hide' or 'shield' the magician and his entire life—including the preparatory procedures he is or will be engaged in—from the being(s) he intends to evoke. It is a stone of mystery and power—as far as the Fallen are concerned, and one which they fear almost as much as they do the Blasting Rod, the Sword of Art, or that most horrifying of all magical instrument, the Knife with the Black Handle.

The procedure to follow is the one I have used myself throughout the decades, and which I have taught privately to my students. It has never failed to work, and to work as intended. The Blood Stone is to be purchased, purified, and consecrated thus:

Ritual Preparation of the Blood Stone

Let the magician buy, without haggling over the price so ever, a natural Blood Stone. That is, one that has not been artificially fashioned or polished or worked upon by anyone. It will appear a medium flat green in color, and will have a streak of flat red running throughout its length (the wider and more pronounced the red streak, the better.) This red streak symbolizes blood: the blood of the opposing enemy that has been shed upon the earth as a result of battle, and stands as both a warning from, and declaration by, the magician that he will enter into battle with the Fallen, regardless of the personal price he must pay, or whatsoever may befall him. Such is the extent of his temerity and Valor in the issue before him. It is such a one from which devils flee. This purchasing should be done during the day of Mars, during an hour ruled by Saturn. At the same time let him buy a convenient length of pure white linen, of medium weight, a new, unused, pair of scissors, and a container of mountain spring water (it should be water that has only been filtered, and contain no preservatives of any kind.)

On the same martial day (or one following if he cannot accomplish all on the first day of the purchasing) during a Saturn hour, let him take the stone, place it upon a stone surface of some kind, and pour over it a liberal quantity of the mountain spring water. As he does so, let him recite Psalm 51.

Let him pour—without any blessings, aspersions, or consecrations—another quantity of water over the new scissors, and sprinkle the white linen with another quantity of the water as well. Now let him cut a section of white linen from the length he purchased, and several narrow strips from the length also, and place the stone in the large section, wrap it close around the Blood Stone, and secure the linen 'pouch' with the linen strips such that the 'pouch' cannot open without him purposely doing so. Let him next take the remaining linen and burn it to cinders so that it may never be used again for any purpose: not even by him. Likewise let him take the scissors and utterly destroy them so no man can make use of them anymore. Now let that remaining quantity of mountain water be taken outdoors. And while facing the **East**, let him return the last of that water to the earth, in as reverent and humble manner as he is capable of mustering within him.

Let the magician carry this secret stone with him from the first moment he decides to perform an Evocation to Physical Manifestation, regardless of the grimoire from which he decides to operate. *Let this stone remain on him at all times, day and night, never leaving his person, until the very moments immediately before he enters the Circle of Art to Conjure in the Evocation itself.*

By doing so, not only will the magician remain free from the machinations of the evil and Fallen, but he will prevent the Slingshot Effect from occurring *prior* to the operation. In addition, this simple procedure will have attracted the attention of those beings he intends to summon, such that they will be ready to attend onto him when the Great Work of Evocation begins.

The stone can also be used during those interludes between Evocations or other High Ceremonial Experimental Magical Work should the Operator have cause to think he is being interfered with during such times. In such cases, he has only to take the pouch and place it on his person, keeping it there at all times, until the undesired effects he has been experiencing have ceased.

I have covered much more here than I told the gentleman about during our telephone conversation. But of necessity, our discussion had to be limited, and so I wished to address the matter in a more fully responsible way here.

Yes, this has been a strange paper to be sure. But I remind the reader, it is no less strange than the act of Evocation to Physical Manifestation itself—as he or she will find out when they enter the Circle for the first time, to summon those from Hell itself.

Devotion, Magical Momentum, and the Magical Journal

I received the following letter from an individual whom I respect greatly, and whose magical institute and philosophy I admire and hold with equal respect. The issues he cites are so important, that I felt his letter should be reprinted here in its entirety. Those readers desiring to truly follow a magical curriculum would do well to read his comments carefully, and to implement them in their *daily* lives, ***exactly***.

In this letter, he brings out several important matters dealing with a daily devotional period (when necessary) in order to maintain that all-important concept and reality: that of magical momentum. In like manner, he points out the absolute need for the creation and maintenance of a Magical Dairy (Journal or "Day Book") and the reason why such a device is so important. In point of fact, as he explains, it was Aleister Crowley who, in contemporary times, pointed out the need for such a written record in addition to his explaining the 'why' behind this need, and how it should be used. Of course, Crowley was right.

Like the writer of this letter, I am not a "big fan of Aleister Crowley" and for my own reasons. But his own true spiritual unfoldment—brought about by the system he hammered out for himself—cannot be denied by anyone, nor should it be. Additionally, his contributions to Magic are without parallel in the last century (and certainly in this one as well, so far!) Thus, his comments about the deciphering of one's own Magical Journal are extremely important and should be heeded by all.

In fact, I highly recommend *Aleister Crowley and the Practice of the Magical Diary*. Its instructions in the creation and continuation of the "Journal" as I refer to such a record, are very valuable and absolutely necessary, indeed.

Personally, I used very similar techniques throughout the years, taught to me by Regardie, to get to the point I am at in my own Spiritual Unfoldment: for what this may or may not be worth to the reader. In addition, I have maintained **daily** private "notebooks" or "diaries" of magical and other personal data since March 1963, and have learned as much from them as I have from my Magical Journals. This might very well be something for the reader to consider as well.

So enjoy the following letter, take it to heart, and continue to do what you do so well—WORK!

Dear Dr. Lisiewski,

> I was reading your weekly columns when I noticed your suggestions to students wishing to begin their esoteric studies and Kabalistic practices.
>
> Your emphasis on the Day Book, or record of personal practice is of inestimable value to each student. Through a daily dedication of briefly writing down what they have done and the results obtained they create a habit that will benefit them in many

unseen ways. In addition to the simple act of discipline, it shows their real dedication to the Work.

Did they do something, anything that day?

As a father of two young children, husband, and author, I know the difficulty there can be in carving out the needed time to do our 'ideal practice'. Yet, if one's schedule for a day or week does not allow for an hour of unbroken work, even simply saying a regular set of prayers, and sitting for ten or fifteen minutes twice a day, while performing Square Breathing continues momentum created by other exercises, until our regular schedule can be resumed. Such a simple yet demanding practice also demonstrates to us that 'simple' is not the same as 'easy' nor does something have to be complex in order for us to benefit from it. In short, we must daily do something if we want to progress in any discipline—and magic is the highest of disciplines.

While not a big fan of Aleister Crowley, the mentor of your friend and teacher Israel Regardie, Crowley states some things that are important in themselves. In particular he points out in *Magick in Theory and Practice* that from one point of view, magickal progress actually consists in deciphering one's own record. Without a record we have nothing to decipher and seriously hamper our progress.

In addition to the Day Book, or Magical Diary, individual notebooks are important. I am finally completing two notebooks I keep, one on esoteric theory and the second purely on magical and mystical techniques and methods. Each book is dated as to when it was started. A quick look shows me that it was over 15 years ago for these two. In addition there is a book consisting only of the *Sepher Yetzirah*, written out completely by myself, along with pages dedicated to each Hebrew letter, and additional commentaries from various sources.

Very often when I write articles or books these notebooks alone are the source of information, as they are a distillation of decades of practice. A practice that once seemed so overwhelming, and now is as the alchemists say, "children's play."

Thank you for pointing out these critical points to your readers and students, and best wishes to them on their Path of Return.

The Daily Devotions

We who practice Magic and the Occult Sciences are so pragmatic. We are so intent and fixed on changing our worlds within and without through the process of exteriorizing our interior growth, that all too often we fall into a mechanical trap—and one of our own making. We may begin our daily life by performing the Lesser Banishing Ritual of the Pentagram (LBRP) and might even follow it with the Banishing Ritual of the Hexagram (BRH) complete with all of the Signs, or involve ourselves in some other set of physical-mental gestures and performances. All in an effort to set the tone for the day; to give us the edge before entering the world without. At least, this is what we tell ourselves as we enter our daily ritual period.

But if we take a little time for introspection, and sincerely allow that material which is directly below the surface of our consciousness to rise into our awareness, do you know what we generally find? We find **fear**. We discover that we are really performing our daily magical or occult rites to ward off those things that go bump in the night; that night which exists in the darkest recesses of our minds. Perhaps this inner fear is a remnant of the days of the cave: of that time when the darkness without called the darkness within us to the fore. Maybe it is this that we are continually trying to combat in our safe, sterile, daily lives of humdrum duties and activities.

But yet maybe today, to a large measure, we have also invented mental bogeymen to enable these fantasies to fuel our lives with an excitement we wouldn't have without them. Maybe—just maybe—our fears are primarily anticipatory. They do not exist in the world outside as empirical fact. And to insure that they never become fact; to make absolutely certain we don't run into any **real** trouble during the day, we ritualistically begin our daily lives by responding to this combined ancient and manufactured 'call to fear.'

Why do we do this? In order to repel the possibility of such fearful things and events we imagine **MIGHT** happen from ever really happening to us in the world without. And so we enter into our daily secret practices so we can feel safe and sure that the minute we set our foot outside our front door we will not be overwhelmed by a uncaring world and parasitic society. Or worst yet, that the evils of that world and devils of this society do not come to our very doorstep. In fact, we do not need a Judas-Goat or a Brutus: we have provided them for ourselves, by mixing the biologically-based fear produced in times of genuine crisis by our natural, inner survival mechanism, with that anticipatory fear we manufacture for ourselves, and which is due in large measure to the bland, sterile, 'hooray-for-me-and-the-hell-with-you' continually pleasure seeking society we have helped to create. It's time to step back. It's time to look deeply into our own minds and hearts, and discover or recognize, and own up to what is really within us. What we are really made of. What really moves us. What lies at the very center and core of our being. And maybe that time is today.

The Daily Devotions are just such a practice. They enable us to begin the long, hard, and arduous process of interior self-discovery. Call them prayers if you like, it doesn't really matter. The devotions, in whatever form they may take, are exercises in Self-Discovery. They are designed to move us away from our own self-centeredness and move us toward our True Self-Centeredness: to that place within where Man meets God, and where our life meets the Life that is all, governs all, and exists in and through all. These meditations if you like, enable us to shift our consciousness away from the fantasies of self-excitement, recognize a genuine biologically produced fear reaction, and toward the **actuality** of Self-Realization. And in the process these devotions enable us to put things—both within our hidden, inner nature, and in the world without that we fear so much—in their proper place.

As usual, the devotional means of doing this are left to the discretion of the individual. I recommend however, that the individual at least consider the "Four Adorations" that appear in Regardie's *The Twelve Steps to Spiritual Enlightenment* as prayers to be used on a daily basis. While simple and easy to commit to memory, they are filled with an energy and vitality that quickly communicates the beauty, complexity, unity of the universe, of all life, and of God, to one's mind. In a short while, these adorations will instill such a fervor within the individual and so elate and exalt the mind, that contact with the Absolute Spiritual Nature—not the supposed spiritual essence mouthed by moderns—will be felt and at long last known. Not long after this, the intensity of this exaltation will become so great, and occur with such a fiery intensity, as to blissfully consume the spirit, mind, emotions and eventually the body of the aspirant, in a Holy Glory that can only be experienced, but never described in words. (For those who may be Thelemically-minded, the equivalent of the Christian-based Adorations of the Twelve Steps can be found in Regardie's *The One Year Manual.)*

After beginning the day with these devotions, the student *will* find that his or her view of the world, society, and life in general, undergoes a transformation. The self-manufactured fears are no longer present as a motivational force for ritual performance. Instead, any daily ritual work that is later entered into is seen—and most importantly, **felt**—as an exteriorized expression of the Indwelling God Head within. Now, the rituals are propelled by a new and vital energy—not the energy of an unconscious fear complex; but rather, by an energy that is a mode of expression of the Divine within. The rituals are no longer needed for self-preservation and safety, but as a means of Self-Expression; of translating and projecting the inner fire of the Indwelling God Head into the world without. And since there are three other adorations beside the Morning Adoration given in the Twelve Steps and in the One Year Manual, the recall of the morning's quiet during these additional devotions will strengthen and sanctify the interior nature of the practitioner all the more.

What do you think the results of such a change in daily curriculum will be? Of beginning each day with a sincere Daily Devotion, taking an introspective break, and then performing that LBRP or/and BRH that you are so use to? Ironically, the change will bring about the very purposes these two rituals were designed to bring about, but in an entirely new, balanced, and unified way. This is the paradox. Our pragmatism, founded in our own fears, worries and concerns, has failed to give us that measure of safety and protection for which we initially performed them. But when performed from an interior, sanctified base, we find that these safeguards are not only enlivened and activated to an extent we never experienced previously, but we find an abundance of other truly spiritual AND material gifts flowing to us on a daily basis. Interesting, isn't it?

The reader would do well to consider this simple injunction: begin your day with a Daily Devotional Period; one that is repeated three more times during each day, and then—and ONLY then, after taking some time for introspection—perform that barrage of rituals to which you have devoted yourself. I assure you, you will not regret making this simple change in your daily magical or occult work.

"Stressing" and its Use in Magical and Mystical Processes

Many years ago, Frater Albertus taught me a simple method of entering more completely into mystical states of awareness. In later years, I found this technique to be of inestimable value in gaining deeper insights into magical and mystical written material as well. Additionally, as the years went on, I found that it could also be used with great profit in acquiring knowledge of any kind. That is, it easily lends itself to the process of obtaining that not-so-obvious knowledge that underlies all learning efforts. Thus, while the average reader of this book may initially apply this technique to his magical practices and mystical exercises, he would do well to become so familiar with it that he can apply it at will to any new learning or analytical endeavor. The process I am speaking of here is one I simply refer to as "Stressing." Here is how it works:

Let's take a simple admonition:

(Original Phrase) — *"It is good to do Good."*

This barebones phrase can and often is used by students as a mantra if you will; one that enables them to focus on the essence of the concept(s) behind the phrase. Fair enough. And if recited over and over, it most certainly will deliver up **some** understanding of just those thoughts and emotions that underlie this meaningful series of words. Now, let us introduce this so-called "Stressing Process" and apply it to these six words and see what else can be gained from them.

(1) *IT* is good to do Good
(2) It *IS* good to do Good
(3) It is *GOOD* to do Good
(4) It is good *TO* do Good
(5) It is good to *DO* Good
(6) It is good to do *GOOD*

Rather than repeat these six words in a monotonous, repetitious way as originally given in the original phrase above, and thereby allowing the mind to flirt hither and thither, we do the following. *During each repetition, successive words are stressed in the order they appear in the phrase.* That is, on the first repetition, *IT* is stressed. In the second repetition, *IS* becomes the word stressed. In the third repetition, ***GOOD*** is stressed. etc. This procedure forces the mind to associate and explore hidden connections and meanings embedded in the words themselves. These are then married to the overall concept(s) embraced by the phrase, producing an entirely new coalescence of abstractions and ideas that would have previously gone undiscovered. Of course, such discovery can only lead to an exponential growth of new understanding and personal insights, enabling the individual to attain to that which he desires, and all in a more complete and holistic way.

If this innocent process is given a fair trial, I am certain it will give to the Practitioner what it has given to me and those to whom I have taught it: a further technique for exploring the Inner Realm of their own nature. One that will add to their ever growing armory of practices that will eventually allow them to become who they already are.

The Art of True Healing and The Middle Pillar Ritual

In 1937, Israel Regardie issued a small hardcover volume entitled, *The Art of True Healing.* In 1964 it was reissued in a second revised edition, and reprinted through (at least) 1970 by Helios Book Service in Cheltenham, Glos., England. This small volume was not presented as a sophisticated, complex magical treatise; but rather, as a practical, workable system for reestablishing physical health, obtaining mental equilibrium, the physical necessities of life and finally, as a method by which Union with Godhead could be achieved. And all this through a carefully designed technique using relaxation, rhythmic breathing, and mental imaging, along with the intonation of certain Hebrew Names of God.

At the root of this system of "therapeutics" as he called it, was the release of neuromuscular tensions through rhythmic breathing and imaging exercises; *vital preliminaries* to using the latter imaging and intonation techniques. For it was through this wedded combination of relaxation, rhythmic breathing, mental imaging, and intonation, that enormous spiritual currents could be 'called up' from within the deepest nature of the individual to effect health, or 'called down' from universal planetary forces; forces that will 'charge' the aura of the individual to such an extent, that the unconscious mind of that individual—acting as a powerful electromagnet—would attract to that person just those things and conditions of life that would enable them to grow in every material sense.

But first, must come the release from those unconscious stresses and pressures that plague each and every cell of the body throughout its physical reign on earth. For only in this way can the spiritual forces flow unimpeded—through the psychic nature—and then into the physical constitution of man, bringing about a new Heaven and a New Earth; at least in the individual sense. This small book is—in my opinion—Regardie's crowning glory. For it sets forth a highly scientific, powerful system of stimulation of the Interior faculties which—when coordinated according to his instructions—can and will result in all those fulfillments the individual of any age seeks in order to live a healthy, happy, successful, and prosperous life. There are some small matters I would like to point out in using the techniques of this invaluable book. Considerations I have found to be of great value both to myself and to others, since I have been using it myself for the past 35 years.

In fact, what I am pointing out here is not 'new' in any sense of the word. Rather, these few matters are simply cautionary notes and bits of elaborations: they deal with issues I have found too many would-be practitioners of the technique fail to observe, always wanting to get onto the 'meat' of the matter. As a consequence of this 'quick-fix' mentality, they inevitably fail. The technique does not fail, but they do, and—inevitably and as expected—then place the blame on the technique itself. Rather than list these few extra cautions and considerations 'in text,' a numbering of them may better suit the reader both now and for future reference.

Please note: since that which is given here are only so many 'notes' to make this Middle Pillar technique work that much more effectively, you will need a copy—an unedited copy—of the Middle Pillar Ritual as given in *The Art of True Healing* in order to actually perform the ritual. Happily, the recently released book,

Foundations of Practical Magic by Israel Regardie, published by Aeon Books, contains this and four other *unedited* classics of Regardie's.

As to the suggestions being offered here, the following will prove helpful to the student:

1. Step I of the *12 Steps to Spiritual Enlightenment,* i.e., *Body Awareness,* should be the first exercise mastered before attempting to use the Middle Pillar Technique itself. You cannot relax what you are not aware of, and this step enables you to become aware of all those bodily sensations that lie on the periphery of conscious; sensations that must be addressed if they are eventually to be released through relaxation proper.
2. Step II of the *12 Steps*—*Relaxation*—should be mastered second. Through the mental imaging alone employed in this Step, great torrents of life-giving blood will flow to all parts of the organism, bringing about a physical relaxation and emotional sense of Peace which cannot be described, but only experienced. This is an *absolutely essential* feature of using the Middle Pillar Technique properly—and effectively.
3. Step III of the *12 Steps* comes next: *Rhythmic Breathing*. For it is through the individual training his breathing reflex to take up the four-fold rhythm of the universe that enormous currents of Life—contained both in the air and in the rhythm—enter his system, energizing his body and mind to a high pitch; a concentration of Life-force that will then be directed into the Middle Pillar Ritual proper.
4. During the actual performance of the Middle Pillar Ritual, be certain you follow the Circulations of light in order and in direction given. That is, in the case of the first Circulation, the light streaming from *Eheieh* above one's head will pass downward, **through**—not "over"—the left shoulder, **through** the left side of the body, up under sole of the left foot to the right foot, and slowly ascends the right side of the body until it returns to the Crown—the *Eheieh*—Itself. This Circulation should take place at **least six times**.

    In the case of the second Circulation, it is to be imaged as a brilliant stream of light or energy descending from Kether—the Crown—down **over** the front of the face and the body, turning backward under the soles of the feet, ascending up and **over** the back until it rejoins the Crown. This Circulation should also be repeated at least six times.

The third Circulation is what I refer to as the "Fountain Circulation." It involves drawing the energy contained in the "Earth center" (Malkuth) upward, through a 'tube' if you will, that runs through all of the five "psycho-spiritual organs" as Regardie terms and illustrates them in the book. As with a waterfall of jet spray, this energy, drawn upward from Malkuth through this 'tube,' violently shoots outward, overhead, just as does water jutting from a garden fountain. This descending spray then envelops the body completely, forming an ovoid shaped enclosure in which the practitioner sits and mediates.

5. When intoning the Divine Names of God as given in the text, *be certain to pronounce then exactly as given by Regardie in the text.* He spells them out phonetically, so you should have no trouble with them. But whatever you do, *do not replace them* by any New Age contrivance, e.g., substituting "IAO" for Jehovah Eloah ve-Daas, the Divine Name of God for the Tiphareth, and hence, for calling down the powers of the Sun. This will end in an imbalanced state, and bring you more trouble than you know what to do with. A word to the wise.

6. When using the technique as given in Chapter V to manifest some material want: after turning the aura to the Kabbalistic color assigned to the planetary force you are **about to bring down**, *at that point*, form or call up from memory the mental image of the want, condition, or experience that you desire those forces to manifest in your life. *Be certain to maintain that mental image throughout all of the intonation repetitions of the Divine Name of that planet, as these intonations are the next step in the process.* That is, with the image in your mind, and with your being aware that you aura has now turned to the Kabbalistic color assigned to that planet, *those same-colored electric-like currents of force that are now imaged by you as converging upon you from all point of the universe, will enter into your mind, 'charging' that mental image you wish to see manifested in your life: the intonations aiding the charging process.* This is a very important consideration, as Regardie did not make it clear in the book (but he

did tell me about doing just this privately, many years ago, so I am passing it along to the reader, now.)
7. A properly performed Middle Pillar Ritual should take between 50–65 minutes. Less, you are cheating yourself. Longer, you are not achieving the 'release' needed to turn the matter over to the force that can manifest it for you. Longer periods will also bring up torrents of anxiety: very uncomfortable states, from having not having effected complete release. Why? The enormous energy that is still circulating within your aura will stir up unconscious fears. This will not only cause anxiety and apprehension, but will interfere with the object of your desire either not manifesting, or manifesting at a slower rate.
8. Immediately after the ritual, do your best to put it out of your mind **completely**. Do **NOT** dwell upon it! Shift to some other activity, preferably some physical activity such as running, swimming, playing ball, etc. It must be some activity which not only keep your mind off the ritual, but which will 'burn off' any excess psycho-spiritual energy that remains in your aura.
9. When performing this ritual for some material purpose, do **NOT** engage in other magical activities, e.g., the Lesser Banishing Ritual of the Pentagram, the Banishing Ritual of the Hexagram, Divination, Invocation, and certainly, not Evocation to Physical Manifestation! Your goal here—your immediate objective—is to manifest something in your life that is of critical importance to you. As such, you must focus all of your mental, physical, psychic, and psycho-spiritual energy upon that **one** goal…no matter how long it takes.

Trying to 'mix' it with other daily magical practices to 'save time' or 'keep up with your magical development' will get you nowhere in all of them. As I have said so often, *focus on one objective at a time*. Magic is not an expediency or method of instant gratification, by any means. Good luck to you.

Talismanic Magic

This is one of the most popular, yet least understood branches of Magic *today*. If you listen to the instructions give in most of the New Age books on the subject, you are told, in essence, that all you have to do is get some colored paper (or light gauge cardboard if you really want to be 'exotic'), some colored ink pens, and either devise some " personally meaningful" symbol-set or browse through some old magical texts, transcribe those symbols to your chunk of paper or cardboard, mumble some 'incantation' and *voila*! In fifteen minutes or so, you can whip up a humdinger of a powerful talisman that will bring you all you want in life! Of course you have to "charge" it, usually, by some synthetic, mixed-together technique dreamt up by the writer, carry the "charged" object with you, then sit back, and wait for the manna to fall to you from the heavens! If it sounds like I am once again being disdainful of the mass of Occult writing on the market today, you are absolutely right: I am. But only because I take Magic very, very *seriously*. And I am quite certain that you who are reading these words take it with equal seriousness.

As is the case with so many snares for fools, there is some grain of truth hidden in those Simple-Simeon instructions. But the True Art, Science, and Practice of Talismanic Magic is anything but simple. The prime reason being, your subconscious state of subjective synthesis can and will; could and does, effect the efficacy of the talismanic objects you produce. Why is this so? Because your subjective synthesis does *not* create the power that is placed into the talisman. Rather, it is this interior, magical, subconscious state that both *channels and directs* that power—a power that exists within the deepest recesses of your own being, and in the universe at large that lies outside of you. This is why you must study the Kabbalah so assiduously: so *you* can consciously control the channeling and directing of the various magical forces and processes—including that of Talismanic Magic—according to the dictates of your Will.

But you may ask, "How can something 'subconscious' be consciously controlled and directed? By your having consciously labored to develop that ordered state below the level of your consciousness, the subconscious state of subjective synthesis reaches a point at which it automatically responds to your conscious need—the demand of your Will in any magical act—for both its structure and content, thereby lending itself to your conscious channeling and direction. Quite a mouthful I know, but as with everything worthwhile in life, effort is required in order to obtain what you want; and in this case, that 'want' is understanding.

Yet, as in all branches of Magic, there are other necessary requirements that must be fulfilled if the desired result is to be achieved. It is much like an opera. Can you imagine what a production of, say, Mozart's *Don Giovanni* would be like, if all of the participants were on key, save for one or two? Taken together, they would sound like a chorus of scorched cats, and defeat the entire purpose of the presentation. The same here. So what are these other requirements?

Generally speaking, they are:

1. The materials from which the talisman is to be constructed
2. The various geometrical forms (sigils, planetary kameas, etc.,) that are to placed onto the talismanic material
3. The method of transferring the power from the deepest strata of your being and from the outside universe into that object that will become your talisman

Concerning to the materials. As stated in so many Medieval and Renaissance texts—Agrippa not being the least—the material to be used is that which is in harmony with the power to be summoned and infused into the talisman. And that material in **all** cases is to be a **metal** (Agrippa also deals with stones, gems, and the like, but they are of no practical concern to us here.) That is, that metal which has been classically and Kabbalistically assigned to the Planetary force being called upon. Yes, if you are going to produce a Talisman of the Sun, then gold is required. It could be a blank, gold medallion upon which are to be inscribed the appropriate sigils, etc. And the higher the gold content of that medallion, the better. If the talisman be of Venus, then a high-grade copper disk would do. In the case of Jupiter, then a disk made by melting pure tin metal and pouring it into an appropriate mold would be called for. The same with the metals of the other planets. Only in the case of Mercury do we encounter a problem: that of its metal. While magical grimoires such as the Goetia assign a metal combination to this planet, the fact is that only the orange glass poured from the metallic element, Antimony, strictly corresponds to this planet as "Fixed Mercury" (it should come as no surprise that the early magicians were well versed—if not very well skilled—in those areas of Alchemy that were needed for their effective working in Magic.) But this alchemical consideration is quite deep, and cannot be covered here. (I will however, be covering this thoroughly in an upcoming book on Alchemy.) Still, an effective talisman of this planet can be produced by using **"parchment paper,"** and an appropriate orange-colored **oil paint** with which to draw the sigils decided upon for this particular talisman (only "parchment paper" is recommended owing to the process that produces it. Unlike the fabrication of standard paper, the technique used to produce this form paper is less chemically severe, and produces a fiber-base material that produces quite good results.) In this case, the use of a paper-like material does not function as some trite 'expediency,' but rather, as a necessity. It will work well, but not nearly as well as a talisman of Mercury made from the orange glass of the planet, as I previously mentioned.

Geometry plays more of a role in Magic than many realize. For 'form' can denote the 'content' and action of a given thing. That is, the form of a thing can determine that which it can contain, while providing a matrix within which a specified action can take place. Let me give you an example from physics. In Electromagnetic Field Theory, the 'shape' or geometry of an electromagnetic field determines the magnitude of energy flow within that field—its 'content' if you will—as well as the action that takes place within that field and beyond. Meaning, the way in which energy is transferred from point to point: both within the field, and the object that field is directed upon in order to produce an effect. This metaphor has great application in Talismanic Magic; for those lineal forms—sigils, kameas, and so forth—that are chosen, determine both the content and action of the talisman. So it is advisable to choose classically ascribed, historically-dated figures whose very antiquity enables them to act as a repository or 'source' for the energy that is to be transferred to the talismanic object. One such text which offers such figures is the *Clavicula Salomonis*, or the *Greater Key of Solomon the King*. Ironically however, this profoundly important workbook of Magical Evocation to Physical Manifestation has been used in modern times only for this purpose, and as a guide book in making the magical impedimenta. Nevertheless its figures are very important and powerful in Talismanic Magic, when used correctly. The Practitioner would do well then, in searching the texts of the Dark Ages, the Medieval era, and the Renaissance period for such forms, and knowledgably applying them to their talismanic construction.

Finally, we come to the method of transferring the power from the deepest strata of one's being, and from the outside universe into the object that will become the talisman. There are few legitimate, effective methods for actually achieving this, despite the numerous hodgepodge found in most New Age books. The two methods others—myself included—have found to be very effective, are the Middle Pillar Ritual devised by Israel Regardie, and the direct use of the *Clavicula Salomonis*. It is beyond the scope of this present section to delve into the latter, as effective and powerful as this method is. In effect however, it involves using a talismanic design given in the Clavicle that has a correspondence with the particular demon being summoned, and having that being transfer its power into the talisman. In this way, the power of his Office is transferred to the object, putting that power under the control of the magician.

The first method, that of the Middle Pillar Ritual (as found in Regardie's original, unedited book, *The Art of True Healing*, and which can be found on the used book market) can easily be used to incite a given planetary current, have that current flow through the psychic and physical natures of the magician, and from them into the talisman. It should be remembered however, that this is not some "quick fix" method of power transfer. Why? Because the Middle Pillar Ritual must first be mastered before it can be used for any purpose: and this mastery takes time. When I first began to study under Regardie in September 1971, he directed me to perform the Middle Pillar twice a day for a period of six months, using white light only. That is, the color of my aura was not to be imaged in any other color until the mechanics and details of the basic ritual performance were under my conscious control. Only after that was I instructed to image my aura in a different color to 'call down' the force of a particular planet in order to achieve a certain purpose. This practice lasted another six months, using a single color, until I became adept not only in the ritual itself, but in the other vital components of the ritual. Namely, in relaxation, rhythmic breathing, and concentration. These general guidelines may be of some assistance to you, the reader, such that your magical efforts—in Talismanic Magic and in other areas of Magic in which you may decide to use this particular ritual—are truly effective. Once again, we see that there are no "instant gratifications" in any branch of Magic: only careful study, hard work, more careful study, and yet more hard work.

In the space of this short presentation I have tried to give you more than some vagaries regarding the theory and operation of practical, effective, Talismanic Magic. I trust these words will be of some use to you in your ever-changing process of becoming more than you are; and always, according to the dictates of your own God-Directed, God-Inspired Will.

Chapter Seven

The Effects of Magic

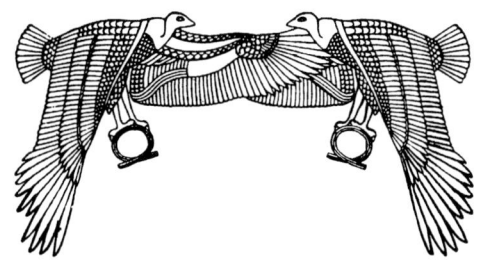

Attainment of Ecstasy

The attainment of the states of ecstasy and the Divine Bliss during the act of Ceremonial Evocation to Physical Manifestation, are not induced through the use of some invocation, prayer, or conjuration, supposedly designed to "exalt the consciousness." Indeed, these states are a natural follow-through of the Ceremonial act itself. Anyone who tells you it is necessary to "exalt" your emotional nature by reciting the Invocation of the Bornless Ritual or the like in order to attain to these states, is simply talking through his hat, or is regurgitating what his New Age cronies have mouthed to him. Such devices do nothing but distract the mind from its intended purpose: the summoning of an infernal entity to physical manifestation.

As the Experimental Magician will find, when the final conjurations of the evocation converge in his or her Sphere of Operation, the ecstasy and Divine Bliss will follow automatically, effortlessly.

For your own sake, concentrate on the details of the Operation, and let your physical, mental, and emotional actions 'flow' through and from you, with the same ease with which you breathe. You will achieve this natural 'flow' by focusing upon what you are doing, and upon nothing else. Then, and only then, will you experience complete success in your evocation.

The Nature of Physical Phenomena in Magical Practice

Over the years I have received hundreds of reports from readers of my book, *Kabbalistic Handbook for the Practicing Magician*. Almost to a report, those letters explained how applying a full Kabbalistic Analysis to a ritual as 'standard' as the Lesser Banishing Ritual of the Pentagram (LBRP) has produced seeming physical phenomena of the type described in that book. Most stated that the difference between doing the LBRP (or other ritual) with this analysis and without it, was the difference between day and night. In fact, approximately 82% of those who corresponded with me over this matter have actually turned back to Golden Dawn (GD) practices, simply because they now understood that all they had to do was finally learn the Kabbalah properly, and then apply it to their ritual or ceremonial performance in the way suggested in the book. This opened the entire GD curriculum to them in a way they have never experienced it before, and they were grateful for this bit of advice my book gave them on the matter.

One thing that concerned and delighted them about using Kabbalistic Analysis, was the physical phenomena experienced both during and after the ritual. Their concern lied primarily in wondering if the phenomena could somehow effect them in their daily lives; that is, outside of the ritual and in a negative manner. The delight of course, was in the stimulation that their physical senses received when performing a ritual; a ritual practice that was now based in their growing and expanding subconscious state of Subjective Synthesis. Put plainly, their unconscious mind now knew what it was expected to do, and carried out its part of the ritual almost flawlessly in most cases. In view of the number of comments received on this matter, I thought it was time to give a brief explanation of the phenomena being experienced by those who take the "time and trouble" to do things properly. That is, those who learn the Kabbalah as they should, and who then apply it to their ritual practices before they enter the Magical Chamber to carry out the physical components of the performance.

Concerning the Sense of Smell

In the main, I have found that odors produced from such rites are physical. That is, they can be and are detected by others (it is not uncommon for my wife to return from the university and ask me where the odor of roses or sandalwood came from, even though I did not used any suffumigation in performing some simple ritual.) It is my view that such odors are brought about by the presence of benevolent spiritual beings who are attracted to the ritual site. It is also very possible—as I see it—for such odors to be produced by one's own Holy Guardian Angel (HGA) depending on how close one is to performing the Abramelin Operation. If one has performed this Operation and was successful, it is then common place for the HGA to produce such beautiful scents during the performance of *any* ritual, regardless of how seemingly 'minor' that ritual may be considered. These odors will linger and eventually travel throughout the entire dwelling, lasting many hours—even an entire day and night. It is a physical sign of 'approval' and a form of blessing.

Concerning the Sense of Touch

No few readers have explained to me that while performing their rituals, they experience the feeling of being physically touched every so often, while in the Circle. The touching primarily occurs on different parts of the face, arms, and hands, or on the back of the neck. It is not as if the hair on these parts of the body was rising up. Rather, it feels as if someone—or something—is making a gentle—but firm—sustained contact with that part of their body. This caused quite a few to worry that something malevolent was penetrating their Sphere of Operation, and could do harm to them in some way. Rest assured, if the Circle is properly constructed, purified and consecrated, *nothing* can transgress its boundary. I have already seen finger marks on my own arms from such occurrences. Large, slender markings that wrapped around my forearms and left a visible impression even after the ritual, although only the slightest of pressure was made by the agent that produced the marks. I have also seen the same on my face after a given performance.

In my opinion, this 'touching' is a type of guidance one is receiving from some spiritual entity desiring to instruct the individual in correcting some part of his physical movement in a ritual (if on the forearms or hands.) Or to turn his head in a given direction in order to become aware of some component of the rite or its result that one would not ordinarily be aware of. That is, if one is tracing an LBRP incorrectly, this touching on the arm or hand startles the magician into an awareness of that part of the body and what he is doing with it such that the incorrect motion(s) can be corrected. If on the face or back of the neck, one is being encouraged to look more closely at what is happening around him or in the areas off his center of immediate awareness. There are usually surprises in a sub-quarter when this occurs.

There is another sensation that can be ascribed to the sense of touch that I have written about and which many have experienced and asked me to account for in more detail. And that sensation is that of a *wind stirring in the Magical Chamber*. It is, in fact, quite common, and (to me) indicates that the energy (intelligent or otherwise) that is being contacted and summoned is moving from the astral plane into the physical plane. The natural resistance between the two planes produces a field of force that stirs the most susceptible physical elements it first encounters: air molecules. The result: a wind-effect is produced. Simply note the effect as it occurs, be all the more conscious of your physical movements and gestures during the ritual, and record the phenomena in your Magical Dairy. There is nothing to fear here either.

Concerning the Sense of Taste

This is not a typical effect, but it does occur. At times, the magician will notice either a sweet or bitter taste in his mouth. I have noticed this is always in agreement with the nature of the Operation being worked. That is, if one is operating to (counter)attack, a bitter taste arises. If the Operation is one of cleansing and purification, a sweet taste arises. In either case, there is nothing the individual has to concern himself with. It is simply another indication that the intended energy is being summoned, and the rite is working as it should.

One note here regarding Invocation and Evocation to Physical Manifestation. In the former, a sweet taste will always arise. In the latter case; in dealing with any of the Legion of Seventy-Two or the Fallen, a bitter taste will always be experienced. Do not let it distract you. Simply note it and continue on with that which you have chosen to do.

Concerning the Sense of Hearing (Sound)

Phenomena of this nature are highly problematic, owing to the areas of the Magical Chamber in which they will *always* be found to occur: *outside the Circle*. It is not at all uncommon to hear loud hisses, squealing (primarily from corners of the room) grunts (usually in one of the Four Quarters) whispers, loud raps on the walls, or a loud pounding sound as if a heavy man were trudging slowly up the steps leading to the Magical Chamber and therefore toward you, or—the one that bothers me the most—the incessant sound of something scratching at the walls; a sound reminiscent of something trying to claw its way out of some confinement. I have seen areas on walls actually damaged by such forces; and owing to this, I label them as physical in nature.

It is my suspicion that—due to their occurrence outside the circle—these sounds are produced by malignant beings trying to dissuade the magician from continuing his work, probably due to the pain and agony his performances are causing it or will cause it if taken to completion (Evocation to Physical Manifestation.) While such phenomena most certainly do occur in daily magical ritual performance, it is nothing compared to the magnitude and frequency of occurrence that is present when it occurs in Evocation to Physical Manifestation. In any event, use extreme care, pay close attention, and use due diligence not if—but when—sounds arise in the Magical Chamber. For you can be certain, "Something (truly) is afoot!"

Concerning the Sense of Sight

Without doubt, this is the most disturbing phenomena of all. And as with sounds, these visual events always occur outside of the Circle. However, they seem to be more dependent upon the nature of the Operation being performed. That is, Evocation to Physical Manifestation will produce visions of men and beast, etc., while Invocations will produce visions of angelic beings. In my own case, I will never forget the circle of small angelic figures that held hands and formed an inner circle within the circumference of the physical Circle of Art in which I was operating. These faceless, white beings simply stood there, the absence of their faces disturbing me to no end—at first. However, as I continued this certain magical practice daily over a 4 month time period, I became quite use to them. So much so in fact, that I hardly noticed their presence as I went about my intended Work.

Daily ritual practices usually produce floating, twinkling lights, and rays of light shooting along the walls of the Magical Chamber. In my opinion, these latter type of visual events are akin to one sharpening a knife on a stone of flint: 'sparks' are produced as the knife is sharpened by rubbing it against the flint surface, a nature consequence of the act of sharpening. The same here: the ritual performance constitutes a type of 'rubbing' against the barrier that separates the astral from the physical; a rubbing that is brought about by one's physical movements and ritual gestures. These types of occurrences are nothing to be concerned about. That is, unless of course, you are involved in Evocation to Physical Manifestation. THEN you had better be more than careful, because such twinkling and floating lights indicate that the manifestation is occurring at a rate much more rapid than usual, and some very unexpected and unpleasant results can come down on you quicker than you will realize.

There is also Astral Vision to be discussed, but I will leave that for another time. While only a cursory outline, I trust this paper will provide some insight—and provide some guidance—for those who have written to me regarding the production of physical phenomena during magical practice.

The Nature of Physical Phenomena in Magical Practice
Part II

Previously I discussed the nature of physical phenomena arising from various magical practices as that phenomena effects the sense of sight, hearing (sound) touch, taste, and smell, and speculated as to the possible causes underlying such occurrences. The purpose in doing this was not only to quell the concern of those who actually performed a full Kabbalistic Analysis on their ritual performances prior to doing them and who thus received dramatic physical effects from those rituals, but to provide a reflective base from which all of us might further examine our ritual work to see if there were attributes of our Work that we might have overlooked, or simply dispensed with without further investigation or thought. I am happy to say that from the number of responses from readers, the first purpose was fulfilled quite well. Additionally, the second intention also produced results. And the two most prominent results so produced will now be discussed in this small paper.

My very dear friend and colleague, Mr. Mark Stavish, Director of the Institute for Hermetic Studies, sent me the following which you may find useful:

> "Water—my experiences with water almost always occurred on the top of my left hand. It would be a drop. Sometimes two or three, but rarely." Mark further stated, "Jean Dubuis (a famous Occultist, Alchemist and Teacher who influenced Mark greatly) said that water, rain, was the means of transferring energy to the earth. So if you created a large energy sphere, then water or rain would often occur.
>
> "During the period when I attended the Wilkes-Barre, PA Pronaos (AMORC) with my great-uncle, each month we noticed that on the FIRST and THIRD Thursday of each month *for over five years,* that regardless of the month or even overall weather conditions, there was always some degree of humidity, rain, or moisture in the air on those nights. It became a joke."

This is an interesting and telling point, because it adds a new dimension to the physical phenomena of both sight and touch; it is also a clear example of an astral force impinging on an occult operation or magical rite to such a magnitude, that a crystallization of an invisible material substance (in this case, water content of the air) results. If anything, this physicality of magical and occult work is a further demonstration of what can occur when such work is properly executed. If the reader will use Mark's further example as an additional call to arms in the analysis of their own work, he or she may be able to recall and understand all the more those seemingly innocuous occurrences they may have experienced but overlooked or disregarded for want of a possible explanation.

Mark's comments helped me in this regard, for there was something I overlooked completely. Something which taught me (yet another) valuable lesson in magical matters. In 2001 I was involved in some highly experimental magic. That is, I was trying to apply what I hypothesized were general working principles from some medieval grimoires to certain rituals I was striving to construct. Rituals that—while medieval in principle—were echoed and addressed by none other than Eliphas Levi in his classic, "Transcendental Magic." This extrapolation and attempted synthesis required a formal "Working." That is, a repetition of the ritual performance over a 14 day period, a fair experimental run as I then saw it. The ritual involved certain principles of the Water and Fire Elements.

During my daily practice, I noticed an extreme increase in humidity in my Magical Chamber. I noted it, but as such physical manifestations are common, I did not think too much about it. But on the 7th day, I began to realize that the humidity level became so high, I could not don my ritual vestments without extreme discomfort. I did take humidity level readings in the Chamber, and found that while they did rise daily, on the 7th day they reached 97% and were absolutely suffocating. There was also a dramatic daily temperature increase in the room; but on the 7th day, the temperature in the room reached 92° Fahrenheit (F) (the average daily outside temperature at that time of the year—the winter time—being 37° (F), and the average temperature in our house being 69° (F). Additionally, all heat was turned off in my Magical Chamber, as I prefer to work in as cold a condition as possible.)

Still, I was determined to carry out the performance over the calculated 14 day period, so on that 7th day, regardless of the 97% humidity level and the 92° temperature in the Chamber, I conducted the rite. Within one hour of finishing the performance, I heard the sound of water running, and a loud hissing sound. The sounds blended together in such a way that I could not tell where they were coming from, and quite frankly, began to panic. But the unknown factors did not last long: both toilet bowls—one in a half–bath on the first floor of our house and one in the Master bathroom on the second floor—had blown their gaskets and plungers and overflowed at the same time. In addition, the 1 year old hot water heater in the basement had "ruptured" as the plumber later told me, leaked water all over the basement, and had its heating coils destroyed by "…apparently an uncontrolled energy surge…" (Note the presence of the Water Element in the first case and the Fire Element in the second.) But that was not all. For when my wife attempted to do the laundry, the automatic washer overflowed, soaking the floor and everything in sight, including a new carpet in the laundry/utility room. And all of this occurred within the span of 3 hours after the performance of the ritual on that 7th day. All total, there was over $1,000 worth of damage done due to my not backing off the ritual, analyzing the inordinate physical phenomena I was receiving, and making adjustments to the performance accordingly.

The point in all of this is that the forces we work with in Magic and the Occult may not be 'real' in the sense by which they are defined and quantified by physics; but they have an energy component or capacity that is most certainly able to effect the forces that do effect the physical world, and we can and will pay for it if we are not as careful and vigilant in our work as we can and should be. As the old saying goes, "A word to the wise is sufficient." I trust the reader will benefit from my folly.

Magical Saturation & Supersaturation: Just What are these States?

I briefly addressed a 'side issue' that arose in which a reader asked for a recommended course of magical study and experimentation for beginners. I did this because all too often beginning students—as well as those who should know better after a few years of work—glorify the vistas and panorama that truly is Magic, but without realizing there are many, many hidden conditions—or wide and deep 'pot holes'—on the Magical Path. And the one addressed in that question is a real doozy; especially since it is not addressed in ANY contemporary magical texts of which I am aware, save one, the title of which will be given at the end of this discussion. (The subject to be presented here is thoroughly addressed in certain mystical texts; but I will refrain from giving them here, because it is much to early for those texts to be of value to most. And for those who are nearing the point at which they need these books, they already know of the mystical texts to which I am referring.)

The first condition to which I refer is actually a normal, healthy phenomenon that allows the psychic nature of the Practitioner to adjust safely and completely to the ever growing magnitudes of magical energy they are calling down (or up, if you prefer) as a result of their magical study and practice. I call this state or condition, *"Magical Saturation."* It is a state which can—very quickly—lead to another but not so desirable state which I term, *"Magical Supersaturation."* Regardie did not differentiate between the two. Rather, he referred to both states as a condition of *"Spiritual Dryness."* To make matters worse, it is a condition I have never encountered in any so-called New Age writings. Thus the student is literally lost when the day comes and he or she begin to babble the Names of God or the Barbarous Words of Evocation like a blithering idiot. Briefly, this *Magical Saturation* can be summed up as, 'too much of any good thing causes problems.' But yet it must be remembered, this is a natural and healthy state, and *cannot* be avoided forever.

To be specific: in the state of Magical Saturation, the psychic nature becomes so overloaded with magical energy that it—cannot—just like a sponge—absorb anymore. When this happens, it just closes down, and uses this 'down time' to assimilate the massive influx of magical energy to which is has been exposed. That is, it literally integrates this high frequency, highly refined energy into its own psychic structure and functions. As a consequence, during this state, you cannot even think of doing any magical reading or practice: the very idea of even attempting such simply shuts your mind down. Of course, if you can't even do any magical reading, trying to do any ritual work is even more unthinkable: you just can't bear it anymore.

Now, in both theory and practice, you can push past this first state. At least you can the first few times it occurs. But even then, you can do so only for a short time. If you do however; if you push past the Magical Saturation stage, you will then enter another period—one of Magical Supersaturation. This is a very negative period in which it is difficult to even think somewhat deeply about anything—and that includes all those daily humdrum matters that are a part of every life. That is why it I term it a "not so desirable state." As the realistic and accomplished Magician knows, life is still tough enough, even when one is operating their Magic flawlessly, bending conditions and circumstances to their own will, achieving psychic and magical growth by leaps and bounds, while also enjoying the awareness of their own perfect Spiritual Unfoldment. Then along comes *Magical Saturation*, and now you have to tough it out by using only your normal reason, logic, social and life skills, etc. In other words, you have been reduced to the level of the average 'Joe' in the street. Lots of fun, huh?! But when Magical Supersaturation occurs, you're caught: you can't even use these most basic, evolved, human functions correctly. That is, you can't think clearly, reason correctly, act and react properly, evaluate effectively, all the while feeling like you are walking in some slow moving daydream state. In short, everything in your life—including you—seem very surreal. And you can bet this will lead to more life troubles than you care to count.

The first time Magical Saturation happened to me was in January 1973, one month after getting married, and after eight years of increasingly intense Magical work (including two full blown Evocations to Physical Manifestation) and sixteen months after going under Regardie's tutelage. I didn't know what happened: I could not even form a mental image of a pentagram let alone trace one in the air. My tongue literally refused to pronounce any of the Divine Names, let alone intone or vibrate them. Regardie's advice? "Get used to reading some Agatha Christie novels, Joe, or start watching the boob-tube until the Dryness passes!" And it did—6 months later. If I had pushed past this first state into the state of Magical Supersaturation, the time it would have taken for that state to fade away would have only increased in length. In fact, I did push past into Magical Supersaturation at one point: it was thirteen long months before I could even broach the idea of 'working Magic' once more. And the life problems I experienced as a direct result of this 'pushing past,' were beyond belief.

Can this first state be avoided? No. The state of Magical Saturation is a normal reflex reaction to the Work as I stated: it must occur so you can go on to higher forms of Magic and grow mentally, emotionally, and psychically, while enabling your Spiritual Nature to unfold quietly, normally, and fully.

Can Magical Supersaturation be put off? Yes, but only so long. But that "so long" is anywhere from years to decades. But it will occur too, and NOT as a result of your backing off and allowing the state of Magical Saturation to occur and do its job within your psychic nature. Why must this second state occur anyway? Because it will only occur...eventually...when the 'time is right' for you. That will be the time in which you are on the verge of the Great Crisis: The Dark Night of the Soul and the Abramelin Operation.

But these are matters that cannot be addressed here. They are decades away for most, and for those who are nearing the Great Crisis now, nothing I say here will be of any value to them. Why? Because they will already be in such sympathy with their Holy Guardian Angel (HGA) that he will lead them in the specific way they must approach, endure, survive, and Attain to the Knowledge and Conversation of him.

There is one contemporary magical text that deals with ideas and topics directly related to the Dark Night of the Soul (or a variation of it as I read it) and its role in Attaining to the K&C of the HGA. In fact, it also deals with matters of more important immediacy that precede the entire HGA operation. It is a remarkably lucid, well written and intense book, written by a man who has no doubt Attained (I say this, because only one who has passed through the states of the process would know of the things he brings out in his contribution.) I unreservedly recommend this book. The student must, however, study it carefully and think upon its contents. It is my suggestion though, that under no circumstances should the student run right off and attempt one of the versions of possible ways in which one can Attain to the K&C of the HGA. Because that is what this book is about. In my opinion, it uses many—but not all—of the principles behind the Abramelin Operation, applying them to the Operation itself, and to other possible avenues through which the Experience could be Attained.

I would also counsel those who choose to use this modern book as a guide in eventually attempting the classic Abramelin Operation (which it also covers, although only briefly) to purchase a copy of *The Book of the Sacred Magic of Abramelin the Mage,* and use it as the main study, preparatory, and working text for the Operation itself. The modern text would them be used as a reference and guide in clarifying and explaining certain areas that Abramelin does not make quite clear. In this way too, it is an invaluable document. The book I am referring to is entitled, *21st Century Mage: Bringing the Divine Down to Earth* by Jason Augustus Newcomb. In my opinion, this is not a "New Age" book. It is incisive, clear, thorough in its content considerations, and above all, well balanced.

Chapter Eight

Magic, Mysticism and Alchemy

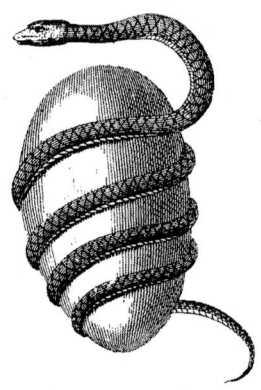

Magic, Mysticism, and Alchemy —
Is There an Essential Connection Between Them?

Throughout magical literature, extending as far back as the writing of Albertus Magus if not earlier, we find an attempt to make Alchemy fit into the magical scheme of things. Indeed, even the Golden Dawn has its own few 'practical' experiments in laboratory alchemy, not to mention its extensive 'spiritual' view of the matter, as it pertains to the supposed 'perfection' of the magician's inner nature. But try as they may, regardless of the time period or the writer, Magic and Alchemy are two distinct, separate disciplines. Any attempt to unite them in the bonds of Holy Occult Wedlock are only so many vain attempts to justify some a priori system of desired thought; one that is completely devoid of the extensive study of alchemical theory and of laboratory experience. To a lesser extent, a few mystics have also made an attempt to marry their mystical tradition to the Science and Art that is Alchemy, albeit they have been more 'honest' in their doctrines, insisting that the symbolism and words of Alchemy are only so many gateways leading to the spiritual splendour of man's innermost being. That is, they have not appreciably attempted to demonstrate the relevance of their mysticism as it applies to the laboratory model of alchemical experimentation.

On page 111 of *Ceremonial Magic & The Power of Evocation*, I stated a *Magical Axiom* (Axiom 9) which reads: "Do not reject the religious tradition in which you were raised, nor the common-sense found in what religionists call the Commandments of God. The use of these percepts is crucial in devising an effective subjective synthesis and producing a corresponding coherent, integrated subconscious belief system. It is also the one fundamental axiom every Practitioner of magic rigorously avoids, which accounts for more magical failure than is realized."

Quite a few readers have asked me if this axiom is truly necessary, and for me to be "honest" in my private answer to them. They wondered if the advice given in this axiom is absolutely necessary in order to achieve success in their ceremonial evocations, and even if it is a necessary ingredient in their having success in their daily magical ritual performance. Or, if it is not some type of unconscious projection of mine; one based, perhaps, in my own need to "make peace" with my former Catholicism.

In his very insightful book, *Shadows of Life and Thought*, A.E. Waite deals with this issue, although in a somewhat stilted way. Nevertheless, his argument is telling. And in the end, it is correct. In fact, it was Waite's influence that taught me this lesson and that indeed, it had to be applied to my own magical work and life. When I finally did so; when I achieved an intellectual and emotional honesty with myself over this matter, the results that stemmed from my magical work increased by a factor of at least one hundred.

The matter boils down to a very simple state of affairs. Most of us are brought into this world and 'educated' in some system of religious thought. More often than not it is in one of the major, recognized forms of religion such as Judaism, the Judeo-Christian ethic, Hinduism, or some such structured 'approach to God.' And for one reason or another, those of us who have taken up the practice of the Occult in general or Magic in particular, have done so due to some basic disagreement or conflict with either the tenets, the formality, or the widespread hypocrisy that underlies these forms of religious orthodoxy. But consciously recognizing this alienating condition does not neutralize that subconscious (unconscious) part of our mental fabric and psychic nature that has made our early days of the creed's acceptance, its own. As surely as your subjective nature has a need for material gratification and worldly fulfillment; for acceptance by others and for love; it has an equal need for each and every other sustaining, unconscious thought-pattern being satiated and gratified: it has become a matter of maintaining psychic equilibrium. As such, these needs have a direct and powerful effect on the extent and effectiveness of the state of subjective synthesis that you create in order to work your magic effectively. Lighting a candle to some saint, saying a prayer central to that early Faith, or attending a church or synagogue—if only for a few minutes once or twice a year—will serve to strike the required balance within this part of your hidden nature. After a while, you might not only find yourself not objecting to doing these things, but you may find that you actually enjoy doing them as well. "Impossible! I don't need those lies and that nonsense in my life anymore!" you say? Don't fool yourself. You can try, and you might get your conscious mind to agree with your hate of this part of your past, but you won't deceive that Secret Self hiding behind the dim horizons of your consciousness. Try making Peace with this part of yourself and see.

It may help if I give you an example. As I stated in *Ceremonial Magic*, I was born into a Roman Catholic family and raised in that Faith. And while I cannot abide the Catholic church in its present form, I yet consider myself a Christian, and more exactly, a Catholic! How can this be? Quite simply, I found the philosophical teachings of Pierre Teilhard de Chardin, a Jesuit Priest, theologian, philosopher, and paleontologist—and whose complex writing unify certain aspects of Science and Religion—to have a profound impact upon me. Together with the New Thought Philosophy, the two enabled me to form my own eclectic system of thought; one which is in perfect agreement with my own subconscious state of subjective synthesis, and which allows my magical efforts to succeed splendidly. To this day, I do not attend any church services, nor am I likely to. But with the views of de Chardin and New Thought welded into my own subjective synthesis, there is no need for me to take such a measure. I pay homage to that Part of God that is important to me in another way, daily.

Give this seemingly minor consideration some thought as you can, and try to hammer out a system of 'religious thought' for yourself. One that will allow you to "Light a candle to the God of your childhood," and which at the same time, will allow you to practice your magic in ways that others can only dream about.

Magic vs. Mysticism — You May be in for a Surprise

Regardless of how far back we go in time to examine the doctrines of Magic and Mysticism, we are faced with one inescapable conclusion: both of these avenues of psychic development and spiritual unfoldment run parallel to each other. More often than not they are in direct competition with one another; if not in the literature of any given era, then in the spirited public and private debates of their adherents. It is a property of human nature that those who follow a given way feel theirs is the 'best' philosophy, the 'only religion ordained by God for man,' or that theirs is the "One True Church." This human propensity is completely understandable and might even be acceptable, if the conclusions that followed from such views did not bring with them such utter blindness and base ignorance when considering the essential natures of these two *seemingly* disjointed paths to God.

Recently, one of my private students in Magic experienced his turn in assuming that his way—the way of Magic—was the "best" of all possible ways, and that Mysticism was only so much backwater in the spiritual sea that eventually 'helps' in leading one, first to Attain the Knowledge and Conversation of the Holy Guardian Angel (Attain to the K&C of the HGA) and then, to more distant shores that lay beyond this exalted first port of arrival. After obtaining my student's permission—and with the reader's permission here—I would like to address this seemingly obtuse issue in an effort to possibly help those who have either asked this question of themselves, or who will inevitably do so at some point in their own magical futures.

Experience has taught me—and this includes my own experience from my younger days when Israel Regardie was mentoring me in Magic—that at the outset of his or her magical career, one concludes:

1. Magic is the most exalted way. Not only to manifest one's desires upon earth, but as the ultimate avenue by which one can approach and eventually experience God
2. That Mysticism is a parallel road; but one that lacks the dynamics possessed by Ritual and Ceremonial Magic. That is, while Mysticism is 'interesting,' only the Rites of Magic can completely fulfill one's material and spiritual desires

As the years wear on, and as additional magical and interior experience is gained, these first views are modified by the practicing magician almost automatically. Eventually, he or she realizes that this modification has taken place, and now the individual becomes consciously aware of their new conclusion which tells them:

3. Magic can and even should be *combined* with mysticism in order to realize the ultimate goals of worldly accomplishment and spiritual unfoldment.

In other words, the pure magical approach has left them wanting in some interior or exterior way. So the student begins to explore the realm of Mysticism, and makes many and varied attempts to fuse the two into one eclectic, workable, satisfying whole. Through this fusion, he or she (still) anticipates their using Magic in order to fulfill their worldly desires, but now also hold to a new impulse: that Mysticism will lead them to God by a more or less direct route. More time passes. Not atypically, another decade or so in which this synthesis is attempted.

It is during this intense exploration that the individual may discover Mysticism is actually a structured or layered discipline. That is, as I see it, this discipline can be found to consist of:

1. **Mysticism** — the 'standard variety,' such as is found in the work of those Rosicrucian societies that are so well know today. The student eventually discovers that this form of Mysticism actually consists of a combination of 'weak' Magic

and watered down Higher Mysticism (see below). But in actuality, this particular mystical approach cannot be condemned or discarded out of hand, since its aim is to develop the **PSYCHIC**—as opposed to the truly **SPIRITUAL**—nature of the individual, the latter of which is already perfect and simply needs the proper mode of interior **AND** exterior activity through which to express in both the interior and exterior worlds.
2. **Higher Mysticism** — an extremely pragmatic, truly **Psycho–Spiritual** involvement meant to manifest the Will of the Mystic in the here and now by forging a *conscious link* with that part of God that is both within and without the Mystic. It is best illustrated, studied, and practiced by focusing on the doctrines, teachings, and methods of what is called "**New Thought**" or "**Mental Science.**" (The wirings of Frederick Bailes, Ernest Holmes, William Walker Atkinson, Judge Thomas Troward, and Raymond Holliwell are the most powerful examples I know of in this type of Mysticism.)

But even here is a cautionary note to be remembered. And this is, the writings that define the very core of this "Higher Mysticism" can be divided into two Schools of Thought: the **Pragmatically Psycho-Spiritual** school, and the **Philosophically Religious** school, the resulting **'philosophic-religiosity'** of the latter being directed into material advancement of the individual; but *only THROUGH* his or her further spiritual unfoldment. That is, the latter approach brings desired material results, but as an *effect* of the aspirant's **true spiritual unfoldment.** This unfoldment is really a conscious ascent (in varying degrees) to Godhead in Kether (not in Tiphareth) literally, which brings the power of Godhead down into Manhood, and therefore enables manifestation of wants and desires on the material plane of Malkuth through the refinement of Yesod.

But for the hard pressed individual who wishes to follow this type of 'practical mysticism,' the **Pragmatically Psycho-Spiritual** School of Thought (as given in the writings of Bailes, Atkinson, Troward, and Holliwell) is the **only** way to proceed—at first. That is, after providing for the material wants and desires, an elevation and perfection of this school's approach leads one to the **Philosophically Religious** school through the writings of Ernest Holmes—which involves a conscious ascension to Godhead and bringing that power down into Manhood. This final step then, comes to be understood as the preferred way to proceed yet further in these matters.

3. **High Mysticism** — the Mysticism in which the **Love of God** is the sole aim: **both in giving and receiving that Love**, such as is found in the writings of St. Ignatius, Evelyn Underhill, and in those most appropriate and current of all instructions, given in the writings of Pierre Teilhard DE Chardin. (For those desiring an approach to "High Mysticism" other than that of the Christian School of Thought, writings based upon Native American, Australian, African, Taoist, Buddhist, Jewish, Hindu, Islamic, and ancient Greek Visionaries can be found in, *The Essential Mystics: Selections from the World's Great Wisdom Traditions* by Andrew Harvey).

Thus, in the end, after the elevated, Higher Mysticism of the Philosophically Religious school is reached, the individual's quest is usually transformed into that of **High Mysticism:** the highest form of Mysticism, and the final level meant to expand the Seeker's **Soul** (the **consciousness**) directly into God—thereby attaining **conscious Union With God** in the purest sense, while he or she is yet in this world—and this, essentially, by applying the ancient maxim that has curiously been adopted by Magic as its creed, "*Invoke often! Enflame thyself with Prayer!*"

But ironically, 'something' happens near or at the end of this period: as if the Seeker was being given some final test. Something that leads the utterly exhausted Magician-Mystic to finally conclude that:

4. Magic *completes* Mysticism

This conclusion is based upon two fundamental premises:

- The idea that *one should not attempt to elevate himself to Godhead, but rather, the he should (only) attempt to bring the*

Godhead down into manhood, a view espoused throughout contemporary magical literature

- *That one's exterior Magic should be 'balanced' by the interior method of Mysticism.* That is, Magic is conceived as being a more primarily outward—and therefore 'dynamic'—expression of one's spiritual nature and Will, while Mysticism is viewed as being its interior, 'static' counterpart

Why does the student's first conclusion seem warranted? *Because in the course of ritual and magical work with the standard practices of The Lesser Banishing Ritual of the Pentagram, the Banishing Ritual of the Hexagram, the invocation of the Elements and performing such rituals as the Middle Pillar, working with Talismanic Magic, etc., the magician comes to establish a relationship with the forces of those practices and (hopefully) uses those forces and those relationships as springboards in attempting to Attain to the K&C of the HGA.* In short, the practitioner sees him or herself as being involved in a *dynamic* activity through their magical work. And this is where their reasoning 'goes wrong.' For while it is true that ritual and ceremonial practices can eventually lead one to Attain to the K&C of the HGA, **this attainment is NOT the end of what has been** called in the literature of the field "The Great Awakening." *Rather, it is only the beginning of it!* After the Great Event of the Awakening however, the individual—being led by his HGA—will find that:

Mysticism completes Magic: it is not the other way around

He or she may therefore (eventually) find that further travel on the Path and exploration of the deeper mysteries of one's own being does not occur through further ritual or ceremonial performance; but rather, from a serious and *complete* 'turning inward.' A turning inward that is the hallmark of *Mysticism*.

As to the second conclusion: the idea of 'balance' is both misinterpreted and misunderstood by the Practitioner. They come to believe that this 'balance' possesses some sort of 'flexibility.' That is, he or she feels they can somehow 'shift' from one to another—or alternate—between Magic and Mysticism. Or to put it plainly, that one can *use* either one to offset problems that arise from not getting the 'proper' (or the desired) results from the other. They fail to understand that—as in the physical world—balance is a very tenuous matter indeed. They would do well to visit a child's playground and watch children at play on a seesaw. The fulcrum possesses one and only one point at which the device will do what it was intended to do. And that *single point*, is the *point of balance.* It is the same with Magic and Mysticism. This confused thinking regarding 'balance' occurs because the individual attempts to use a metaphor in 'reasoning out' a course of practical action, while failing to **understand** the concepts and meanings behind the very words they used to 'reason out' that course of action. As a consequence, they make fundamental errors in communicating with others—and worst of all—with themselves. One thing is for certain: whether the individual chooses to follow Mysticism or Magic, or use the former as the gateway to the latter, a study of language itself is one of the best investments they could make with their time. The most traditional and best place I ever found to start such a study is by reading *Language in Thought and Action* by S.I. Hayakawa.

For thirty-five years, I too believed the self-induced arguments above, proclaiming to myself and others that "Magic completed Mysticism." But after the Attainment and what proceeded, I found out otherwise, as have so many others who have had the same set of experiences. The two—Magic and Mysticism—do not run together on parallel lines, necessarily intersecting at some or any point. In effect then,

Magic is *A* precursor — but not the ONLY precursor — to Mysticism.

Am I therefore advocating that Magic is a 'waste of time' and one should dash straight off into the glorious realms of High Mysticism? Of course not. For those of us who are (or were) drawn to the Magical Arts and Sciences, Magic is as important; as necessary and as crucial an undertaking and practice as it is for us to breathe. But as in the case of all living and growing things, it must be remembered that *personal change* brings with it new vistas and new worlds to explore, as well as other means through which those worlds are explored.

In the final analysis, when we enter our Magical Chambers daily to perform our magical work, we should keep one ear always tuned to that saying uttered by, I believe, Percy Bullock, one of the members of the early Golden Dawn: *"In the end, we all become Mystics."* The bottom line is: he was right.

Magic, Mysticism, and Alchemy — Is There an Essential Connection Between Them?

Dating from the earliest Mystery Traditions of Egypt and Mesopotamia, and echoed throughout the ensuing centuries by 5th century Pagans and Christians, even to the time of Albertus Magnus in the 13th century and the 16th century writings of Paracelsus, we find concerted attempts to make Alchemy fit into the magical and mystical scheme of things. Indeed, even in the best known school of the latter day Western Esoteric Tradition—the Golden Dawn—we find a few 'practical' experiments in laboratory alchemy, not to mention its extensive 'spiritual' view of the matter as it pertains to the supposed 'perfection' of the magician's inner nature. But try as they may, regardless of the time period or the writer, Magic and Alchemy always seem to emerge as two distinct, separate disciplines. Are attempts to unite Magic and Alchemy in the bonds of Holy Occult Wedlock only so many vainglorious exercises, meant to justify some a priori system of desired thought? One that is completely devoid of the extensive study of physical alchemical theory and its laboratory experience?

To a lesser extent, a few mystics have also attempted to marry their mystical tradition to the Science and Art that is Alchemy, albeit they have been more 'honest' in their doctrines, insisting that the symbolism and terms of Alchemy are only so many gateways leading to the spiritual splendor of man's innermost being. That is, they have not appreciably attempted to demonstrate the relevance of their mysticism as it applies to the laboratory model of alchemical experimentation.

What, then, are the values of Magic or Mysticism as applied to Alchemy? Indeed, do they really share some common ground? Or, are these three esoteric disciplines distinct, unique efforts, which are to be engaged in separately at any given time?

During my study with Frater Albertus at the Paracelsus Research Society (PRS) in Salt Lake City, Utah, from 1975 through 1980 in which I completed the entire Seven Year Cycle of Theoretical and Laboratory instruction in Alchemy which he taught, it became evident to me—and to all of my other classmates—that even to breathe the word "Magic" during those classes was to invite the most horrendous ridicule from Frater Albertus. And attempts to perform simple, private magical rituals even in one's own room while at the Society's compound, met with the strictest of disciplinary measures, not the least of which was the possible permanent expulsion from the PRS. As an example. During my "Quarta" (4th year) class at the PRS, I performed my (then) usual daily magical regimen in the early morning hours, prior to class. The dressing down I received in front of my classmates from Frater was one of the most humiliating experiences of my life. When I complained to Regardie about this some months later, he chided me again, severely, stating, "Working any Magic while at PRS is out! You should have known better by now! Frater told me about this! He had a conniption because he sensed what you were up to, and you deserved what you got! I learned that lesson a log time ago, and respect Frater's wish while there: 'do your own stuff on your own time, not on mine!' and he is right in demanding this!" Yet Frater not only 'tolerated' Regardie and his well known magical background, but the two actually became fast friends and colleagues—after a style. After completing the 7 Year Class Cycle at the PRS, I questioned Francis once again on that incident of three years earlier, and what could have possibly angered the old Alchemist so much. This is one matter Regardie would not be direct with me on, saying only, "You'll figure it out in time."

It took twenty years after that last seventh year class for me to realize that Frater's anger was actually the Key; or rather, *a Key* in seeing that a connection does exist between Magic, Mysticism, and Alchemy, and in using that Key to understand the roles that Magic and Mysticism play in alchemical practice. For in Frater Albertus' world, his *preferred mode of influencing alchemical experimentation was through Mysticism, and not through Magic. Further, since the entire PRS was designed to blossom as a consequence of this mystical marriage between the two—between Alchemy and Mysticism—the performance of any magical ritual while there served to plant so many thorns among the flowers, and interfered with the blossoming that was going on daily.*

So how is it then, that if Magic is so far removed from Alchemy—and Mysticism so harmoniously congruent with it as demonstrated by Frater Albertus and his famous Paracelsus Research Society—that Regardie and Frater—and later myself—were able to 'make peace' over our approaches to Alchemy, and even work together long after the seven years of formal classes ended? If it seems as though I am trying to draw a correlation and therefore a relevancy between Magic, Mysticism, and Alchemy, you are right: I am. For in fact:

Alchemy is the 'proving ground' for those activities termed "Magic" and "Mysticism." It is neither a separate discipline nor a disjointed esoteric activity. Rather, it reflects—in the Laboratory of Malkuth—the extent and level of psychic development and spiritual unfoldment respectively, that the Alchemist has achieved by virtue of his or her Mystical or/and Magical practices.

*As such, the active exploration of Alchemy by the Magician or/and Mystic through study and laboratory experimentation, produces a third field of Occult activity: a 'Philosophical Effort,' whose crowning glory is the Summum Bonum of the Philosophers: The Stone of the Wise—an actual **physical object**, produced through alchemically processes. This Stone enables the Philosopher to physically transmute his or her exterior world, incite yet greater spiritual transmutation within their own interior world, in addition to using the Stone to confer **physical immortality** upon the (now) Adept Philosopher.*

We know that both magical practices and mystical exercises are designed to drastically change both the outer and inner worlds of the adherent, and that therefore—eventually—the matter of one's spiritual unfoldment must and will be addressed through such efforts

What is happening here, is that whether one first chooses the magical path or the mystical path, or begins to develop the psychic faculties first through magical practices and then 'grows' into the mystical way of attainment, the spiritual *unfoldment* that occurs will enable the alchemical processes to produce the "Paraphysical" (above or beyond physical) results they are intended to produce in the laboratory. However, the aspirant will find that the *Path of the Mystic* will produce the intended results much more completely and more quickly, *if* the individual *naturally* grows into the mystical *after* having exhausted the magical.

Am I saying that the Path of Magic will produce lesser alchemical results if persisted in, and the move to Mysticism is not made if the *natural inclination* to do so arises? That is, will the alchemical results be slower in coming, and will those results always seem to lack some 'maturity' if the Mystic Way is utterly rejected when its time of arrival dawns upon the magician? Yes, I am. And while this may upset many a magician, I did not make the rules in these matters: but I have observed them at work countless times, and have tested them upon myself and others over four–plus decades, and am *certain* of what I have just written. This is why so many magicians throughout history have abandoned serious alchemical studies in the end: their results were always left wanting, forcing them into a 'spiritual' interpretation of those results, and in fact, of all of Alchemy.

By the same token, one cannot force him or herself to move from Magic to Mysticism, simply because they are desirous of the results Alchemy promises. That is, the 'growth' from the former into the latter must come *naturally*, as a consequences of having taken Magic *as far as they are capable of taking it* in their own particular case. In like fashion, the individual who chooses to travel the Path of the Mystic at the inception of his or her esoteric studies, must not expect to reach the Promised Land of alchemical results any faster than the person who is **naturally** drawn to Magic as a first effort. This 'original' mystic-type will find that they too must pass through the same trials, tests, and tribulations of inner growth just as must the magician; and so consequently, will not reach the prized Crown of the Philosophers any faster than their brethren magicians.

Above all remember, it is both absolutely absurd and an utter waste of effort for the magician to 'perform' some magical rite before entering into a particular alchemical experiment. Such attempts to 'transfer magical energy' to the experiment are as ineffective as they are ludicrous: it simply does not work that way. Conversely, it is equally foolish for the Mystic to enter into some depth state of meditation or contemplation prior to that same (or other) alchemical experiment, in order to 'spiritualize' themselves and the experiment to the point where the promised alchemical results manifest easily, quickly, and completely. Such is trite "New Age" propaganda. The long and the short of it is:

*Perfected alchemical results are the products of a gradual, inner growth that leads the Seeker to ever higher states of consciousness; states in which some Unity with Godhead is attained. And these states cannot be forced, coerced, or demanded: they must be **earned** through the techniques of Magic which bring about psychic **development**, and through the practices of Mysticism which encourage and assist in the **unfoldment** of the aspirant's true spiritual nature.*

All those involved in the fields of esotericism have heard of the *"Three Alchemical Essentials,"* i.e., the *Salt, Sulphur,* and *Mercury* of the Alchemists, and that they are—in fact—more than "principles. They have also heard of the *"Three Alchemical Processes"* of *Separation, Purification,* and *Cohabation,* and may even know that these manipulations are much more than allegorical ideas applied to the Three Essentials. Many of these others may even know that the Salt is another word for the *body* of an alchemically prepared substance, the Alchemical Sulphur is actually the *consciousness* of that substance, and that the Alchemical Mercury is the *Life* of that substance. Still others may be aware that the Salt exists throughout all Three Kingdoms of Nature—the Vegetable, the Animal, and the Mineral—as a compound having the chemical properties of a base, while the Sulphur is that which exists as an oil throughout these Kingdoms. Further, some may also know that the Mercury has different 'vehicles,' depending upon the Kingdom from which it is derived. That is, its vehicle is an alcohol in the Vegetable Kingdom, the blood in the Animal Kingdom, and an Alkahest in the Mineral Kingdom.

But what remains to be discovered through the *apparent* mechanical manipulations of the Three Essentials by the Three Alchemical Processes, is the concealed Quintessence of the Essentials, and the secret forces behind the Three Processes. This is the task of the *Philosopher,* and not that of the Magician or Mystic.

Rest assured however, that the latter two can most certainly enter into the Kingdom of the Philosopher if they but persist in the Great Work, according to the paths presented to them by that part of the Godhead that lies at the very core of their being.

The Nature of Truth and its Role in Magical and Mystical Attainment

Listen to those who people the world around you: "The truth of the matter is..." or "If the truth be known..." Perhaps you heard "Ours is the true magical order because..." then again, "To tell you the truth..." This word, "truth" is bandied about so much in daily life, and used with such flippancy and carelessness, that it and the concept for which it stands has become utterly meaningless. It has not only lost all of its impact, but the very essence of its interior meaning has dissipated into the casual sayings in which it is buried. Like thousands of other potent and important words, it has fallen into that class of useless verbiage that conveys nothing, acting as filler to connect verbal space by those whose intellect is as empty as the hollow words they use. You know the type I mean. The, "Well, like ya' know, like ya' know, like ya' know" crowd. If my appraisal of this situation is correct, what then is this thing called truth? Why is it important, how can we come to know it, and equally important, how can we use it properly in moving to magical and mystical states of attainment?

In my opinion, the ultimate nature of that which we call "Truth" consists of the *conscious apprehension of an Interior (subjective or subconscious) state or experience that can be tested in the Exterior world (Malkuth).* What does this mean? It simply means that those interior experiences or states of awareness that we consciously experience during our magical rites or mystical practices **must** possess key elements that can be tested in the outer world of daily life. If any such consciously apprehended Interior experiences or states cannot be so tested, *they are to be discarded as a mental or psychic aberration; one that can and will lead to those two greatest threats to the magician or mystic: self-illusion and self-delusion.* Let us examine more closely what is meant by "conscious apprehension" so as to remove any confusion.

Learn—>Understand—>Comprehend—>(Practice)—>
Experiential Knowledge—>Apprehension

Let us take an example. Suppose you are looking for "Truth 2." In our search for this "Truth 2," knowledge which is comprehended is placed into practice through such techniques (in our case) as magical rituals, ceremonial actions, or mystical introversions. This 'practice-element' leads to an entirely new form of knowledge which I refer to as "Experiential Knowledge." That is, a knowledge which gives deeper insights and establishes new connections with similar ideas (that are part of, say, a "Truth 1") which the student has previously comprehended and made his own through earlier practices. This new Experiential Knowledge of Truth 2 will gradually be so assimilated by the mind of the student that he reaches a point where he *consciously apprehends*—makes that new Experiential Knowledge—*a living part of his own Interior life, both consciously and subconsciously.* Thus, he has *consciously apprehended* something that was initially an Interior (or subjective) experience or state, but which now is also an integral part of his daily magical or mystical consciousness as well.

But it cannot and must not end here. *For in all cases, Truth—the genuine article—will always present to the conscious mind of the student, elements of itself that can be put to the test in the Exterior World of men and matter.* If the test succeeds, then the individual has most certainly attained to "a Truth." If it fails, then it must be rejected as a self-illusional or self-delusional ploy of his lower nature, created and offered to turn him from the Path of Spiritual Unfoldment and magical growth or mystical attainment. Likewise, if no such elements of the "Truth" present themselves for testing, then the unveiled lie of the lower nature is to be eradicated and discarded as quickly and completely as possible.

It is important to understand here that this simple "Truth Concept and Test" as I term it, is not some secret society or magical order concept to be used only for magical and mystical ends. Far from it! In fact, while we use this device as a mainstay in our magical and mystical endeavors, we can and should also use it in our daily affairs of living, working, and moving through the world of men and their society.

If you study the above with a careful eye, you will be able to answer for yourself 'why' knowing the Truth is so important, 'how' you can come to know it, and will be able to devise proper ways of 'using' it in you own magical or mystical efforts. Why will you be able to apply this simple "Truth Axiom" to your own specific, particular magical, mystical, or life-cases? Because now you know what Truth 'looks like.' Don't you? Think about it.

Thought there was more to this 'Truth' business, didn't you? There is not. As with all things that are ultimately based in empirical reality, the Truth is always simple. It is only man, with his need to unnecessarily complicate and make complex the simple things, and to bend things to his own will through his stylized interpretation, that problems arise. Guard yourself accordingly. Let no one tell you your own Truth: discover it and make it your own through your conscious apprehension of it.

Self-Honesty and its Role in Magical Attainment

"Self-Honesty": a term and concept mouthed by few, believed in by less, and practiced by fewer still. But what is this quality and how does it impact one's own magical attainment, psychic development, and spiritual unfoldment? If we look at the words composing this term, we find of course, the two seemingly innocuous words, "self" and "honesty." We think we understand each word, so why is it so difficult for us to put the two together to form one *working* quality that can benefit us in *each and every area of our lives;* not only in the study and practice of Magic? Essentially because we really don't know what the "Self" is. That is, we have had few, if any, genuine **realizations** of this most central aspect of our lives. By the same token, we have somehow managed to transform the moral function of "honesty" into a condition that has become an expedient *tool* used to achieve the success we desire, obtain the thing we want, and avoid situations and conditions we fear or shy away from for one reason or another. In short, while we retain the use of the word "honesty," we have replaced it with the mental concept of *"cleverness."* We then compliment ourselves when our lack of *experiential knowledge and understanding* of the Self is applied to the techniques of cleverness, and we obtain the trinket of our choice.

Yet why is it that when we obtain our most recent 'heart's desire' we feel so ill at ease; have trouble sleeping the same night we received our latest delight; and walk around day after day, feeling at odds with 'something' within us. Why is it that this latest 'necessity'—the product of our very lack and cleverness—is soon abandoned by us, being ever so quickly replaced by the desire for yet another bauble that we rationalize in a split mental second is *really* the thing we were after in the first place? Why? Because deep within us is a conflict; a state of being that tells us our lack of experiential knowledge of the Self, united to the tricks of cleverness, have gotten us something we *thought* we desired or needed. But since the object of our fleeting lust did not fill the bill of contentment, we keep looking ahead to bigger, faster, more expensive, more of the same, without recognizing the root cause of our trouble.

This root cause is really two-fold: lack of experiential knowledge of the Self, and a confusion between **need and desire**. In a very real way, the first—that lack of experiential knowledge of the Self—brings about the second. As a result, we can't see the forest for the trees, and can no longer distinguish genuine need from pure desire. But rest assured, your subconscious mind knows the difference. And no amount of rationalization or cleverness will fool it into believing that a need is a desire, or a desire, a need. ***It is the unconscious awareness of this difference that*** *thus establishes the internal conflict within us.* And the process will continue, wasting our time, our energy, and our very lives, unless we do something about it, and do that something **now**.

It is an emotionally painful process to be sure; but only because we have fallen into a pattern of action-reaction that has become a 'comfort zone' for us. Regardless of the real-world problems this lack of Self-Honesty creates for us, this comfort zone has become our friend and ally: someone or something we automatically rely on to fill that emptiness inside. An emptiness that—as you know—is never really filled, but only cluttered with more confused needs and desires. So how do we extricate ourselves from this endless cycle of return and unfulfillment?

The most effective way I know to remove oneself from this useless pattern of confusion, unhappiness, and lack of genuine result, is through the process of *Self-Disidentification*. This rather easy process does take some time to **master**. But its effects are so immediate and positive, that the serious individual who employs it will usually see dramatic results within days. For it is through a coordinated series of verbal and inner self-dialogues, coupled to certain mental awareness states, that this dis-identification is brought about; a condition in which one becomes so consciously aware of his Self as pure consciousness and Will, that all other aspects of the personality become subservient to it. When this happens, this *experience of Self* is immediately and effectively able to distinguish between genuine need and the pure desire, and order them in such a way that the individual's direction and efforts in obtaining them become maximized to the extreme. The result? This new Self-Honesty now enables one to obtain just those very things that truly make the individual happy, content, and emotionally justified while using the processes needed to effect their obtainment. In a magical sense, when one uses the process of Self-Disidentification, it is not unusual for things lusted after to fall away, things genuinely needed to appear easily and in a short time, and those objects that are truly desired to be handled in such a manner that they too manifest in the life of the individual in a surprisingly short interval. It all becomes a matter of eliminating the useless, re-prioritizing, and effectively directing and using one's forces, while maintaining a feeling of self-integrity that appeases the objections of the subconscious mind that arise when cleverness is replaced by the simple quality of—Self-Honesty.

How does one go about such a Self-Disidentification? The best methods I ever found are those given in the book, *The Act of Will*, by Roberto Assagioli. Not only does this relatively small volume discuss these simple but powerful techniques, but it discusses the Will as a complex psycho-spiritual function, much in keeping with my own view on the Will being the result of shifts in consciousness.

In terms of Magic, once the experience of the Self becomes a daily event, and the honesty that differentiates between needs and desires is in place, the individual's reprioritizing and directing of his or her magical force insure that the best comes into one's life at all times.

Those who are serious in their study and practice of Old System Magic such as I advocate, would do well to investigate the writings of Roberto Assagioli, and incorporate them into their life stream. Those who do will forever be grateful to this genius who wedded the originally cold, austere principles of psychoanalysis to the truly spiritual phenomena of the Self and its Will, and who did so in the most holistic way conceivable.

Wisdom and Power of the Ages — The Time of Its Re-Emergence is at Hand

The Word is everywhere today, and it is spreading. The Wisdom of Old System Magic cannot—and will not be hid any longer under the New Age bushel of dogma and pseudo-doctrine; of lodge and Order; of personalities and badges; of half-truths and deceits; of ignorance and fear. As a light that has been hidden by a great darkness must eventually and inevitably put that darkness and its shadows to flight, so too has the light of Old System Magic broken through, once again, into the conscious minds and intellectual strivings of those who would call themselves Magician. After one hundred twenty-plus years of distortion, mutilation, and rejection, the sacred images and words of the Grimoires—those Grammars of Magic—created by the Fathers of Old System Magic, are once more reaching the furthermost corners of the mind of those who have eyes to see and ears to hear. This is the message my friend and colleague, Mr. Mark Stavish, Director, Institute for Hermetic Studies, has summarized so beautifully and eloquently in a post he recently sent to me. Many were the conversations and numerous the hours he and I spent hammering out this magical point and that magical reckoning, all of which led to his quoted letter below.

Too many people expect something for nothing when they enter Magic. Still more expect a great something for even less work—or is it from the lip service they give that masquerades as 'work.' It doesn't work this way as I have said countless times in my writings, and as Mr. Stavish echoes and delineates in additional detail below. From such insights and experiential knowledge as Stavish demonstrates in his letter, one also learns that there are no guarantees in Magic (or in anything in life, for that matter.) All that exists are probabilities; probabilities whose potential for manifestation increase exponentially as the individual follows the simple process of:

Learn—>Understand—>Comprehend—>Apprehend

and whose techniques I have explained so many times in my books.

I invite my readers to read Mr. Stavish's paper below, and to pay its contents very close attention, and give its messages special heed. For if this is done, many of the problems that beset you can and will be cleared up in the twinkling of an eye. That is, after you *Work*, and achieve an **Apprehension** of its content.

Mr. Stavish's paper follows…

Dear Dr. Lisiewski,

Our discussions regarding operative magic, with emphasis on Talismans, seems to always lead us back to two very important points. One you discussed several weeks ago in your Magical Thought of the Week, concerning the Element of Fire, and its role in all occult work. Fire is the most important of the Elements and often the least understood or used. Only the Element of Fire can initiate our consciousness to new levels, as it is a direct expression of the energies of the Higher Self, the Holy Upper Trinity of the Tree of Life, our Holy Guardian Angel or true inner initiator.

Along with this is the question of 'paying the price' of success in whatever it is we do—magic, alchemy, professional or personal life choices. The price we pay is the mark of our commitment to the goal we seek to realize. How often haven't you been told by someone who contacts you, "I'll do anything! Anything to learn magic, alchemy, etc." only to ask a few questions and realize that the person who has come to you asking for your time, knowledge, and experience places more emphasis on their monthly cable TV fee, martial arts instruction, or monthly visit to the tattoo parlor or body piercing than in actually learning occult arts. They are not willing to do whatever it takes, only to SAY whatever it takes. As such, they will not pay the price in time, money, intellectual or emotional power, in other words—commit the energy—it takes for success.

A simple example anyone can prove to themselves is in what we have mentioned so many times. Energy follows the mental plan. The mental plan follows our actions. Precision in the plan and actions bring precise results. Take making a talisman for example.

Anyone who has taken the time—often only a few extra minutes, a half hour at most—to draw a geometrically exact polygon (i.e., a pointed star) on their talismans can feel it take on the energy as it is being made. The act of will, or focused consciousness, the extra concern, desire for precision, beauty, and actual results, makes the talisman alive long before it is ever consecrated or dedicated to use.

The student goes from being an experimenter to an Artist, and results are guaranteed because of the well established mental framework with which it was prepared and executed.

The price was paid, and the 'purchase' made. The Artist owns it because they have created it and deserve it.

You have mentioned to me that when you were doing some magical work you knew what items you needed, heeded the instructions of the grimoires and did not haggle 'over the price of a black cock' went your way and the desired effects came forth. Some have wondered why this is, but we know it and it is simple. Emotionally the desired ends were more important than the money it cost for the wand, vessel of brass, or what have you. This is no different than the person who makes the sacrifice to take out a loan, go to college or technical school, and reach a goal rather than sit in fear of a thousand things that could rise up from their subconscious and keep them from doing it.

Today we see a similar thing in the so-called occult community. People who would dare to call themselves students of the Art, blaspheme its holy name by whining and complaining about their lack of this, that, or the other thing and why everything should be handed to them at no cost to themselves.

They dare use the word—FREE. We know there is nothing for free in life. Everything has a price. While they, the end user may not be paying it, someone else is. This kind of 'spiritual welfare' mentality is poison to success. While discretion must be used in what one is paying for, how much, and why, in the end, even a fool separated from their money will quickly gain wisdom if they are serious about the Path and not concerned about what it takes from them.

How often haven't we heard the phase, "But I can't afford...!" In other words, that acronym you are so fond of quoting, "**B**ehold the **U**ltimate **T**ruth (B.U.T.) B.U.T. I am not willing to spend that much time, money, or both to achieve my goal, nor am I willing to do what I need to do in order to make the time and/or money available for achieving the goal, and want someone else to do it for me." B.U.T., B.U.T, B.U.T! There are no "B.U.T's" as we both know so very well, nor are there any "I can't!" There is only an *Act of Will*, an act of *choice*—I will, or I will not. In magic, there is no 'can' or 'cannot' nor is there any 'B.U.T.'

Book Eleven of the Hermetic texts says:

19. Consider this yourself. Command your soul to go anywhere, and it will be there quicker than your command. Bid it to go to the ocean and again it is there at once, not as if it had gone from place to place but was already there. Order it to fly up to heaven and it will need no wings, nor will anything impede it, neither the fire of the sun, nor the ether, nor the whirlwind, nor the other heavenly bodies, but cutting through them all it will soar up to the last body. And if you wish to break through all this and to contemplate what is beyond (if there is anything beyond the cosmos), it is in your power.

20. See what power you have and what speed! You can do all these things and yet God cannot? Reflect on God in this way as having all within Himself as ideas: the cosmos, Himself, the whole. If you do not make yourself equal to God you cannot understand Him. Like is understood by like. Grow to immeasurable size. Be free from every body, transcend all time. Become eternity and thus you will understand God. Suppose nothing to be impossible for yourself. Consider yourself immortal and able to understand everything: all arts, sciences and the nature of every living creature. Become higher that all heights and lower than all depths. Sense as one within yourself the entire creation: fire, water, the dry and the moist. Conceive yourself to be in all places at the same time: in the earth, the sea, in heaven; that you are not yet born, that you are within the womb, that you are young, old, dead; that you are beyond death. Conceive all things at once: time, places, actions, qualities and quantities; then you can understand God.

21. But if you lock up your soul in your body, abase it and say: "I understand nothing; I can do nothing; I am afraid of the sea; I cannot reach heaven; I do not know who I was nor who I shall be," what have you to do with God? For you cannot conceive anything beautiful or good while you are attached to the body and are evil. For the greatest evil is to ignore what belongs to God. To be able to know and to will and to hope is the straight and easy way appropriate to each that will lead to the Supreme Good. When you take this road this Good will meet you everywhere and will be experienced everywhere, even where and when you do not expect it; when awake, asleep, in a ship, on the road, by night, by day, when speaking and when silent, for there is nothing which it is not.

Herein is the important point. Once we enter our Path, IT decides what our price of continued advancement will be, in time, talent, and treasure, and it will require, demand, and take all three from us until there is nothing left to stand between us and our goal.

You have often said that magic and alchemy are the hardest and most difficult paths there are, and filled with more sorrow, despair, broken dreams and bodies than any other. This I can attest to, and as you so very well know for yourself, once we have accepted this—THEN the Golden Dawn of Illumination arises within us, not before, and not with hidden fears buried deep inside. Once we accept it, then the Good rises up to meet us, and It—the God [Good] is everywhere.

Magic, Higher Mysticism, and Quantum Physics — They Have More in Common than You Think

In our work in Magic and Higher Mysticism (New Thought) we are often confronted with such statements as, 'the way we view the real world is a reflection of our magical practices' or 'the nature of our thought patterns determines our perceptions of reality.' Yet again, we hear the oft touted maxim, 'We are at where we are in life by right of consciousness.'

While those who have not experienced altered states of magical consciousness and the mystical levels of awareness upon which such proverb-like expressions are based simply smile at such ideas, even those who know the truth of these declarations from their own experience will—at times—wonder about the ultimate nature of those very experiences: those experiences that have indeed brought them to where they are in life at this very moment. More often than not we attempt to shore up our lack of essential understanding by turning back to the very magical text or mystical book that produced the effects—whether Interior or Exterior—that we wanted and received. We return to them again and again, seeking some type of succor that will someday, somehow, eliminate those reoccurring doubts that linger in the corners of our most secret thoughts.

But always, there is that nagging question; that wondering if indeed what we have achieved or received is truly due to the virtue of our magical or mystical efforts. We quietly wonder if those achievements and that worldly gain is not simply due to some coincidence, synchronicity, or some other type of 'happenstance,' and that in reality, our spiritual work is not just so much fluff and flutter. It happens to all of us; and usually, more often than makes us comfortable. Put another way, we furtively wish for some 'hard core' evidence 'out there' upon which we can hang our hat of dubious wondering; and in doing so, put our doubts to rest, once and for all.

Modern science—and especially Physics—has been amassing more and more *physical* evidence that may very well quell—once and for all—the hidden doubts and secret fears of all those who tread the magical and mystical paths. Curious, isn't it, that a branch of science devoted to the study of physical law, could not only aid us in our understanding of the spiritual, but give us insights in how spiritual law works. From the speculation of the existence of the "God Particle," to Einstein's equations in which he searched for a Unified Field theory, to the postulation of Black Holes, and now, to the study of Quantum Mechanics, more and more hard core, physically measured data is explaining the dual nature of matter, energy, light, and indeed, of the entire manifest universe. One very recent book in particular, *Quantum Enigmas,* published by none other than the prestigious Oxford University Press, may be of serious interest. Below is the review of this book as it appears on Amazon.com.

> The most successful theory in all of science—and the basis of one third of our economy—says the strangest things about the world and about us. Can you believe that physical reality is created by our observation of it? Physicists were forced to this conclusion, the quantum enigma, by what they observed in their laboratories.
>
> Trying to understand the atom, physicists built quantum mechanics and found, to their embarrassment, that their theory intimately connects consciousness with the physical world. Quantum Enigma explores what that implies and why some founders of the theory became the foremost objectors to it. Schrodinger showed that it "absurdly" allowed a cat to be in a "superposition" simultaneously dead and alive. Einstein derided the theory's "spooky interactions." With Bell's Theorem, we now know Schrodinger's superpositions and Einstein's spooky interactions indeed exist.
>
> Authors Bruce Rosenblum and Fred Kuttner explain all of this in non-technical terms with help from some fanciful stories and bits about the theory's developers. They present the quantum mystery honestly, with an emphasis on what is and what is not speculation.
>
> Physics' encounter with consciousness is its skeleton in the closet. Because the authors open the closet and examine the skeleton, theirs is a controversial book. Quantum Enigma's

description of the experimental quantum facts, and the quantum theory explaining them, is undisputed. Interpreting what it all means, however, is controversial.

Every interpretation of quantum physics encounters consciousness. Rosenblum and Kuttner therefore turn to exploring consciousness itself—and encounter quantum physics. Free will and anthropic principles become crucial issues, and the connection of consciousness with the cosmos suggested by some leading quantum cosmologists is mind-blowing.

Readers are brought to a boundary where the particular expertise of physicists is no longer a sure guide. They will find, instead, the facts and hints provided by quantum mechanics and the ability to speculate for themselves.

So for all those of us who must wrestle with the doubts and uncertainties underlying the states of consciousness we experience during our magical work and mystical practices, and who need to understand that most powerful of all energy sources in the universe—*the human mind*—I unreservedly recommend this book.

Take the time and given the attention to understanding your own mind and its role in our work by looking at what some of the "High Priests" of science—the Physicists—have to say about their *experimental* discoveries underlying that mind of yours. Consider carefully turning your attention to this field of study, rather than seeking out some sappy, whiz-bang weirdo book whose tenets cannot be empirically tested, and whose 'message' is designed to confuse you all the more and add to your growing collection of doubts about your work—and yourself.

Chapter Nine

Questions & Answers

QUESTION: Can you give us more templates for making charges? For instance, how would one phrase a charge to easily and quickly remember everything read, heard, or seen? How would a charge for better health be phrased, etc.?

ANSWER: While it is clear you are thinking things through and getting the gist of Old System Magic, please don't continue looking for 'recipes' and 'instant answers' to questions that you (or any individual) can only answer for yourself (or themselves). Remember: one size does not fit all! The charge 'templates' I gave in my books and on my website were intended to spur a mode of thinking; one that uses the individual's own Subjective Synthesis in order to compose an effective charge that has a personal meaning for that individual. *It is into such a personal charge that the summoned or evoked force is then effectively channeled through.*

You see, charges that work for me will not (necessarily) work for you or for anyone else: this is the individuality behind all effective magic, and what people do not want to hear. They are so use to instant gratifications and quick fixes, that they simply cannot get it out of theirs heads that such things do not exist in Old System Magic. It is as simple as this: *individual efforts* must be made if the magician is to succeed in this ancient art and science. I do suggest the following as an aid to entering the mode of thought required when "Designing a Charge," as I term it.

Sit down with pencil and paper, quietly, undisturbed by others, and carefully consider the ends you seek. Next, you must contemplate what those ends mean, i.e., what the fruits of those ends will net you in this world—and this in their very *essence*—and *how that essence can be captured by a series of words and phrases that are a product of your considerations, contemplation, and internal promptings.* Your Subjective Synthesis will help you in this, if it is well built and polished. If not, you will have trouble in that you will miss the mark in the wording of the charge and you will know it. Things just won't 'look' or 'feel' right to you. In either case, I recommend you perform a complete Kabbalistic Analysis on the desires, using the simple techniques I gave in the *Kabbalistic Handbook for the Practicing Magician.* Making such an analysis will 'forcc' the Subjective Synthesis into recognizing the desire. As a result, it will give you just those right intellectual impulses that will cnable you to write an effective charge for whatever—and I do mean whatever—you desire. Take no short cuts: that is what Old System Magic is all about. It works because you work. That is why it is so effective.

QUESTION: Does it really matter that I paint the magical implements even though they come from the old grimoires? I mean, all I have been taught for years is to use qabalistic colors on everything including the circle and now you say to throw that all out and use just plain stuff? Are you serious? I want to learn old magic but I just can't get these ideas of modern magic out of my head! What can I do?

ANSWER: Yes, it really matters if you paint your Old System Magic impedimenta with all those Kabbalistic colors because in effect you are mixing systems, and the effort will blow up in your face. You will bring about a Slingshot Effect of the like you (perhaps) never saw before, and will wonder what happened— that is, after you pick yourself up and crawl out of the circle, should you be fortunate enough to be able to crawl: either literally or figuratively.

I am serious about making a complete, clean break from that which never netted you anything. You and I know the magic taught today does not work: that is why you are starting to study Old System Magic. You need not justify anyone's *a priori* (meaning, independent of experience) system: you need results—pure and simple. Please follow the directions I gave above under Preparation for Old System Magic. What is given there is not a "template;" it is a process I have hammered out over a forty-four year period of study and experimentation in Magic, and which I have taught to others for well nigh on twenty-five of those forty-four years. And it works.

If you are serious about extricating yourself and building the life you want—and I believe that you are—follow the counsel given previously about breaking all ties to previous occult work. After the smoke of the extrication clears, you will not regret what you did, or what you went through in order to extricate yourself.

QUESTION: I know I am getting ahead of myself here but is there any grimoire you recommend for beginners? I would really like to get on with this business of evocation but don't know where to start. Any advice?

ANSWER: I suggest you stay as far away from Evocation to Physical Manifestation as you can, and for quite some time. Why? Because it is obvious you are not prepared for it. In the first place, there is no such thing as a 'Grimoire for Beginners.' There are grammars that are easier to work from, but even they demand much from the Operator. And secondly, '...getting on with the business of Evocation...' belies an attitude in which Evocation is seen as some kind of weekend activity you engage in to straighten out your life: a life that you made a mess of because you *reacted* to something instead of *acting* on it. There is a significant difference between the two. No doubt you reacted without thinking, or reacted from a completely emotional basis. That is not how Evocation to Physical Manifestation is to be approached. Yes, you have life problems. Yes, Evocation to Physical Manifestation can be a tremendous help in removing those problems or straightening them out. But to go into the Ceremonial act as a 'quick-fix' remedy will avail you nothing except pain and absolute failure.

You will note I always write, "Evocation to Physical Manifestation." I do this purposely to differentiate this Ceremonial action as expounded by the grimoires from that flippant absurdity preached by the New Age. And the real type of Ceremonial action is unbelievably serious and dangerous, simply because you are not projecting some psychological complex into the circle. No, this is the real thing, for in the Ceremonial act of Evocation to Physical Manifestation you are going to Call Forth or Summon Up one of the Fallen, and they are living beings whose nature is chaos itself raised to the nth level. They have existed since the Creation of the world, have infinite mentality, are unimaginably devious and cunning, and are always antagonistic to the one summoning them. Not out of a personal hatred for the Operator, but simply because their nature is such. In Part II of Studies in the Grimoires we will deal with the *Heptameron* proper. And while it is the 'simplest' grimoire to work from in many ways, it nevertheless has the same dangers and inherent difficulties of, say, the *Clavicula Salomonis*, the *Grimorium Verum*, or the *Grand Grimoire*.

So relax and get such thoughts out of your head for quite some time. "*Magic is done from the inside out, not the outside in*" as I constantly tell my private students. You must achieve a certain growth within your consciousness before you can handle—and channel—the enormous forces you will be contacting. This takes time. Time and WORK! Be guided accordingly.

QUESTION: I have been studying *Ceremonial Magic and The Power of Evocation* but at the same time there is some doubt as to whether the *Heptameron* will be the right grimoire for me. Have you ever known of anyone who has put forth all the effort to gather the things needed for the ceremony, and after properly preparing everything, turned out to have a failed evocation?

ANSWER: You are confusing having a strong, well-defined subconscious state of Subjective Synthesis with having a *belief* that magic works. The 'belief' and the actual subjective state are completely opposite. This highly defined, energetic subconscious state can only be built up by hard, conscious work in studying magical texts, the kabbalah, and weaving the results of *your own* experimental magical work in with that subconscious structure.

How do you do such "weaving?" By analyzing your experimental magical results. And how do you do this? By using—for example—the technique of Kabbalistic Analysis as described in *The Kabbalistic Handbook for the Practicing Magician*.

The study component of developing your Subjective Synthesis must undertake the following the sequence:

Learn—>Understand—>Comprehend—>Apprehend—>Apply

You must study the material to 'learn' it. But learning is not a single, absolute state in and of itself. It's a *process* by which something new eventually finds its way into your *subconscious mind*. Hence the different 'levels' of the process as given above. As to "Apprehending" the material: this is a peculiar feeling that comes to the student after so much exposure to it, an uncanny awareness that they 'know it cold.' And as to the "Apply" step, well, that speaks for itself, doesn't it? You then test the strength and structure of your Subjective Synthesis by applying it to your ritual and ceremonial work.

I have never known anyone who put all the effort into a grimoire—as that grimoire called for—and who did not get the result they sought. Magic is not a quick-fix, instant gratification expediency designed to quickly get you out of some mess you got yourself into because of laziness, greed, lust, jealousy, plain 'bad thinking,' or foolishness. It is a process like any other in life, and must be adhered to on its own terms: just as you automatically 'obey' the Law of Gravity and its 'rules' without complaining about them, so too must you apply that attitude to Magic. Then, and only then, will the Magic work for you as you want, and give you what you desire.

QUESTION: Can we barter with a demon? Make a pact is it were?

ANSWER: In fact, very few of the grimoires mention anything about such an exchange. Neither the *Clavicula Salomonis*, the *Lemegeton* (including its most famous book, the *Goetia*) the *Grimoire of Armadel*, *The Secret Grimoire of Turiel*, *The Sworn Book of Honourius the Magician*, nor *The Enchiridion of Pope Leo* to name the most well known, state anything about 'exchanging' something with the demon for what you want from it. In fact, as I wrote in

Ceremonial Magic and the Power of Evocation, it is by the Divine Bliss that overtakes the Operator during the height of the evocation, that the demon is brought to obedience. This occurs because—in fact—that part of God within the magician becomes the One who demands from the demon through ITS human agency, the magician. And in so doing, the demon's fulfillment of this demand 'sanctifies' the Fallen One, by allowing it to serve the Will of its Creator.

When the magician reaches a certain state of development, *God's Will becomes his will, and his will becomes God's Will: the two are—in that moment—identical.* Hence there are no reasons for bartering; an act which simply establishes an unnecessary and very dangerous link between the demon and the magician.

QUESTION: If there is NOT a DIRECT path to a particular Sephirah, how then do I apply the Kabbalistic Cycles method successfully? Can you give me a Specific example?

ANSWER: You simply consider the effect of the planet ruling the hour in question, remembering that the effect of that hour will have four times as great an influence as opposed to the influence of the planet ruling the day.

Always begin a project; that is, take the first physical action of putting pen to paper (or the modern day equivalent) during a fortunate Path-Planetary influence, such as on a Monday during a Mercury hour. You can then continue any time once the project is initiated (during a favorable influence such as given above.) When it comes time to submit your work for approval, again, choose a fortuitous hour-influence such as a Monday during a Mercury hour, or a Friday, during a Jupiter hour, etc. *But be careful here! You must be certain to remember when the idea for that project first came to you!* If it occurred during a very unfortunate influence—say, during a Mars hour on a Saturday—and you were not aware of this and began the project during a fortunate influence as given above, it will bear no fruit whatsoever. Conversely, if the idea initially occurred to you during a fortunate hour, but you began it during an unfortunate influence, it will go nowhere. In fact, in the latter case, the writing will be hard, things will go very wrong throughout the project, and you will be left with nothing.

People frequently misunderstand the Kabbalistic Cycles and think they are absolute guarantees of success. Their thoughts run pretty much along the following lines: "Well, as long as I do B, C, and D at the right times, 'A'—the actual inception of that project—will take care of itself." Or they are not even aware that the *time the idea came to them is the crucial first component of the project*. The Cycles are infallible and will work every time. Apply it to events in your own past, and you will quickly come to see just how incredibly accurate those Cycles are.

QUESTION: For about two years now I have been seeing the numbers 11:11 or 1111 in the strangest of places and at odd times. These past few years of my life have been hard and trying. I don't just see the numbers on clocks, but in odd places as well. I would like your opinion on this, as to if you feel it is my mind simply making these events happen, or noticeable, or perhaps it has more meaning?

ANSWER: I would not dismiss these observations out of hand, but do some studying of Numerology in an effort to (perhaps) find some thread that could lead to either an answer or a tentative answer. If the mathematics of numbers—called Number Theory, a very advanced form of mathematics—was expounded by none other than Pythagoras and other Greek Philosophers and Mathematicians, then it should be good enough for any who—like Pythagoras—advanced metaphysical meanings and explanations behind these Real Numbers: including the Integers, Rational and Irrational Numbers, not to mention the number 0 (zero) and the idea of 1 (One.) I recommend starting your quest with the following books.[1]

The Greek Qabalah: Alphabetic Mysticism and Numerology in the Ancient World, by Kieren Barry

The Theology of Arithmetic, translated by Robin Waterfield. (A very important book attributed to the famous 4th century Iamblichus. It deals with the mystical, mathematical, and cosmological symbolism of the first ten numbers.)

The Pythagorean Sourcebook and Library, compiled and translated by Kenneth Sylvan Guthrie. (Another very important book for many reasons, when studying Pythagorean and Neo-Pythagorean writings.)

---

[1] See also *The Meaning and Philosophy of Numbers* by Leonard Bosman, foreword by R.A. Gilbert.

QUESTION: I noticed that in the *Heptameron* there are no instructions on preparing and consecrating some of the materials used, such as the parchment, pen, ink, etc. I would really hate to work with unconsecrated items.

ANSWER: The items you mention can be effectively asperged with holy water and suffumigated by passing them through the smoke of the Dominican Brand incense, which is used generally in the Heptameron Operation as you know (of course, you would also use the Benediction of the Perfumes, Exorcism of the Fire, etc., as given in *Ceremonial Magic and the Power of Evocation.*) After suffumigating in this way, the particular ink, parchment, and pen (only these three items) used for a given Operation could also be passed through the Perfume of the planet you will be working under.

It is also far better to devise your own words of purification that are in agreement with the nature of the Operation than it is to take such words from a 'canned' source such as the Clavicula Salomonis (unless you were working from the latter grimoire, of course.) Consecration of the items will actually occur through their use in the ceremony.

As to the robe, it is well nigh impossible to obtain the 'ideal' robe such as described in the *Heptameron*. A good quality, white, lined robe is all you need. It too would be asperged with holy water, and suffumigated with Dominican Brand incense. The Oration to be said when the Vesture (robe) is put on would also be used at that time, which dedicates the robe and the act of donning it to the Operation. As such, it is a form of consecration, and a very powerful one indeed.

QUESTION: I have the book *The One Year Manual* and I have searched for an original version of *Twelve Steps to Spiritual Enlightenment*. I am not keen on the Thelemic-based Adorations in the One Year Manual but I can not find the Christian-based Adorations. Where could one find the Christian-based Adorations to use as a part of their program?

ANSWER: As to the Adorations, either create them yourself—based upon your own inner promptings that come during your meditations—or extrapolate meaningful verse, thoughts, and ideas from one of the following three books, and weld them into an Adoration that exalts your own mind and Spirit. (It is so easy to automatically rely upon others for that gold that lies hidden within us. But it is there, and should be mined by one's work in the Spirit.)

I have found the following three books to be a great help to me, and a constant source of inspiration that aids my own spiritual unfoldment dramatically, safely, and continuously. The books I so highly recommend are: *Christ in You*, Anonymous; *Meditations with Teilhard de Chardin;* and *15 Days of Prayer with Pierre Teilhard de Chardin.*

QUESTION: Many grimoires speak of controlling fire, levitation, teleportation and control over any of the other elements in a physical sense, by gaining the power from a spirit. In your experience, have you found this to be so?

ANSWER: When a grimoire tells you a spirit can cause fire, move a person from one place to another, turn coins of the realm into gold, or whatever the case may be, the meaning is neither allegorical nor symbolic: it is factual. Read the grimoires EXACTLY as they are given. DO YOUR WORK, and take their counsel INTO THE CIRCLE where you can test their claims. When you do this; when you achieve experiential knowledge for yourself.

QUESTION: What determines exactly what asking for "too much" is? Say someone evokes a Spirit to physical manifestation with the desire to ask for money, how much would be too much? Is there that much difference between asking for a few thousand dollars verses a few million? And would their personal reasons for asking for something determine the slingshot effects? If the operator asked for something that truly was important to help them get to where they want to be in life, would that reduce the slingshot effects?

Would it be possible to add into the "charge" to not cause any negative effects? Wouldn't the spirits be bound by the charge if the operator were to add that little clause in there?

ANSWER: No, it is not possible to "add into the charge..." anything that would somehow eliminate any "negative effects" as you term them. Why? First of all, in even thinking about adding such a condition to your charge you are sending a clear cut message to your subconscious mind that you are afraid you will fail in the Evocation to Physical Manifestation proper, and as such, want to escape the responsibility for your failure. Your fear of failure may be due to your inexperience, your lack of preparation, or knowing that you willfully took shortcuts in preparing both the implements of the rite and yourself. Your unconscious mind will most certainly communicate this to the demonic entity involved, and you can be sure it will happily—and effectively—play upon that, such that your fear reaction will cause you to fulfill the ancient admonition, "As your belief, so be it unto you."

The key is to build and polish your subconscious state of Subjective Synthesis as carefully and as completely as possible, so that these needless fears of the lesser self are not factored into the actual Operation.

Your subconscious state is a totality of consciousness that embraces not only your subconscious state of Subjective Synthesis, but a constellation of other thoughts and ideas about an equal number of infinite issues and things, all of which interact with each other to make you unique in terms of who you are! So what applies to you does not automatically apply to me or anyone else. My suggestion to you here is to use your time *productively*, and begin a magical regimen that will lead you where you desire to go, and work at it. Then and only then will the answers to your theoretical conjectures—that are unique to you—appear on your mental horizon in the twinkling of an eye.

QUESTION: However I noticed something that surprised me regarding the order of the last two programs. I see that you have as reward for those who *successfully* complete the "Advanced Program of Magical Attainment" a bonus program for "Attaining to the Knowledge and Conversation of the Holy Guardian Angel". I had the impression from my seeking along these lines that it was advised that one reach K&C of the HGA before ever attempting Evocation to Physical Manifestation of a lesser/infernal entity. And your comments elsewhere of the merging of the Divine with the Operator during the evocation being quite the key to it all had me connecting this with the HGA.

ANSWER: For all of their "advice" and insistences, I have never met one who has attained the Knowledge and Conversation of the Holy Guardian Angel (Attained to the K&C of the HGA) in any genuine way: save for some psychological 'phenomenon'. In fact, the Evocation to Physical Manifestation of an entire assortment of demons is—in my experience—a prime requisite to attempting the Abramelin Operation. If one cannot gird his mind and soul by achieving the Divine Bliss—by momentarily uniting with God—in an evocation, how can such a one possibly endure the State beyond the Divine Bliss that accompanies the Vision of the Holy Guardian Angel? EVOCATION TO PHYSICAL MANIFESTATION IS *PREPARATORY* TO ATTAINING TO THE KNOWLEDGE AND CONVERSATION OF THE HOLY GUARDIAN ANGEL: it is not ancillary to it. And you will find that when you subdue the Princes of Evil of the World who will parade before you during the Three Days of the Attainment, you will no longer need to engage in such vanities as Evocation to Physical Manifestation any longer. You may do so if you choose, but I am willing to wager you will find the Truth and the Power that lies within you to be more than sufficient to deal with any condition, and will no longer need such a trifle as Evocation to Physical Manifestation. You will also find that the Word that proceeds from your mouth will be enough.

QUESTION: You stated that the magician should make their own altar however you didn't seem to give a definite answer as to whether the magician could buy an altar. Because you have mentioned before that it is acceptable to buy a sword of art could it also be acceptable to buy an altar as well? Can I buy rather than make all of my magical implements?

ANSWER: Although both the Altar and the Sword are magical weapons (or "Impedimenta" of the Art) they serve vastly different purposes. The Sword divides, separates, and thus threatens to induce further chaos into those whose natures are already unstable and chaotic: those beings known as the Fallen Angels. It can be made by another if one's skills are not up to it. Nevertheless it must be consecrated by the Operator as a declaration of his intent to use it to separate, divide, and thus introduce further chaos into those beings who are already in a continual state of chaos.

The Altar, on the other hand, is that place whereupon a sacrifice is made and upon which a desire rests. It is symbolic of the Cross of Redemption upon which Christ made His Sacrifice; His desire being the redemption of all mankind. In the case of the magical Altar, the sacrifice made upon it is that of the self of the Operator being offered up; the desire, that which he is seeking to obtain through his 'self'-sacrifice. As such, the construction of the Altar by the Operator is absolutely essential if it is to represent the 'best' that the self (the magician) has to offer up at the time of its making. Make the altar yourself. Make it the best you can: spare nothing in its design and construction. For upon it rests not only your sacrifice, but your desire.

QUESTION: I am preparing to do my first evocation to physical manifestation this winter outside. It's pretty secluded and generally quiet around here. My concern and question is, will I be the only one to hear and see the Spirits or do I run the risk of my neighbors hearing moans and groans? Also, Is it possible to do a physical evocation of the "good" angels (Michael, Gabriel, etc.) are there any good books for this?

ANSWER: Noises and groans are just that: noises and groans, and can be heard by anyone who has the ability to hear. I completely reject contemporary nonsense that claims all of these sights and sounds that one experiences during a ritual or ceremonial action occur solely in the mind of the Operator.[1] And neither will be those generated by your magical efforts if you practice Old System Magic the way the Fathers of the Grimoires intended. So get use to it: any disturbances that effect the senses—both

---

[1] Acoustic, visual, and even environmental phenomena are associated with spiritual breakthroughs into the physical world, be they by "good spirits" or "fallen angels". Hekate's appearances were preceded by "bellowings of the ground". The Mithric Liturgy, a method of self-initiation found in the Greco-Egyptian magical papyri describes a complex series of events, including a shaking of the earth, all that proceed the appearance of the divinities. The classical understanding was that these phenomena were a result of the normal rhythms of the physical world being disturbed by the break-through of the gods into the material domain. One sees similar notions in both the Jewish and Christian scriptures with earthquakes being common listed along with flashes of light, darkening of the sky, lightning, and storm winds. To be clear, such phenomena is not meaningful in itself, but is a sign that the rite is proceeding accordingly, and should they not occur, then something is wrong.

physical and para-physical—can and will most definitely be detected by others outside of the Rite proper.

Under no circumstances is it possible—in my opinion, based upon my experience—to "evoke" an archangel to physical manifestation. The divine nature of these beings is so exalted and above that of man's, that our senses could neither comprehend nor tolerate—let alone endure—their manifestation. Indirect physical phenomena caused by their presence is most certainly possible, however. But a visible appearance? Not as far as I know. As to evoking other "good" angels as you term them. Yes, this is most certainly possible: the appearance of one's Holy Guardian Angel (HGA) at the culmination of the Abramelin Operation is one such example.

QUESTION: I recently obtained *A Treatise on Angel Magic* (by Adam McLean, Samuel Weiser, Inc.) that lists the Archangels of Kether to Chesed with their corresponding seals. The book is based on "The Treatises of Dr. Rudd" or *Mss Harley 6482* (written in late 17th century) at the British Museum. In turn, Mr. Mclean states in his introduction that Dr. Rudd based his materials on the following earlier works.

Nowhere in Mr. McLean's book (and correspondingly *Mss Harley 6482* does it state how to use the Archangelic Seals during invocation (hold it, put on the altar, wear it like a lamen); nor how they are to be made (metal, parchment, plain white paper).

ANSWER: Mr. McLean's books are extremely valuable contributions to Old System Magic. He is an excellent researcher, highly logical, and impeccable in his analyses of the source material he writes about. You should realize that much of Old System Magic is based upon manuscripts, the original authors of which 'assumed' certain levels of common understanding on the part of those who would come after them. However, time and tide change many things and certainly, they have changed the understanding of those who read these magical tracts today as compared to those who read them when they were first issued centuries ago. As such, there is sometimes a great deal of difficulty in understanding the requirements necessary for working these documents correctly—such as the difficulties you list in your question. Nevertheless the material is there, and serves as important information for those who are involved in what others (and I) call "Experimental Magic."

Now, how does one go about 'filling in the blanks' of such manuscripts, such that they can be made workable? This is the province of Experimental Magic as I stated. Such an activity assumes that an individual who engages in such experimentalism possesses several qualities:

That the Experimental Magician has a broad knowledge-base in the classical material of the field, i.e., in the many grimoires, and understands them from both a theoretic and operational perspective. This means understanding the thought-stream which lies behind the grimoire(s). Of equal importance is:

1. That one possesses a great deal of practical experience in either Invocation, Evocation to Physical Manifestation (or both) or in any other area in which one may be involved in, e.g., Divination by means of the Magic Mirror (see A.E. Waite's, *The Book of Ceremonial Magic*).

2. That one can withstand—in all ways—the brunt of those inevitable failures produced during the course of the experimental work. That is, it is necessary to endure the events that will come from the Slingshot Effect.

3. That one's mind possesses enough analytical ability to be able to sift through—not only the number of results that will be experienced—but the diversity of those results and of the details that compose them, and be able to synthesize them into an ordered, structured, eclectic whole.

That the subconscious state of Subjective Synthesis be so built and polished, that it can be relied upon to penetrate into the theoretic basis of the grimoire(s) being studied, and so gain insight into the nature of the missing data needed to operate from that (those) text(s). This penetration is effected through an Interior type of Concentration: not "meditation."

It is not enough to think that a sound knowledge of kabbalah will give the magician the tools needed to work in Old System Magic effectively and successfully: it will not. Why is this? Because as I pointed out in my books, Old System Magic is not founded upon kabbalah[1], no matter how loud the prophets of the New Age insist it is. kabbalah simply embraces certain concepts of Old System Magic and claims it as its own; as if it actually created those concepts. It did not. An example of such a claim by some modern writers on kabbalah make is that of assigning the Seven Planets of the Ancients to seven of the Sephiroth. Some writers would have you believe this assignment were unique to kabbalah. Again: it is not, the early writers of kabbalah simply extracted these assignments from classical astrology and placed them under its own umbrella of attributions, and this has continued on ever since. Hence, as the Practitioner of Old System Magic will find out—if he or she has not already done so after only a minimum of work—much of what is passed off as kabbalah cannot be trusted to deliver up the keys to the missing information in any given grimoire or manuscripts of Old System Magic.

---

[1] Old System Magic, or the Magic of the Grimoires, academically known as "Solomonic" magic, while it uses a great deal of Jewish references is not directly traceable to Jewish sources as its roots, but more likely to Jewish sources for its gloss. Such is the same with many of the so-called "Egyptian" systems of magic being promulgated today. Francis Yates explains it as such in *The Occult Philosophy of the Elizabethan Age*: "If one re-reads the *De occulta philosophia* attentively one will notice that in each of the three worlds Agrippa brings in Hebrew names and formulae... Agrippa probably believes that he is both strengthening natural magic and celestial magic by bringing them into contact with powerful Hebrew magic, and also purifying these magics, making them safe by associating them with holy Cabalist influences... Agrippa's occult philosophy is intended to be a very white magic. In fact it is really a religion, claiming access to the highest powers, and Christian since it accepts the name of Jesus as the chief of the wonder-working Names... The function of Cabala as Agrippa saw it was not only to provide the highest 'supercelestial' magic, but to guarantee the safety of the operator against demons on all levels. The fear of demons had haunted [Marsilio] Ficino, but Cabala eliminated this fear. It is an insurance against demons, a guarantee that bold attempts at unlimited knowledge and power will not lead to damnation. Though the genuine Hebrew Cabalist might be shocked by Agrippa's interpretation of Cabala solely as white magic, yet this interpretation served a purpose in fortifying man for intellectual and spiritual endeavors." (p.55–56)

Only by Interiorized Concentration and Experimentation as discussed here, can those missing pieces of data be reclaimed.

I would also recommend a book to you that Regardie was very fond of. At his suggestion, I worked with it from 1980–1981. I found it to be valuable—to a point. Nevertheless, it did open up the gateway to the Unconscious in a safe and sane manner, and provided me with some very deep, accurate, and vital information of both a magical and personal nature.

You might try working with it yourself. The book is entitled, *Inner Guide Meditation: A Spiritual Technology for the 21st Century* by Edwin Steinbrecher.

QUESTION: Do you believe that there are devil's that are actually friendly towards humans?

ANSWER: In some traditions, there are infernal beings that are supposed to be friendlier to man than are others as you cite; and certainly, in all cases there are ways for controlling and dealing with them. However, I can only speak from my own experience—and from what a few others who have done extensive work in this area have confided to me. And that is, that the very term and definition of "demon" indicates their fallen nature, and as such, they are not to be trusted in the slightest. Remember, these are beings whose nature is so chaotic and continually shifting between extremes which we cannot even imagine: they cannot be other than they are. In this way, they are most certainly damned.

There may have—or even be—times when they appear to be 'friendly' to man. Such experiences may have left a marked impression on the one doing the Evoking or Invoking, thereby inducing him to 'conclude' that certain of the Fallen are indeed "good natured." Or could such behavior be a ruse perpetrated by the demon to obtain just such a conclusion, and have that view then disseminated in the world of men? This too is something to consider. You must also remember that if they are "good natured," why do we take such elaborate protective measures during our interaction with them? Surely the Circle and the Sword of Art, the Blasting Rod, and the Knife with the Black Handle to name only a few.

As for myself, I am the excessively cautious type, and so treat all of the Fallen as potential enemies teetering on the verge of actively becoming treacherous and destructive. I do not trust any of them beyond the level of direct control I exert over them during the rite.

QUESTION: Why are you so hard on the New Age? After all, it has brought magic into the public view more so than ever before.

ANSWER: As I pointed out in my third book, *The Kabbalistic Handbook for the Practicing Magician,* my argument is not with the material that actually comprises this so called "New Age" phenomenon. Far from it. If you study the texts from what I term Old System Magic, you will find their contents are what these New Age books are all about. In fact, if you read Donald Tyson's annotated and edited version of the *Three Books of Occult Philosophy,* and pay special attention to his Introduction, you will find that what is called "Golden Dawn" material is really material taken from those Three Books. But specifically, the original GD material came from Barrett's, *The Magus,* which is the butchered version of the Three Books.

Another example—and one which lent the "Hermetic" to the term, "Hermetic Golden Dawn"—can be found in Stephen Edred Flower's classic, *Hermetic Magic.* As Mr. Flowers points out in that splendid book, the true Hermetics came from the Graeco-Egyptian magical stream, being locked away in scholarly works, the like of which have only recently been discovered and treated seriously in translation. Most certainly, there is nothing wrong with utilizing those original forms of magic as contained in the early grimoires of the Dark Ages, the Medieval era, and the Hermetic approach of the Graeco-Egyptian line. But when this material is extracted from those sources and patched together into a flippant "system" meant to "do Magic" in some slip–shod, quick–fix, hodgepodge way, then yes, I am most definitely against it! Why? Because such rubbish not only gives magic a bad name, but it produces terrible results, the likes of which can—and which all too often do—create more misery and difficulties for the serious student of magic than if he or she had not attempted them at all.

I hold to what I have written previously, the individual must develop his or her subconscious states of subjective synthesis by learning the Kabbalah, learning to research the material being worked with, analyzing the ritual or ceremonial act to be performed (as for instance, through what I call a "Kabbalistic

Analysis") and in the process, building an eclectically balanced "system" of interior (psychic) thought patterns along with ritual and ceremonial actions that will work for that individual. "One size fits all" does not, has never, and will never apply to Magic.

QUESTION: I am getting the results I want but also some slingshot effects, I just have one main question, how is it possible for me to get full big results and sometimes quick without the actual visible manifestation, I am doing everything correct as far as I know but there is a manifestation but it isn't physical, not visible, but after a couple of days I see forms moving about me especially late at night, why is this happening and why am I not getting a full manifestation or physical phenomenon?

ANSWER: You cannot get "full, big results and sometimes quick..." without the actual physical manifestation. Why? Because you need to attain the Divine Bliss which brings the manifestation about, and which then leads to Control and finally to Command. Evocation to Physical Manifestation is not some mechanical technique as you are (apparently) treating it; for when you say, "I am doing everything correct as far as I know..." you are reducing the process of Evocation to Physical Manifestation— that is, the manner of accomplishing it—to a mechanical action (or technique.) That is, you are performing the Rite as if it were a series of mechanical actions or operations directed toward the result you want. That it is not. And yes, you will get some—or "partial"—results as I have discussed in my writings, and yes, the Slingshot Effect will also most certainly occur. This is just part of the process: a part that results from not having attained Divine Bliss. As to the "forms" you are seeing: they could be many things, but I highly doubt they are spirit or demonic beings, as you indirectly intimate.

QUESTION: In Dr. [Christopher S.] Hyatt's recent *Radical Undoing* videos[1], he made a statement that I personally felt important. He stated that if the aspirant hasn't control over the energy (kundalini energy) of his body in all likelihood his/her efforts will come to naught.

---

[1] *Radical Undoing* is a six-volume set of videos available from The Original Falcon Press.

ANSWER: Dr. Hyatt is most certainly correct: these energies need to be controlled. Remember though, my position is that these are psychic energies, and not the oft touted "spiritual energy". While I have not yet seen the video you cited above, I do know him very well, and know that he is quite hardcore in these matters. Being so, I assume he is referring to a type of psychic energy that has a physical correlation with the human body, i.e., in this case, with the human nervous system. So yes, it must be controlled.

Now, he probably gives techniques for controlling that energy. And in his approach his techniques as they have been in the past…will most likely prove quite effective. However, we must remember, that his approach and the magical approach you refer to via the LBRP are different; much like two sides of the same coin. That is, while the techniques differ, the energy involved may be quite the same.

Specifically, in the LBRP, the expansion of the astral form occurs through Imaging. That is, through seeing and feeling the astral body expand at the beginning of the rite. At first, the expansion is purely 'mechanical,' in that you must strive to image it. Then too, as you do so, you will be adding to your subconscious state of subjective synthesis. Later, as you become proficient in the rite, you will notice that both the astral expansion and the ability to control the energy 'summoned up' or generated by the performance will become automatic. That is, it will become "…a consequence of the rite and (of) an effective subjective synthesis" as you suggest.

You may ask yourself: "Why does it take practice before this automatic state 'kicks in' in such a ritual, whereas in Evocation to Physical Manifestation, the attainment of higher states of magical consciousness and the state of Bliss or Divine Love occur simply by focusing on the actions of the ceremonial act itself?" The answer being, that by the time you have reached the stage where you are truly ready to attempt such an advanced magical practice as Evocation to Physical Manifestation, you will have developed your Imaging faculty and you subconscious state of subjective synthesis to such an extent, that all falls into place…automatically. Hence the need for linear, progressive, slow growth in these matters. Your job…your Divine Task…is to develop your psychic faculties so that your perfect spiritual essence can shine through, fusing itself into those faculties, and manifesting through your body and magical acts into the material world.

There are no shortcuts to Heaven. But there are to Hell.

QUESTION: Is there really a difference between concentration and meditation? They seem to be so much the same. I mean, how do you tell the difference between them realistically and how do I achieve them?

ANSWER: Yes, there is a difference between the two, and it is significant.

Concentration is the fixed attention of the mind upon one idea, thing, concept, physical sensation, internal impulse (either physical or mental) or external condition, to the exclusion of all else. In this state, the mind becomes much like a laser beam that emits—in this particular example—a specific visible frequency of light. In other words, the beam has achieved a state of "coherency," in which all other light–frequencies, save one, are eliminated. The same occurs in Concentration, or at least, should. The achievement of this state of one-pointedness is dynamic, but only in that the mind has determined—in advance—to attain it. Thus, in effect, Concentration becomes an *action* of the mind. The techniques themselves that induce this state however, are both "active" and "passive" at different points in the process. Thus, this state is not—as so many have stated— an exclusively "active" process.

In Meditation, the individual *focuses* **the fixed attention of Concentration upon the single idea, thing, concept, physical sensation, internal impulse or external condition that was the motivating reason for attaining to the concentrative state in the first place.** Here, the very focusing of the mind on the issue or object becomes an "active" process. Once the attention becomes fixed however, the mind then becomes "passive," by *opening itself* to the inspiration, guidance, or *gift* the idea or concept being meditated upon has to offer the aspirant. As such, the process of Meditation is a *reaction* to the flow of inspiration, guidance, etc., that the ideal concept, or image has to offer the individual.

Now, how does one attain to these inner states of *Spiritual*— yes, Spiritual, as opposed to the Psychic states? As to Concentration, there is no better process that I know of than that laid down by Israel Regardie in the first "five steps" of his classic book, *Twelve Steps to Spiritual Enlightenment*.[1]

In Step One, Body Awareness, the individual becomes aware of those physical sensations—mostly subconscious (or unconscious)—that do not simply disturb attempts at Concentration and Meditation, but which outright prevent one from attaining to them. By applying the very definition of Psychoanalysis to the process, that is, 'making conscious that which was formerly unconscious,' those hitherto unknown activities within the body become know to the conscious mind. And in the process, discharge their energy from the body through the mind, thereby quelling their negative influences on the mind as it strives to achieve these states. In short, once they become 'known' to the conscious mind, they can no longer 'surprise' the individual during the 'action–reaction' processes of Concentration and Meditation.

Step Two, Relaxation, induces a deep release of those neurophysical tensions hidden below the layers of the 'automatic' mental pressures and physical tensions and impulses in the body that were rooted out in Step One. Once discharged, the free flow of psychic and spiritual energy, no longer impeded by this new or 'second-level' of resistance, ultimately becomes accessible to the student.

Step Three, Rhythmic Breathing, can be thought of a psychospiritual 'filler' for the tensions and physical impulses of the psyche that have been emptied by the first two steps. In this exercise, the energy of Spirit, contained in the very air, is brought into the body of the individual according to a four-fold rhythm, its life-giving properties spreading from the physical body into the mind and psyche, much as a stone thrown into a pond sends out ripples throughout the entire pond. New levels of physical power and mental clarity are experienced, which soon constitute a new way of living for the practitioner.

Step Four, Mind Awareness, is the most difficult step in the process. In this exercise, the hidden content of the mind is attacked directly. Through the Freudian process of Free Associa-

---

[1] Agrippa believed that magic must be linked to mysticism and as such was a true path to God.

tion, the mind is allowed to empty its secret contents directly into the consciousness. The horrors and hidden machinations contained below the surface of consciousness stream into the conscious mind in torrents. But in the process, these phantoms empty themselves of their pent up psychic energy, thereby reestablishing a free flow of psychic energy to those formerly damned up levels. In short, after this step is completed, there is nothing left within the mind that can disturb the individual in his or her inner quest for effective Concentration and Meditation.

Finally, in Step Five, all of the benefits and development achieved through the previous four steps are brought to bare on the problem at hand: that of Concentration, and this by using a mantra to fix the attention of mind upon the meaning of the words that compose that mantra. Once this phase is mastered, it then becomes easy to apply the technique to the act of Meditation: to focus the fixed attention of Concentration upon an idea, thought, concept, etc., of the individual's choosing, for the purpose of discovering its hidden nature, and the special gift that idea or concept have for the individual.

As you can see, like all else in the Occult in general and Magic in particular, the development of Concentration and Meditation require a great deal of hard work, perseverance, determination, and dedication. There is nothing for nothing in these Arts and Sciences. But the gifts they bestow upon the individual who doggedly pursues them, are beyond the ability of anywhere to put into words.

QUESTION: Even after reviewing the material over and over again (particularly Axiom 3 in *Ceremonial Magic*) there is still something very elusive about the subjective synthesis concept. In a nutshell, from what I've come to understand about this concept, is that the individual (who is a subjective being, with a subjective psyche) takes in the information related to magic and synthesizes it into their own psyche and subconscious. It in turn becomes a part of them. Isn't that just another way of saying "to properly understand" or to "internalize information." It also seems to me as if you are implying that when the individual has built a proper subjective synthesis something is activated within that individual and their subconscious can then in turn create the reality that the individual desires. Am I at least headed in the right direction with these interpretations?

ANSWER: You are most certainly correct in your interpretation and understanding of what the subconscious state of Subjective Synthesis is. It shows you have taken the matter seriously, have struggled by turning inward to 'make it a living part of your own being, and have succeeded. Based upon my own experience—and that of my personal students—I think the reason you feel "...there is still something very elusive about (it)..." is due to two factors: first, the concept itself is new to your normal thought processes, and second, the acceptance of the concept itself is not yet fully integrated into your own Subjective Synthesis. Worry not. Full integration is assured you. You have done a magnificent job here, and are to be complimented for your—work!

QUESTION: I haven't been able to think of a solitary thing wanted personally, and recently had the worst back lash in history from aiding a person to obtain a higher work position.

ANSWER: A person's wants and desires—so very frequently confused—are of course, a matter that is completely up to them. This being the case, I can be of no assistance to you in this matter. As to your backlash. Well, helping people does have its rewards and drawbacks: it goes with the human territory.

QUESTION: I am very new to the study of this art, but I am finding it enjoyable and fascinating. The only wrinkle I am experiencing is the capacity to learn from books. This is not to say that I am stupid. I just find I learn a topic a lot easier from being shown how to do something as opposed to reading about it. I have found that what may take many days to understand by reading, usually can be cut down to a couple of hours if shown. As you can appreciate, this can be a headache when reading a guide on how to use video recorder machines! I especially find it hard to learn when I am reading books written in the earlier half on the 19th century. Trying to understand Dion Fortune or Israel Regardie gives me a headache, and I coming close to giving up the study and maybe moving on to Yoga.

ANSWER: You are much too hard on yourself. It takes time and effort to learn to read earlier writings (including the grimoires) owing to their (in my opinion) more prosaic and fluid style. A good, more recent example is the Introduction to Mathers' *The Kabbalah Unveiled*. If you take it upon yourself to read such carefully and slowly with a good dictionary by your side, I think your command of this more powerful and complete form of writing style and syntax—as opposed to the 'teckie' claptrap found in any field of study today—will improve dramatically.

The very idea of 'jumping ship' to Yoga because of this perceived difficulty of yours is very ill-advised. Why? Because not only do earlier yogic documents employ a similar syntactical arrangement and writing style found in Western magical and mystical writings of the 19th and early 20th century, but they also possess a stilted Eastern-to-Western language composition that makes them even harder to understand. Additionally, if you are thinking about any of the 'contemporary' yoga texts so readily found in any bookstore, forget it: they are nothing but grossly watered down, inaccurate New Age pabulum of the various forms of Yoga.[1] You are definitely on the right path by Working to comprehend Western Magic.

---

[1] What is passed off in the West as yoga, be it Hindu, Buddhist, or Chinese, is often misunderstood by would be practitioners, especially those seeking an "easier" path. For example, according to Hindu and Buddhist teachings, the tantric practices are considered most ideal for this time—the *Kali Yuga* (also known as the 'Time of the Wolf' in some European pagan mythologies), the Dregs of Time—that we live in, and if practiced can bring one to enlightenment in one lifetime, although sixteen is often the number stated. However, few people seem to realize, as they seek to immediately jump into the Higher Yoga practices, that certain preliminaries are encouraged by some schools and demanded by others. It is common to have to undertake the "Uncommon Preliminaries" of reciting the 100 syllable *Vajrasattva* Mantra 100,000 times, performing 100,000 prostrations—just to Vajrasattva, and making 100,000 mandala offerings, all BEFORE undertaking the practices often associated with Tibetan yoga: Inner Fire (*tumo*), Dream Yoga, and what is called in the West, Assumption of the Godform. All of which must be learned from a trained teacher or lama, as there are subtle details that will not be known without direct experience. In addition, the notion of having a proper understanding of the View, or what Dr. Lisiewski calls the "internal logic of the grimoires," is conveyed prior to each stage of practice. In the Nyingmapa sect, the Original Translation School, or first school of

QUESTION: In your opinion using the Kabbalistic Cycles, which day and hour is best to retire?

ANSWER: I would arrange for retirement on a Monday during a Mercurial hour, flow down the Tree, and invoking the nineteenth card of the Tarot, the Sun, representing joy, happiness, contentment, and abundance of life.

QUESTION: Through your site I was inspired to check out the New Thought Philosophy. A thorough study of an essay by Ernest Holmes gave me solid hermetic reasons for forgiving and forgetting the ills of the past and being optimistic about the future. In short, this was truly a life changing experience.

ANSWER: The amazing thing is that what the individual so desires; what he or she so sincerely wants or needs in their life, is all obtainable through this form of Mysticism, and ever so easily. Yet the paradox is that one cannot force one's self into accepting, working, and mastering New Thought simply because the results they require are so readily obtainable from it. Quite the contrary. One must 'unfold' into it. And when that glorious days dawns, then all is made perfectly clear and works almost effortlessly for the individual so blessed with this 'discovery.'

People who are attracted to Magic must persist in it until the day comes when they 'step over the line' that leads from Magic to Mysticism. It cannot be hurried. It cannot be rushed. But it will come. This is what Percy Bullock, one of the original members of the Golden Dawn Society meant, when he said at the turn of the 20th century, "In the end, we all become Mystics."[1]

Buddhism in Tibet, there are nine *yanas* or vehicles, each with its own View, that are then synthesized at the final stage. In short, there is no getting around the required preliminary work that must be done, regardless of system or path, as it is the foundation that all future success is built upon.

[1] For the sake of clarity on this point and its relation to Medieval and Renaissance magic, let me restate the earlier quote from Paracelsus: "The magical is a great hidden wisdom, and reason is a great open folly. No armour shields against magic for it strikes at the inward life of spirit of life. Of this we may rest assured, that through full and powerful imagination only can we bring the spirit of any man into an image. No conjurations, no rites are needful; circle making and the scattering of incense are mere

QUESTION: What is your opinion on the book *Initiation into Hermetics* by Franz Bardon?

ANSWER: All of Bardon's books are anything but "Hermetic." As you are probably all too aware, simply because a book uses a popular (and all too frequently misunderstood or not-understood) word in its title, does not mean its content reflects the subject matter of that term. This is the case with the Bardon work you cite here. I am not a fan of any of his books, including *The Practice of Magical Evocation* which I found to be very ineffective and—in my opinion—ludicrous in its theoretical underpinnings.

QUESTION: The *Heptameron* states "let the master carry the sword." It is clear that the magician needs a sword, however it does not specifically instruct to have a sword made. What if I were to buy a sword during the time periods you say the sword has to be made? Would this sabotage the intended results of the ceremony?

ANSWER: Yes, you can purchase one during the appropriate day and hour as you say. Be certain however, to consecrate and inscribe the Names of Power on it during the same day and hour as well.

No, it would not sabotage your efforts, simply because the *Heptameron* is a 'brief' grimoire, and presupposes the Operator already knows the 'basics' of such things. That is, those things which were basic for the era in which the book was written.

QUESTION: Considering the size of the circle of art. How large do you find a room needs be for a rite such as the LBRP? In the same vain, does an evocation to physical manifestation require a greater amount of room or space for a spirit to successfully manifest?

---

humbug and jugglery. The human spirit is so great a thing that no man can express it; eternal and unchangeable as God Himself is the mind of man; and could we rightly comprehend the mind of man, nothing would be impossible to us upon the earth. Through faith the imagination is invigorated and completed, for it really happens that every doubt mars its perfection. Faith must strengthen the imagination, for faith establishes the will. Because man did not perfectly believe and imagine the result is that arts are uncertain when they might be wholly certain."

ANSWER: Always use a nine foot diameter Circle of Art for every ritual and ceremonial act. "Nine" is the number of Yesod, of course, and corresponds to the subconscious (unconscious) mind, wherein all Magic truly occurs—we only 'see' the results of that 'occurrence' in the outer world (Malkuth.) That is, the subconscious mind should be thought of as the *Causal Agent* of the *External Effect* we wish to produce. There is a great deal of correlation between this concept and the central doctrine of New Thought. That is, with the extremely pragmatic philosophy and practice of the latter.

As to the size of the room. I intensely dislike generalizations, but there are a few that carry merit. And in this case, "bigger is better" is one of those generalizations. There are several reasons for this.

First, while it is a maxim that you can never be absolutely certain what will occur during any rite of High Ceremonial Magic, this axiom or rule is also true in such common ritual acts as the daily performance of the Lesser Banishing Ritual of the Pentagram (LBRP.) This is especially true if you have performed a full Kabbalistic Analysis on the rite, e.g., the LBRP. The phenomena that can occur even from this seemingly simple performance are simply too numerous and varied. Hence the need for a sizeable Magical Chamber when performed indoors or for a large Area of Practice as I refer to the space of practice. It's better to have 'maneuvering room' in order to avoid potential problems, than to be confined to some small space because that is all that is readily (or 'easily') available to you. For instance. Let's assume you are in your Magical Chamber and have just drawn a pentagram in the North, are in the process of stabbing its center and vibrating the Divine Name for that quarter, and suddenly you hear something like a heavy breathing or growling directly behind you (this has happened to me many times during the performance of this ritual.) Now, you are in altered state of consciousness of course, owing to the ritual, and so, are caught off guard. If you are doing the LBRP about your own axis—or in, say, a three or four foot diameter operating space—it would be easy for you to break the bounds of the pentagram-circle formed thus far, and ruin the entire ritual. THEN you will have to put up with the negative energy that such a botched performance most certainly will level on you for at least a twelve hour period. (And don't fool yourself: immediately 're-doing' the ritual will bring nothing but more trouble. Count on it.)

Second, the size of the circle has a powerful effect upon your mind, and hence upon your ritual performance. When you don't feel cramped; when you don't have to worry about bumping into some object in the room; when you have the peaceful assurance that you have a 'buffer space' within the Area of Operation into which you can 'retreat' or use to regain your composure in case the physical manifestation is just too great or surprises you, then will your unconscious mind aid you that much more in the effective performance of your rite.

So what am I saying here? Whether it be the daily practice of some ritual, e.g., the LBRP, or the complex, full performance of High Ceremonial Magic—such as Evocation to Physical Manifestation—use a nine foot Circle of Art.

Quite obviously, it presupposes a Magical Chamber or Area of Practice that is larger than nine feet in diameter. In the case of a Magical Chamber—and depending upon the ritual or ceremonial rite being performed it is wise to add another three feet all around. So the Chamber or Area would be fifteen feet by fifteen feet. In the case of Evocation to Physical Manifestation, when operating indoors, make certain you have plenty of extra room: this is very risky business indeed, especially until you become astute in the process. It is not that the entities being summoned 'need' this extra room to materialize: you will, once the manifestations begin—and I am not joking here in the slightest! That idea; that knowledge of 'extra space' cushions the mind, and enables it to deal with the physical phenomena of any rite or ceremony. And in the case of Evocation to Physical Manifestation, it allows the Operator a psychological edge—a very wide edge—in handling the onset of the ecstasy and Divine Love that will soon overtake the Magician. To give you some example of what I have found to be a highly effective Chamber size for my own work, my Magical Chamber is twenty-eight feet by twenty-eight feet, with a twelve foot ceiling.

I realize this is a problem for many Practitioners. It was for me as well until I bought a house large enough to accommodate these requirements. But simply because something is difficult is no reason to revert to 'easy expediencies.' These intolerable conditions; these hard situations; these 'impossibilities' are what a large part of Magic is all about. And they are requirements—they are not up for debate or 'rationalization,' as many would have you believe in this day of the quick fix and instant gratification. In the case of the grimoires, they are quite direct, clear, and outspoken in what the requirements are. And those ancient manuscripts are also something else—they are right, because they work!

QUESTION: I bought your book on Ceremonial Magic and am getting ready to do my first evocation the way you gave in your book. But I am getting plenty scared, because strange and weird things have been happening to me without warning and I didn't expect this. All of the breaks on all of the wheels of my car suddenly fell off, things around my place are actually disappearing, I hear wheezing noises and rapping on the walls where no neighbor lives (I also live alone) and I keep seeing things off the corner of my vision that dart and flash but there is nothing there. It gets worse too. My bed feels very cold and my sheets have a bad odor, even though I change them and they are fine when they come out of the drier. The mattress has no odor either. Only when I do something to further get ready for this evocation does the smell and coldness return to the sheets and bed. Is all or any of this due to the demons I am getting ready to call on somehow knowing I am working toward calling them up? Please help!

ANSWER: Yes, it is entirely possible that what you are experiencing has a direct correlation to your evocational preparatory activity. While I do not know what your other daily magical activities may be, i.e., your daily magical ritual practices and what effect they might have on your preparatory work, I experienced such things (and worse too!) many times, when preparing for High Ceremonial Magic. In my opinion, when the magician prepares for such a Rite, a call goes out to the beings he or she is preparing to summon. They 'hear' it in their world, and react. Remember: they are not necessarily hostile to you as a human being. Rather, it is a property of their nature to be antagonistic, and so will cause a fuss.

The best and only way I found to combat this problem was to purchase a "Bloodstone," wrap it in a piece of 100% virgin (never used for any other purpose) white linen, and to keep it on my person twenty-four hours a day. This stone, also called,

"Emantile" in the Grand Grimoire, has a way of either distracting the demons or confusing their 'homing in' on you. Either way, it works, and works very well. Give it a try: I think you will find that it will work very well for you too (I have recommended it to others throughout the years, and have never received a complaint.)

Above all, do not be afraid to the point where you abandon the Operation. Continue to prepare, gird your heart with strength through prayer as recommended in the *Heptameron*, and when the time comes, carry out the Operation. The best to you.

QUESTION: You have often mentioned Israel Regardie's book *The Art of True Healing* but copies are often only available from used book dealers. There are more modern editions available so why didn't you recommend them over the older edition?

ANSWER: Aside from more than a few intense personal disagreements I have with people editing the great classics of magic and the occult, I always felt that if you want to understand the original ideas, thoughts, and perhaps even the motivations of a writer, you must study his writings in undiluted form. Therefore, you have to obtain the editions in which only the original author's hand appears. In theory, there may not be anything wrong with a 'modern' writer adding his two cents to someone else's book. But unless those additions are clearly spelled out and delineated, I have great objections to such tampering.

Notice Mr. Donald Tyson's edition of the famous *Three Books of Occult Philosophy*, attributed to Henry Cornelius Agrippa. Not only does Mr. Tyson clearly indicate the edit, but he annotates the entire document perfectly as well, thereby making it a—if not *the*—shining example of accurate rendition in a form contemporary readers can use with advantage. Another example of such exemplary work is to be found in Joseph H. Peterson's, *The Lesser Key of Solomon, Lemegeton Clavicula Salomonis*. There are others to be sure, but by and large, they are not many in number.

QUESTION: Let's assume that a spirit has attached itself to a person's aura/body: Would the spirit get hurt if the person performs the Lesser Banishing Ritual of the Pentagram or any other standard Golden Dawn banishing ritual? What if the intention is not to banish it in the first place, but rather, the intention is just to do such rituals as part of the mage's training in raising and directing energy?

ANSWER: The purpose of any "banishing" ritual is to remove that which is unessential from the magician's sphere of operation, *and* from his or her being. Thus, it is performed in order to clear the immediate sphere of working, as well as to 'refine' the magician's nature. To be more exact, banishing is designed to remove that which is unessential from the Practitioner's physical, mental, emotional, and psychic natures, while allowing for (gradual) spiritual unfoldment, when performed frequently and correctly. As such, it most certainly will—or should, if done properly and enough times—remove the spirit from the magician's 'sphere of influence,' which includes the area of working and his or her being, as noted.

Whether you "intend" the spirit to be banished or not is beside the point. True, if you intentionally intend to banish it, then—as given in the original Golden Dawn documents—you would image (or, "visualize" it as the documents state) the spirit (or 'psychological complex') in front of you, and then banish with the intention of removing it from you permanently. However, you must remember you are dealing with Law. In this case, psychic law, but law, nevertheless. So whether you desire it or not, and since the banishing is intended to remove that which is unnecessary from you, the spirit most certainly will be removed.

Look at it this way. You may be on a roof, repairing it, and are using the Law of Gravity to support yourself, your tools, and your materials on the surface of that roof while working. But if you get too close to the edge, that same law will pull you to the ground at the rate of 9.8 meters/sec^2, no matter what. You didn't 'intend' to get too close to the edge but you did, and the law worked. It's the same here. Law is quite impersonal—whether it be of the physical, psychic, or spiritual variety. It simply, 'works,' but it's up to you how to use it.

QUESTION: I read some recent books about the subject of entity possession. They say that if you invoke demons, they probably will attach to you, since their main concern seems to be to feed on human energy, cause havoc and restrict human evolution to something better. I would like to hear your opinion about that, meaning, is this true or is this just nonsense?

ANSWER: Properly speaking, "Invocation" refers to the act of 'calling down" or 'calling forth' a benevolent, positive, intelligent force or being—such as an Angel. Or, it can refer to the calling down or calling forth of a neutral force, the application of which is up to the discretion of the magician. An example of the latter would be the planetary forces 'called down' by an extension of the basic Middle Pillar ritual. On the other hand, "Evocation" refers to the 'calling up' or 'summoning forth' of a malevolent, negative, intelligent or semi–intelligent force or being—such as a demon. There is no 'neutrality' in this case: the force or being is malignant; but not due to any purposeful hatred toward the magician. Rather, these tendencies are simply are a part of the nature of such a force. So, according to the term used in your question, the short answer is "no," possession is not possible through the ritual techniques of "Invocation." Be advised however, that intense, prolonged periods of Invocation can most definitely lead to the surfacing of anxieties, great depression, and panic attacks. Why? Because regardless of the type of magic (or mysticism for that matter) that you practice, the subconscious mind (or unconscious mind) is involved. And while Israel Regardie was most certainly correct when he wrote in his book, *The Middle Pillar,* that one "...cannot gate crash the unconscious..." rest assured you can rattle those gates sufficiently, and wake whatever lies behind those gates! And this, to your great consternation!

However, such a condition as possession is possible through a badly botched Evocation. But really, even here, only as a theoretical probability. That is, in a badly performed evocation—one in which there is only a partial manifestation of the demon, and where control is not fully established even in such a partial manifestation—the end result will most likely be a negative result (a severe Slingshot Effect as discussed in *Ceremonial Magic and the Power of Evocation*) or no result at all. However, if the Operator succeeds in bringing about a full manifestation of the demon, and either loses control or does not fully establish that control, and attempts are made to command the being, disastrous consequences can result. But even in this instance, those consequences are not likely to end in 'possession.' Rather, they are more likely to produce extreme fright in the magician; a fright which can severely effect the heart, or end in a mental instability that can bring on insanity. Such is the nature of this 'business.'

QUESTION: In your book *Ceremonial Magic and the Power of Evocation*, you insist that those entities are objective. Which is their origin, their genesis? How is the place that they inhabit?, & what is their role and objective in that habitat?

ANSWER: This is an interesting question. It points out that I may not have been explicit enough in my writings to make my position in this matter crystal clear. In Old System Magic, the entities dealt with are—as far as I am concerned and from what my experience has taught me—objective beings; entities that have as much of an objective existence as do you and I. In other words, those spirits evoked from the *Goetia*, the *Clavicula Salomonis*, the *Heptameron*, and so on, possess an existence of their own in their world. They have certain powers or "Offices" as the grimoires term them; Offices that can be used or discharged into another dimension of existence—our own for instance. This is where the strain in evocation comes in: trying to make a 'link' between them, their powers, and our world, so those Offices can indeed be discharged into our four dimensional world; and done so according to the will of the magician.

As to the genesis of these beings, their habitats, duties there and so on, this would depend upon the religious tradition to which the individual was raised in. Notice I said raised in, not the one he or she has adopted or even denied. These matters go far, far down into the unconscious realm, effecting every area of our lives, and are anything but simple cut-and-dried matters. Hence the answer to this is just as I have given: it depends upon the earliest religious tradition given you. To be sure, your modifications of such a tradition by either rejecting or replacing that tradition will have an effect on your unconscious perception of these beings, their natures, Offices, and so forth. But that essential quintessence administered to your unconscious during your formative years, will always be there as a backdrop against which these beings are seen.

QUESTION: In *Ceremonial Magic and the Power of Evocation*, Axiom 2 states that "Every aspect of any Magical ritual, ceremony, or rite, including evocation, must be consciously and thoroughly understood." Where should I look to find the meaning of the "Words of Power" and the God-names so that when I am performing the evocation, I fully understand the Powers and the aid that I am calling upon?

ANSWER: There are many sources from which such an understanding can be gained, to be sure. Several of my favorites are: *The New Encyclopedia of the Occult* by John Greer; *Godwin's Cabalistic Encyclopedia* by David Godwin; *The Golden Dawn (The Complete Golden Dawn System of Magic)* by Israel Regardie; *A Garden of Pomegranates* by Israel Regardie; *The Holy Kabbalah*, by A.E. Waite; *The Mystical Qabalah* by Dion Fortune; and *The Kabbalah* by Gershom Scholem. Each has something unique to contribute to the understanding you seek, and is well worth having in your library.

QUESTION: In your books you have clearly stated that for operations of ceremonial evocation to physical manifestation the operator must evoke on either the bare ground, or on a concrete surface laid directly upon the bare ground. I understand that this is necessary in order to stabilize the evocation of the spirit.

My question comes in with how this axiom fits in with Western Magic and specifically with the practice of daily rituals like the Lesser Banishing Ritual of the Pentagram, Lesser Banishing Ritual of the Hexagram, Middle Pillar, Rose Cross Ritual, etc. Does this mean that I must use the same axiom in the same way for these rituals of Western Magic? Must I have a Magical Chamber in a basement somewhere in order to perform these daily rites?

ANSWER: Ideally, even daily ritual performances should be conducted on the bare ground or on a concrete floor, laid directly over the earthen one. And certainly, for Evocation to Physical Manifestation, this particular condition must be observed at all times. But for daily ritual practice, I have found that by performing the rite with bare feet, excellent effects are easily and consistently achieved. And by "bare" I mean "bare." No socks or even the lightest of slippers of any kind must be worn. Nothing must stand between the soles of your feet and the bare—or even carpeted—floor upon which you stand. Because Western Magic is 'synthetic' and above all eclectic—and not very well eclectically balanced at that—there are variations in its working that can work. This is one of them. If you follow it, I think you will be delighted with the results you receive from your daily Magical practice.

QUESTION: Of all the tarot decks available today, which one do you recommend for path working?

ANSWER: Many of the New Age tarot decks are neither accurate in their depiction of those forces that correspond to the Magical theme they are supposed to represent: thus you will have difficulty in tapping into the energy stream of those forces. That is, many of these modern decks are not reliable in serving as pathways by which one can access the energy wells behind the symbolism; energy wells that (supposedly) correspond to the forces of the Collective Unconscious. Additionally, they do not correspond to those personal subconscious (unconscious) energy patterns that resonate or are in harmony with the universal magical energy and the forces of the Collective Unconscious.

I would recommend that you consider the classical deck, the Rider-Waite deck. I have never known it to fail in either divination, or as a source of study for the inner meanings behind the forces that govern our universe. This deck also serves as a prime model of central meditation themes in better understanding the Tree of Life and its Paths, and as a powerful 'backdoor' approach for entering the Sephiroth by means of the Paths, as I gave in the *Kabbalistic Handbook for the Practicing Magician*.

QUESTION: Firstly you have warned people about starting off too quickly in their magical endeavours (i.e., evocation), and this most certainly applies to me. I wonder if you would give us (or recommend) a course of experimentation; guidelines for us beginners who get a little overwhelmed. Also, for example, how would we (beginners that is) know when we are ready to work for change in the objective universe, and what type of initial experiments would you recommend?

ANSWER: A 'recommended course of study' for a beginner is always a very difficult recommendation to make. There are so many variables involved: the age of the individual, their level of intellectual development, emotional maturity and stability, their natural ability or affinity for the Work, their financial situation (books and equipment cost money!) their living conditions and overall life-situation (married, single, children, no children) to name a few, all impact a potential study curriculum. I have had so many such questions, that I came up with a general "Possible Beginners Program" that could help many, and consists of two parts: a Study Component and a Practice Component.

The practices of Part II do not reflect the readings of Part I in a linear way, and purposely so. Why? Because there is a phenomenon I call *"Magical Saturation;"* a state that very quickly leads to another most undesirable state I term, *"Magical Supersaturation."* Regardie did not differentiate between the two. Rather, he referred to both states as a condition of *"Spiritual Dryness."* This is a condition I have never encountered in any so-called New Age writings. Briefly, Magical Saturation can be summed up as, 'too much of any good thing causes problems.' To be specific: in the state of Magical Saturation, the psychic nature becomes so overloaded with magical energy that it—the psychic nature—cannot—just like a sponge—absorb anymore. When this happens, it just closes down. In other words, you cannot even think of doing any magical reading or practice: the very idea just shuts your mind down. Of course, if you can't do any magical reading, trying to do any ritual work is even more unthinkable: you just can't bear it anymore (this is actually a normal, healthy state that allows you to adjust to the new energy levels, safely.) You can push past this first state, of course. At least you can the first few times it occurs, but even then, you can do so only for a short time. If you do however; if you push past the Magical Saturation stage, then you enter another period—one of Magical Supersaturation—in which it is difficult to even think deeply about anything—even daily life matters. This is a state to be avoided at all costs.

The first time Magical Saturation happened to me was in January 1973, one month after getting married, and after eight years of increasingly intense magical work (including two full blown Evocations to Physical Manifestation) and sixteen months after going under Regardie's tutelage. I didn't know what happened: I could not even form a mental image of a pentagram let alone trace one in the air. My tongue refused to even pronounce any of the Divine Names, let alone intone or vibrate them. Regardie's advice? *"Get used to reading some Agatha Christie novels, Joe, or start watching the boob-tube until the Dryness passes!"* And it did—six months later. If I had pushed past this first state into the state of Magical Supersaturation—which I did, years later—the time it took for that state to fade away not only increased in length, but in terms of the life-troubles it led to. Put briefly, it was thirteen long months before I could even broach the idea of 'working magic' once more.

Can this state be avoided? No. Can it be put off? Yes, but only so long. Why does it occur? Because it eventually leads to the *Great Crisis: The Dark Night of the Soul and the Abramelin Operation*.

Now, the Study Component should consist of:

1. *A Garden of Pomegranates*
2. *The Middle Pillar* (the original edition)
3. *Foundations of Practical Magic*
4. *Kabbalistic Handbook for the Practicing Magician*

The Practice Component consists of:

The Twelve Steps to Spiritual Enlightenment

Notes on the Study Component:

1. *A Garden of Pomegranates* is readily available, in undiluted, unedited form. It is a basic—although rigorous—introduction to the theory and assignments of the Kabbalah. I say rigorous because it contains many associations that are not readily connected to one another. It also presupposes the reader has some knowledge of Kabbalah. Nevertheless, even the basic knowledge presupposed can be gained from a careful study of it. As such, it demands serious attention.

2. I strongly recommend you obtain the *Middle Pillar* by Regardie in its original form from a used book dealer or another such source. The 'modern' versions—or should I say, edited versions available today are—well—best left to the New Age types. You won't regret buying the original from a used book dealer, I assure you.

3. *Foundations of Practical Magic* also by Regardie is, very happily, an unedited collection of five original papers that taken together form the cornerstone of genuine Western Magic. Those five papers it presents are: "The Art and Meaning of Magic", "A

Qabalistic Primer", "Meditation", "The Qabalah of Number and Meaning" and "The Art of True Healing".[1]

4. *The Kabbalistic Handbook for the Practicing* Magician brings into the play the assignment and use of the Tarot in practical Magic along with further meditative techniques; not to mention that most important of techniques, "Kabbalistic Analysis," that must be applied to all Magical ritual and ceremonial practices.

Notes on the Practice Component:

1. The book to be worked from, *The Twelve Steps to Spiritual Enlightenment*, must be purchased as a used book from one of the many used books dealers online, as I mentioned. In fact, the counterpart of this book, *The One Year Manual*, has the same content as far as the mechanics of the "Steps" are concerned; but it bases the Morning, Noon, Evening, and Midnight Adorations on Thelema, and contains other New Aeon inclusions as well. I told Regardie I did not like this latter book at all, and felt it 'defocused' one's attention from the classical (and therefore Christian) basis of Magic. He agreed, but said he did it "…out of consideration for the old boy…" The 'old boy' of course, meaning, Crowley. He was never pleased with it, but felt it had to be done. Hence my recommendation that the original *Twelve Steps* be purchased by the serious student.

Notes on Coordination of the Study and Practice Components:

The student would do well to follow the outline suggested here:
Study "A Qabalistic Primer" first.
Study "The Qabalah of Number and Meaning".
Next, study carefully the book, *A Garden of Pomegranates*.
A thorough study of "The Art and Meaning of Magic"[2] would then follow.

---

[1] These papers can be found in both collected in printed form and individually on the internet.

[2] These papers are indispensable for understanding magic in general, modern magic in particular, as well as the unfoldment of Regardie's own synthesis of magic. However, his paper "The Art and Meaning of Magic" was written at a time when access in the West to materials on Tibetan practices were extremely limited. Regardie's comparison of the Tibetan

Careful reading of the paper, "Meditation", follows next.

"The Art of True Healing" would then be studied very carefully, paying attention to the application of basic Kabbalistic ideas to the Spheres operating within the psycho-spiritual nature of the individual.

A thorough study of *The Middle Pillar* would follow next.

The Kabbalistic Handbook for the Practicing Magician would round out this basic study. Here, Kabbalistic Analysis would be applied to the *ritual content* given in *The Middle Pillar,* and to the **content of the ritual techniques** given in *The Art of True Healing.* In doing this, the student will learn to apply Kabbalistic Theory to Ritual Practice: a process which breathes a unique and powerful life into the ritual performances.

While working their way through the suggested reading, the student would begin to practice Steps I through III, and Steps V through VI of the Twelve Steps, paying careful attention to the Four Adorations and doing them every day. At the very least, one month should be devoted to each of the five Steps: no less. Practice of the Lesser Banishing Ritual of the Pentagram (LBRP) as given in the book, *The Middle Pillar,* and the Middle Pillar Ritual (MPR)—as given in *The Art of True Healing*—would not be attempted until the five Steps cited above are mastered, and all of the reading is done. It is extremely important that the reading be done carefully and thoughtfully, in order to build and strengthen one's subconscious state of Subjective Synthesis. For without this synthesis, the student can expect to receive—at the very best—paltry to partial results from all of his or her Magic, whatever area of Magic in which they eventually engage.

The mastery of the LBRP and the MPR—after having fulfilled all 'prerequisites'—will take many months indeed. But the begin-

---

practice of Chod, or 'sacred cutting', to evocation is in part interesting, but biased by an inaccurate source. In addition, his discussion of demons in Tibetan Buddhism being a projection of one's own mind fails to address the broader spectrum of demonology in Tibetan religious culture. For additional information see: *Chod in the Ganden Tradition* by Kyabje Zong Rinpoche, Edited by David Molk; also: *Oracles and Demons of Tibet: The Cult and Iconography of the Tibetan Protective Deities* by Rene De Nebesky-Wojkowitz.

ning Magician will find that in the final analysis, that attention to these details will bring the full results they have every right to expect from Magic, and do so quickly when they enter into more advanced Magical practices. These then are my suggestions for the beginning student of Magic, or for those who are honest enough to admit they did not begin their development properly, no matter how long ago that may have been. I trust this guidance will be of value to the serious student.

QUESTION: How does one avoid mental suggestion and/or psychic attack from others?

ANSWER: You cannot really avoid mental suggestion or psychic attack if someone chooses to exert such influence upon you. You can only ward it off or 'ground it.'

As to mental suggestion. This is a form of hypnosis. As such, it requires that the subject—or recipient, here—be in a relaxed state. For without the relaxation, access to the subconscious (unconscious) mind is difficult at best. The easiest way I know of to ground such attempts at mental domination and control is to firmly press the fingernail of either or both hands into the sensitive, fleshy part of one of your fingers until you feel a sharp pain. Release the pressure every few seconds and reapply it, each time increasing it until the pain increases. Repeat the procedure while the individual is trying to influence you. You may feel a bit light headed if the attempt to influence you is strong. But without a relaxed state, the success of that attempted influence will amount to zero.

As to psychic attack, his has always been a problem, especially since it is rarely a magical attack proper. That is, when a psychic attack is launched against an individual, it is usually unconsciously—but also can be consciously—generated by an aggressor. If it is a conscious, volitional act, it is typically done using the most primitive forms of 'Magic' imaginable. This is the reason why such Magical rituals as the LBRP and the Banishing Ritual of the Hexagram (BRH) are rarely effective in combating these attempts: the energy of the attack is of a much lower, baser 'frequency' than that generated by the LBRP or the BRH. Yes, I know that the theory of the LBRP and the BRH insist these rituals will take care of all nonessential entities and influences in the area of operation. But they do not when there is such a disparity in 'frequency.' In short, this is another case of, "One size does not fit all."

In such a case then, I suggest the 'old standby' book, *Psychic Self-Defense* by Dion Fortune. Its Christian-based methods do work to reverse the attack, and fulfill the ancient admonition, "A curse, like a rooster, soon comes home to nest." Meaning, of course, that you happily send the energy of the attack right back to the one who consciously or unconsciously generated it.

— Letter Two of this man's Self-Discovery and Enlightenment follows —

Dear Sir,

This is again the occult student from Belgium who asked a question before. I just wanted to let you know that I had a "realization" today while driving home from work. All the necessary information can be found in your EXCELLENT book *Ceremonial Magick & the Power of Evocation,* **but there must be a passing of time before the Intuition and Understanding can rise to the surface of my consciousness after reading your book and questioning the text itself.** And if you don't mind I would like to share my realization briefly with you.

In short it was a misunderstanding of some concepts of your book, and partly due to my poor translation and thus interpretation of English to Dutch. I have never had English at school and learned mostly from watching Star Trek series on BBC (the old series).

This is what I used to do: In the past when I wanted to make a Talisman for "something" I would follow the book by (name of contemporary author withheld) and thus make a few symbols on a paper. Then I would choose a day at the correct moon phase and the correct Planetary Hour. Then I would perform the "Opening by Watchtower Ritual" (this I know by heart) and I would perform a Ritual to Charge and Consecrate the Talisman, but I would read the text from paper or book, and forcing myself to "feel" and "see" the Divine Love filling myself and the Temple. I end then with the Closing of the Watchtower. But is the Talisman really charged this way?

I BELIEVE NOW THAT SUCH AS THIS IS THE NEW AGE OR the MODERN SYSTEMS OF MAGIC THAT YOU TALK ABOUT.

I now realize that this is how it should be: I will make a full investigation about the Symbols that I need to bring me my "something" (using your Kabbalistic Analysis from *Kabbalistic Handbook for the Practicing Magician*.) After taking sufficient time reading about the chosen Symbols and understanding them *completely*, I would engrave them on the object that has been chosen to become Talisman (the correct Cabbalistic material, Color, form etc.) I would then take my time and carefully pay attention to every detail. I would memorize every single Ritual to be performed, the Watchtower Ritual, the Charging and Consecration Rituals etc. Making sure I understand, comprehend, and accept the statements of every detail and Ritual that would bring about this Talisman. Nine day before the Ritual I would begin fasting and meditate daily about the Symbols, Tree of Life, Charging, Consecrations. All my being, all my energies and interests would focus on the Talisman and Ritual. Then I would prepare myself completely until the big moment I would begin the Ritual, and then I believe I would experience the Divine Love without purposely visualizing and trying to "trigger" emotions. This Divine Love would UNDERSCORE the different parts of the Ritual *automatically*. This I believe would make a very powerful Charging of the Talisman, and a true one following the ancient Magic System. Yes, the Divine Love should only be for Evocation, but since it corresponds to your Magical Axioms, I see where it would apply to any area of Magic as well including Talismans and I believe I read somewhere where you said this is so.

The difference is very clear to me now: Contemporary or modern Magick is under the impression that by simply performing a Ritual for this or that, and without due PREPARATION, you just follow a mechanical set up that does NOT demand REAL TRUE EFFORT on the part of the Operator. The New Age way then believes that simple visualization and trying to raise the emotional state by effort would make the Magick work and you would get the results. After all my years of work in this New Age way, I now know that this is not the case. Instead, as you wrote, one must follow a definite laid out set of "rules" and conditions prior to the Ritual that demands time and true effort, like in the Ancient Grimoires. This will make sure the Operator EXPERIENCES the different Energies during the different parts of the Rituals, and thus an act of TRUE MAGIC WILL HAPPEN. The results should follow not because you forced them, but because you EXPERIENCED THEM DURING THE RITUAL, AND WILL follow without any doubt.

QUESTION: Do you believe that Out of Body Experiences or Astral Projection is real and something that can be done?

ANSWER: "Out of the Body Experience" (OBE) as I prefer to think of it, is a genuine psychic phenomenon, and one I have successfully experimented with many years ago. There are many exalted ideas that the New Age has made of it, e.g., an "etheric" body, the "astral" body, the "Body of Light," and others. But even in documents of Old System Magic—the grimoires themselves—we find evidence of this phenomenon.

The most rational books on the subject are *The Phenomena of Astral Projection* by Muldoon and Carrington.

For actual practice, I recommend, *Between the Gates: Lucid Dreaming, Astral Projection and the Body of Light in Western Esotericism* by Mark Stavish. This is a very thorough look at various practices and ideas associated with the mentioned topic. My own experiences in OBE have shown that only my consciousness was projected, along with my emotional and rational content. I never 'saw' a 'double' of my own physical body or any such. Instead, if you try this it will give you an idea as to what to expect when you successfully 'project.' Stand straight up, extend your head forward so you can no longer see any part of your physical body. The resulting 'you' is what is experienced: like a point of consciousness just 'out there' moving about at will. I learned the technique of OBE from an old Rosicrucian. This technique I have never seen in any book, he having taught it to me privately in 1971.

QUESTION: You frequently stress the great influence that the religion we were raised in still has on us even after we've adopted different religious beliefs. I grew up in a conservative Protestant household, and my mother taught me that all forms of Magic were evil and sinful. I was not even allowed to watch cartoons in which the characters were doing magic or casting spells.

I now have a desire in my heart to start doing magic, and believe that God put that desire in me for a purpose, that I might know more about Him. Could this religious upbringing of mine have a negative effect on my ability to properly perform Magic?

ANSWER: I salute and congratulate you for being an individual of such character, that you were able to break out of that insane shell of society called "Religious Orthodoxy." By the same token, I understand how much you must have suffered under the heavy hand of "God, Mom, Country, and Apple Pie,' all artificial constructs designed and implemented by the reigning 'powers that be' to keep you—and the almost three hundred million others in this country of theirs—in 'their place.' I say this, because my own personal history is not that much different from yours, save mine was against a Roman Catholic background.

The problem is this: the bases of all orthodoxies—including those of accepted religions—are nevertheless founded in Truths. Truths that were meant to Teach and Free individuals from the pains of this world: not to extol, "This world is nothing but a vale of tears! Go to church, do what you're told, pray your little prayer book or rosary, and beg; beg! God for that new color television you want so much!" Sounds tawdry, doesn't it? Yet that is exactly what their clerics advocate under the guise of their 'religion.'

And of course it is also demanded of you that you assume that the bread and wine you take as the Sacrament of Holy Communion is truly the "Body and Blood of Christ," even if it comes from the hands of some child molester, alcoholic, sexual deviant, thief, embezzler, rapist, or murderer, who his orthodox organization staunchly defends and has the temerity to yet call, priest, minister, rabbi, or whatever trendy term is currently in vogue.

The fact that you are aware of the hypocrisy, delusional nature, and spiritually very dangerous composition of the orthodox religions of the day, and that your inner eye has found another—and genuine—road to the God you worship and adore, will shield and gradually eliminate most of the negative subconscious impact your earliest religious training had upon you. Mark me well here: it will never eliminate all of it, however. But you can nevertheless 'appease' it by doing as I stated in *Ceremonial Magic and the Power of Evocation:* pay it some small homage at least once a year. Even if that homage is something so slight as lighting a small candle as a 'peace offering' to that buried, recessed, unconscious ideational material within you. At first, your Magic may—but not necessarily will—be effected to some extent by your religious upbringing. Most likely, it will be from bouts of guilt, and the voice of your mother ringing in your ears telling you just how 'bad' Magic is.

As you continue to study and practice, while consciously building and later strengthening and polishing your subconscious state of Subjective Synthesis, that voice will fade quickly and dramatically. When that time comes—and it could come rather quickly—that little 'peace offering' will prove more than enough in allowing your Holy Guardian Angel (HGA) to begin teaching you: quietly, and in off moments. At other times, your HGA will influence you by thoughts that just come to you from 'nowhere,' or through flashes of inspiration, all of which will bear themselves out as being true. And at still other times, by a seeming small whisper of that 'still small voice within.'

Go your own way. Listen to no man, group, organization, church, 'magical order,' or anyone to whom your HGA does not direct you. You will know who those are to whom he points you. But even then, learn to "Invoke Often! Inflame Thyself with Prayer!" and always, let this act be dedicated to the God you envision, and to the Holy Guardian Angel who is forever at your side. Trust no one but these Two.

QUESTION: I am very interested in learning more of the "old school" of magic. However, I do not feel I am at all ready for evocation, nor do I have a tremendous interest in that branch. However, so many of the classic grimoires seemed focused exclusively on evocation. Are there any classic texts that give more focus to other practices, such as enchantments and talismanic magic?

ANSWER: This is a good question. First off, the grimoire, *Clavicula Salomonis* (the *Greater Key of Solomon*) has frequently been used as a "source book" for talismanic designs (although this is not its intended purpose as even a cursory reading of it will prove.) I am even told that some have used the *Heptameron* itself as a source book for talismans. I have no knowledge or experience in using this grimoire from the *Fourth Book of Occult Philosophy* (attributed to Agrippa) for talismanic ends, but such an idea just might get your mental machinery spinning in that direction.

Then there is that vast tome of priceless information in *The Three Books of Occult Philosophy*, by Henry Cornelius Agrippa (edited and annotated by Donald Tyson). Tyson has another book of interest as well. While it is not a grimoire, it is a unique extrapolation of ancient Hebrew and Kabbalistic material that presents a powerful 'process' for working with the "Angels of the Name." This book, *Tetragrammaton* is one you should not miss. In my opinion, it is derived from Old System Magic, and is highly, highly, workable. You might also look at the book, *Albertus Magnus: Egyptian Secrets, White and Black Art for Man and Beast* and Franz Hartmann's, *Magic: White and Black. The Science of Finite and Infinite Life.*

In addition, there is *Hermetic Magic: The Postmodern Magical Papyrus of Abaris* by Dr. Stephen Edred Flowers, an utterly masterful exposé of Hermetic magical principles, theory, and practice, and what I conceive to be its 'companion' book, Hans Deiter Betz's, *The Greek Magical Papyri in Translation: Including the Demotic Spells: Texts.*

Pay special attention to Flowers' Recommended Reading list at the back of his book: it will enable you to amass a library of your own in Hermetic Magic easily and quickly, with the best texts available on the subject. (I did this myself and am very grateful that I took Dr. Flowers' advice on this and certain matters he presents in the book.)

QUESTION: You make note that the physical phenomena of evocation to physical manifestation can be presented as a pounding so hard as to crack cement walls. Now, if such is the case, should I take this into account when calculating the structural integrity of my new workshop? The walls will be wooden, not cement, and I'm sure you understand the differences in their load-bearing properties.

Secondly, my original plans were to create a magic workshop that was 10′×20′. However, after reading the Heptameron portion of your book, and understanding the Circle of the Art, this does not seem sufficient. If other grimoires call for circles larger than 9 feet, I will be severely limited in my working space. I know you are fond of working directly upon the earth, but if you had to estimate the needed indoor space to accommodate the majority of circles that I may be working with as I continue my studies over the next series of years, what size space would you estimate would be sufficient?

ANSWER: By all means, take the structural integrity of the walls—and indeed, of the entire "work shop"—into consideration. You never know how successful you will be in the Manifestation phase of Evocation to Physical Manifestation, and therein lies the problem. When I gave examples in my books of the types of manifestation that has occurred in my own work, I was of course, giving a cross-section of results I received throughout a 35+ year period. The better you become at this Science, the more powerful will be the manifestations. For example. Initially, you may receive only knocks on the walls and howls, or—and the most unnerving of all as far as I am concerned—'loud' whispers and knocks. As the years go on and you continue your practice, you may very well receive hard thuds on the walls and floor that are so loud, they reverberate through you. You will find however, that the more extreme the associated phenomena of the Manifestation phase, the more rapid will be the Control that results from the Divine Bliss which overtakes you, and the more effective will be your final Command. Don't worry. You obviously have taken into account the various parameters dealing with the design and construction of your Magical Chamber. And as such, whatever you settle on will be quite sufficient, I am sure.

Regarding the size of the room due to Circle requirements. In no case will you operate with a Circle larger than 9 feet in diameter: all grimoires settle on this number, and for good reasons. That is, while this number associates the Circle and Magic with Yesod, you will also find that this size Circle gives you 'just enough' room not only in which to operate, but one whose size differentiability allows for your maximum focus on the elements of the Ceremonial Act.

Why is this? Regardless of all the Kabbalistic hubbub about Yesod in this matter, there is another, more sublime and mathematically precise reason for this. One that is locked into the deepest strata of human consciousness. And that is, *this size Circle acts as a limiting condition in the mind*; one that is set by mankind's awareness and use—since time immemorial—of the nine "Natural Numbers" defined in the mathematics of Number Theory. Most notably, the Real Number System: a system that includes the Natural Numbers, the Integers, the Rational Numbers and the "Irrational Numbers." Thus, these "Natural Numbers," 1 through 9, are 'fixed' in the consciousness of mankind, the number "9" establishing the limit of action and therefore of the 'reality' of—in this case—the Ceremonial Act. (The number "0" [zero] is considered an "Integer" and was devised around 1000 C.E. to enable such higher mathematics as Algebra to be invented).

You will find however, that peripheral circle structures, e.g., those that appear in the Clavicula Salomonis, require additional space-consideration such as you have thought about. This being the case, you will find that the 'ideal' size room should be 16 feet by 16 feet, or larger. And here, I do mean, the larger the better. Then you will have no concerns when considering operating from any grimoire extant.

QUESTION: In the *Heptameron*, no specific demon names are mentioned other than for example, "Spirits of the West Wind", yet in your book *Ceremonial Magic,* during the Charge you leave a blank for the "name of the spirit". Where are their names? Are they the spirits of the north, south, east and west winds or are they the 72 grimoire demons?

ANSWER: In the *Heptameron*—a grimoire that predates the *Clavicula Salomonis* and the *Goetia*—the spirits are undifferentiated. (The roots of the other two are, arguably, another matter.) That is, in the *Goetia*, the spirits have been differentiated into individual demons: hence the arising of the 72 Fallen Angels. In the blank space, you simply say, 'Ye Spirits of the _____ Wind' as is appropriate to the Quarter from which you are evoking. Just use this and you will be have no problems in your secret work.

QUESTION: I have noticed over the years that most books out there are written for the 9 to 5 society norm schedule. For those of us who are actually working shift work and not bankers hours, going to school, and not on welfare this can pose no end of problems when it comes to actually doing magical work. Can you offer some suggestions?

ANSWER: I salute you most sincerely, because you are one who has taken responsibility for your own life, and who is working to adjust your life to Magic: and not Magic to your life, as so many who write those "9–to–5" books on 'magic' would have you do. Your questions are absolutely reasonable and logical, because you have considered the problem(s) carefully, and worked to find viable solutions and make those solutions the crux of your life.

First of all, the cycle of the sun does not determine your 'day.' The sun in the sky is only the visible symbol of the Spiritual Sun that lies at the core of your very being. It is that part of God within you that does not know the limitation of time or space, yet which is all of those things (and so many more) at the same time. Most of the 'regulations' you come upon in the Occult and Magic telling you when to do what and what to do when, are laid down by men for a multitude of reasons. Not the least of which is to justify some synthetic train of thought and the equally synthetic system of beliefs that are built upon that thought. Thus, when you arise for your day at 8 PM, let your Morning Adoration prevail. At Midnight, let the Adoration at noon be said, and so on, because after all, it is **your** day and not another's. In all of these things, we must look to root principles; the fundamental underlying tenets, just as we do in physics and mathematics. There is no difference, save for the subject matter itself.

There is only prioritizing, because this forces the mind into choosing between that which is important, that which is wanted, that which is needed, and that which is ego-driven. In short, you must sit down and ask yourself the same questions Frater Albertus posed to me one day during my first year (Prima Class) in 1975 at the Paracelsus Research Society:

Where did I come from?
Who am I?
Where am I going?

Now, the first requires the experience of past-life recall, which is certainly obtainable. Yes, it will take time, but it can be achieved. This will shed light upon who you are now, and so the second question can be answered: at least, initially to a point. This answer will become clearer to you as you progress in your occult and magical work. Attendant to the answer to the second question, you will find your path to the third question and to the answer that can only apply to you. A lot of work, I agree. But then, I had the same agenda to deal with back in 1974. And do you want to know something? I answered my 'Three Questions.' You can too.

"But what do I do now?" you ask. I have a suggestion. In the meantime, you may have to do what I did: decide on a program of occult or magical study and work, and set to it, letting nothing get in your way. Let me give you an example.

When I was an undergraduate in physics at university in 1971, I was very poor. The room I lived in had so many cockroaches that I had to put sugar around the baseboards at night to keep them off of me while I slept. In addition, the room was 2 ½ miles away from campus. I had no car, there was no bus service to that area, and I had no cooking privileges in that $45 a month room. Regardie had set me to do the Twelve Steps, and so—while handling my academic schedule and struggling to say alive—I set myself to the task. Since he required that I do the exercises "…three times a day, Joe. You got to really get into it!" I walked back to that room twice during the day to perform my Twelve Step work, returned to the campus for my studies, went to my part-time job, and took care of whatever else was required of me on any given day. Prioritizing forces you to do something else; something that requires you to think, prior to setting your priorities. It requires you to choose what things are important to you.

QUESTION: You have exhorted the student in one of your books to follow the commandments of God as if his life depended on it. It's hard for me to see why this is important when it is well known that Crowley was a drug addict, adulterer, and "the most evil man in the world" and in spite of this, he was able to experience true spiritual unfoldment. I want to "follow the commandments of God" as you say, but I don't want to fall into meaningless dogmatic and Puritanical posturing. Thank you very much.

ANSWER: What we label "good" or "bad" are purely societal conventions that are accepted en masse at any given point in human history. For instance, it was not only acceptable to own slaves in ancient Rome, but it was considered 'good' to have them, for these captive people were indicators of status and rank in the Roman world. Today of course, we cannot even comprehend such a thing, let alone think of bringing it back into 'vogue.' This is only one very obvious example. If you think it through, there are countless others.

There are variations on these themes of 'good' and 'evil.' For instance: the taking of one's own life is not only considered to be against the Law of God, but it is also decreed as being against the law of man as well. That is, it is a crime under the legal statutes of most 'civilized' countries. Yet, there is 'physician assisted death' along with a "Living Will" that allows you to terminate your own life under certain conditions. And what are those conditions? Those that this society—at the moment—feels are 'acceptable.' So to say that Crowley was such and such and draw the conclusion that he was 'evil,' is a completely moot point. If anything, he upset the status quo so greatly, that he was called "The Wickedest Man in the World." And yet this same man who was hated by so many, remains misunderstood by most, and who despised people in general, yet wrote some of the most meaningful, haunting, and beautiful poetry I have ever read. For me, one of his two most beautiful poems, "Jean," captured the transiency of human existence, the grandeur of Creation, and the inevitably of man's fate. It ended so appropriately: "…for the end of science and the end of art, is just…my ear, against your heart." And this, from "The Wickedest Man in the World?" Don't be so quick to take up the judgments that radiate so easily from the mouths of others.

Make no mistake about this: Spirit—the Life of God as it manifests Itself in Man—takes no notice of the ever-shifting conventions of man's definitions of 'good' and 'evil.' It is there for the 'sinner' as well as for the 'saint.' After all, didn't Christ Himself say, "I will go into any house where I am welcome," and "All are welcome at my Father's Table, whether they be Jew, Gentile, Pagan, or Roman." And wasn't it He who sat with sinners, saved prostitutes from being stoned by the 'righteous' crowd, and walked with the dregs of the society of the times, all to the chagrin of the Sanhedrin? It is all too easy and convenient to become so enmeshed in the conveniences, contrivances, and reigning mores of the times, such that you can label one individual as 'bad' and another as 'good.' All such designations are relative in the history of mankind, and are inconsequential to Spirit. *But we humans need some type of moral referent system if for no other reason than to have something which enables us to maintain a personal mental, emotional, and spiritual equilibrium amidst the ever-changing mores of the times.*

The "Divine, Universal Moral Code" to which you refer is what I call the "Eternal Verities" that exist in all people. They are those instinctual, yet spiritually-motivated humanistic attitudes which are the "Mark of God in Man" as I term them, and which constitute those precepts that all religions try to lay claim to as their own but which, in fact, predate all such man-made organizations. They consist of the need and desire to care for each other; the feeling of compassion; the feeling of empathy; the need to help; the desire to share; even that impulse to lay down one's own life for another: another, who may be a total stranger to the one giving up his own life for that stranger. There are more to be sure, but these few listed here are suggestive of those others that fall under this "Mark."

The Ten Commandments are vitally important because they are about as complete and reasonable a set of well-established and thoroughly tested written-down values as can be found anywhere, although the essence of their contents are far from Judeo-Christian in creation: earlier Babylonian, Syrian, Persian, and Egyptian sources contain very similar exhortations of humane behavior in abundance.

The choice of which moral code to consciously follow is a matter that is strictly up to the individual. There are no 'right' or 'wrong' answers here, nor are there any canned solutions (although for those of us reared in Western society, I do recommend the Ten Commandments as I stated.) As in all things in life, the choice—and the responsibility for making that choice—is an individual one. For myself, I choose to follow the Ten Commandments, seeking to understand their meaning as they apply to my own life and affairs. At the same time, I try to follow the Teachings of Christ and understand them in a way that is both meaningful and useful to me. I do this by studying such works as the Manresa, different versions of The Bible (both Old and New Testaments)—and the writings of Pierre Teilhard de Chardin. Additionally, I have found the Psalms to be a veritable font not only of inspiration but of practical advice, as well as a source of power for use in magical rituals and ceremonial work. At the same time, I make no judgment on the choice of the moral systems followed by others. For those interested in this very difficult problem of 'good' and 'evil,' I recommend the following books:

The Christos, or the Problem of Good and Evil by Vitvan (School of Natural Order, Baker, Nevada, 1951)
Lessons in Truth by Emilie Cady (Unity, Kansas, 1939)
The Loves & Fishes by Heward Carrington (Scribers, New York, 1935) and
The Perennial Philosophy by Aldous Huxley (Harper, New York, 1944)

QUESTION: From looking at the results of your Kabbalistic cycle program, it looks like your using the day/night method. This conflicts with all older writings (Talmud, Chaldean, Egyptian, etc.) that says that the cycle is night day. I know this may sound silly but if the night comes after the day in these systems, then the night is the 'next' day. i.e., Monday begins at sundown Sunday night and from sundown till sundown is Monday which is divided into the night and day and then into the 12 parts per half.

ANSWER: Now I'll be blunt. The idea of which came first: the day or the night, is equivalent to your saying that the chicken came before the egg or the egg before the chicken. Obviously, we are looking at the same phenomenon, but from a different viewpoint.

As to Egyptian, Chaldean, and Egyptian systems you are not living in a culture versed in those systems and therefore cannot work them fully. This, owing to their substantive content having been lost to the ages. Yes, there are bits and pieces here and there. And certainly, there is no end of modern-day books spouting 'secret' knowledge of these systems. However, only for Egyptian—actually Graeco-Egyptian writings—do we have dependable scholarly sources from which modern treatments have been culled or adapted. Dr. Stephen Edred Flowers' vitally important contribution, *Hermetic Magic* is such a work, having as its reference the scholarly writings of Professor Hans Dieter Betz. Further, trying to 'adapt' elements of those systems—a kindness for your actually 'mixing' systems'—by blending them with some form of Western Magic, will result in your receiving partial results—or no results—from your magical work, at best. This is not to mention the very real probability—not simply, 'possibility'—of your experiencing no small measure of the Slingshot Effect.

Also, I sense you have not worked the Kabbalistic Cycles System that I proposed, and therefore you cannot comment on its effectiveness from your own experience, anymore than you can comment on any of the ancient systems you named (Graeco-Egyptian, excepted.) 'Right' and 'wrong,' 'good' and 'bad,' 'good' and 'evil;' such words and their attendant concepts are relativities as I discussed in Question 3 above. What you are really saying, is that you feel more comfortable with a night system, for whatever reason you claim. But—as in all things—the choice is yours. My suggestion: Go with what you think is best for you, and be prepared to shoulder the consequences—whatever they may be.

QUESTION: Can you refer me to a source which will help me to correctly pronounce the names of god from the prayers and conjurations of the *Heptameron*?

ANSWER: I recommend *Godwin's Cabalistic Encyclopedia: A Complete Guide to Cabalistic Magic* by David Godwin.

QUESTION: I have practice magic for a long time(a majority of it has been New Age unfortunately) and after all the time, effort, sweat, tears, confusion, etc. I still haven't experienced anything magical or really mystical in the profound sense, I am only 24 years old, so I still know I have a long way to go, but I have reached my wits end, I feel so lost. Anyway my question is this, should I attempt the Abramelin Operation to gain the K&C of HGA, because I know without doubt that once I have my Visitation I will no longer be so confused. I was also wondering if its possible to do the Abramelin Operation first and then start practicing magic. Your answer will be very helpful.

ANSWER: Under no circumstances, should you attempt this exalted Operation! If you have not succeeded to any perceptible extent with more minor practices (Evocation to Physical Manifestation being considered one of those 'minor practices' here) what makes you think you are ready to attempt this most difficult and dangerous (from a number of perspectives) Work? *The Attainment of the Knowledge and Conversation of the Holy Guardian Angel* is a *working* that lies at the summit of the Magical or Mystical Mountain. And as with climbing any mountain, you have to make your way slowly, cautiously, carefully, taking one step at a time. You must insure that your subconscious state of Subjective

Synthesis has been properly built and polished; you must be extremely familiar with your own Interior nature, and with the *psychic mechanisms* by which you project that magical force, i.e., that force that is either called down or summoned up from within your being and projected into the world of form: that is, into Malkuth. Your psychic faculties must be opened and developed, and you must be able to tap into them—and control them—at will. Additionally, you must understand your physical body, and have conscious knowledge of the many sensations and processes that are going on within it. And you must be seasoned in the experience of your own mind: both the depths to which it can plummet, and the heights to which it can attain. And finally, you must be adept at controlling that Interior point within yourself at which your Spirit, Mind, and body, meet.

No, you are not ready for the Abramelin Operation. If you attempt it, it is my opinion that one of two eventualities will befall you: you will receive no result whatsoever, even if—and it is an extremely doubtful "if"—you were able to take it to completion (owing to what it does to your entire being.) Or you would tax your physical and mental constitution so greatly, that you would wind up with some type of a severe and serious breakdown. Be warned! This Operation is nothing to fool with, and is never—and I repeat, NEVER!—to be taken lightly!

QUESTION: One particular line in your charge for the *Heptameron* reads, "completely fulfill my words of Charge given here within the space of thirty days." Why thirty days?

ANSWER: In theory, you can shorten the time to a 'fortnight' (2 weeks) if you wish, but I would not advise it. Your generation—coming over from New Age fad magic—must simply learn to remove your insistence for instant gratification and the quick fix, and allow the *process* which is Evocation to Physical Manifestation to occur. But beyond your overcoming this "I want it now" attitude, there are other, more realistic reasons for your adhering to the recommended time requirement.

In several grimoires, you will find the span of 30 days as the length of time the spirit should be given in order for it to fulfill your Command. Why this length of time? Because as I stated above, this Ceremonial act is a *process*. That is, it is a natural process that is marked by gradual changes. For during this time—when the spirit will be working to manifest your desire—there will be a continuous interaction between you and it. At times that interaction will be conscious. That is, you will feel an inner excitement or a state of anxious, profoundly fearful apprehension; as if something external were drawing enormous amounts of nervous energy from you. What is worse, you will also feel that you cannot control these states of fearful apprehension. Or you may have a powerful feeling of your being attracted to some thing 'out there' or that 'something' is being attracted to you. At other times this interaction will be unconscious. That is, you will receive conscious glimpses that something which you 'cannot put your finger on' is happening around or within you, or you will find yourself all out of sorts for some unknown reason. Or you will become extremely irritable in an unusual way: a way to which you are not accustomed. You may also have panicked feelings that things are just 'not right somehow,' and the anxiety generated by these nagging feelings will send your apprehensiveness to heights you never previously experienced. But worst of all, will be that deep, inner sense of some unknown, unnamed terror; a terror that is within or (literally) 'behind' you at all times during the 30 day period.

All of these conscious and unconscious states mark the gradual changes that are occurring in your external world as the object of your desire is either being brought to you or is being created for you by the entity you charged with the task. Since this desire is part of your psychic nature, and since the psyche is that Interior Realm in which the Magic is actually performed, you will thus feel the stages of the desire's manifestation within you.

In reality then, the 30 day requirement is not given out of consideration for the spirit: the Fathers of the Grimoires established it out of consideration for the Magician. In short, it was given out of consideration for you, since you will be on an emotional roller coaster ride—one you cannot possibly understand at this point—until your desire is made fully manifest.

And don't take the attitude, "I don't need that long! I can handle it no matter what this guy says here!" Because the fact is, you can't! How do I know this? Because until and unless you experience the real thing: Evocation to Physical Manifestation by adhering to the strict requirements of the ancient grimoire you are working from; until you attain that manifestation of the demon, and struggle through the Control of the process wherein you are flooded with such a Divine Bliss that you don't know if you are conscious or not; until you face a reality that you only dream (or fantasize!) about now, you cannot possibly know the extent and magnitude of the changes that this process produces. You will need every second of that 30 days—if not longer.

QUESTION: *The Kybalion*, is it useful? Is it possible for me to use the 10 axioms and your principles set out in *Kabbalistic Handbook for the Practicing Magician* to enhance my practice in Egyptian Ceremonial Magic, or is this dangerous?

ANSWER: Yes, *The Kybalion*, by Three Initiates, is a most useful and insightful book. It has more direct utility in what I refer to as "Higher Mysticism" or "New Thought" than it does in Magic proper. However, the insights gained from it produce unusual states of awareness, these 'second generation' states having direct relevance to Old System Magic. It is a most worthwhile treatise on matters Occult, and in my opinion, belongs in the library of every sincere student of the Mysteries.

If you do purchase a copy, please buy the hardcopy version. I say this for two reasons. First, I have seen paperback editions that were abridged or 'abbreviated.' That is, they were shortened, obviously to increase the profit of the publisher without any regard whatsoever for the material in the text. This is not true for all paperback versions of course, but "...if in doubt, don't..." and hence my recommending the hardcopy version: I have yet to see any of its various productions shortened. Second, you will find yourself referring to it many times. And with the absolute shoddy quality of many if not most paperbacks published these days, a sewn hardcopy will last you throughout the years.

The principles of magical operation set down in *Ceremonial Magic and the Power of Evocation* and in the *Kabbalistic Handbook for the Practicing Magician* are most certainly applicable to Hermetic Magic. Please be certain of one thing however. If you practice Hermetic Magic as, for instance, laid down in Dr. Flowers' masterpiece, *Hermetic Magic*, practice only that form of Magic. Do not mix systems by applying techniques from Old System Magic to other systems.

If you are using Dr. Flowers' book, please be certain to use the 'Hermetic' Glyph of the Tree of Life—the Pagan version—he discusses therein. Do NOT mix it with the Western version of the Glyph that is so popular today. There are different Path geometries or Sephiroth-Path configurations in the Hermetic Glyph, and it is absolutely imperative that you use those configurations—and only those configurations—for your work in Hermetic Magic.

QUESTION: I found *Twelve Steps to Spiritual Enlightenment* by Dr. Regardie in the hardback 1969 original version. The Adorations are very nice. In fact I have been using the Adoration at Dawn contained in this book for almost one year now. They seem to flow off my tongue better than any others I have found.

ANSWER: In many ways, Regardie's book, *Twelve Steps to Spiritual Enlightenment*, is a treasure trove for the aspiring magician. The Adorations are just one of the gems in that hidden treasure as you have discovered for yourself. These Adorations will, in time, become singular devotions in themselves; devotions that will gradually enable your spiritual nature to unfold in a safe, sane, and balanced way, thus preparing you in an ideal way for the practice of Old System Magic.[1]

There are also a number of the Steps in this book that will prepare the individual in a rigorous manner for the practice of Old System Magic. However, this book cannot be used as a complete, 'stand alone' set of spiritual exercises to aid one's advancement. That is, not without bringing the individual to his spiritual and emotional knees; a condition that does not have to be experienced. Regardie himself agreed with me on this point when he told me that if he had time he would "...redo it completely, Joe. I now see too many things in it that could be changed..."

QUESTION: Your system seems more or less to equate progress and success in magic with reaching a state of mystical saintliness as the only way to control the powers and intelligences in magic. Perhaps you are right, but most people drawn to magic are people handicapped psychologically and tormented in life in general. A person who is born in a right family and environment

---

[1] See *Prayer* by Dudley Wright, Introduction by Allan Armstrong, for a fine survey of the nature, purpose, and effects of prayer.

and is raised in a psychoanalytical correct way becomes a real human person—as opposed to a dehumanized non-person or "alien"—with a huge set of abilities (solid self-image, true and intact self, free from inner collision, ability to love, connected with his body, etc) that allow him—especially in our age—to achieve almost everything without needing any magic (perhaps because he is lucky to have the magic of an Unconscious that works for him). My question is whether magic is an eclectic system only for those who are already lucky in life from the beginning because otherwise I cannot see persons "prisoners of childhood" to really have the necessary inner structure and tendency to respect cosmic law and thus avoid tears from mistakes in magic. I do not mean that the lucky ones do not do any work but it is only work in a correct and comfortable current after having been "selected" by life. Even Crowley, as important and competent as he was, I know from sources other than books that in the end his body completely disintegrated and rotted and pieces fell off, a tragic end in life. So magic exists but for who?

ANSWER: Your question is a good one. What is more, is it is a completely fair one. All of us are "handicapped psychologically" in one way or another. The idealized individual you describe above does not exist and never has. That imaginary person is, instead, a 'theoretical model' that so-called modern day "Psychoanalysts" have invented as a justification for that which they cannot justify nor prove: their own 'theories'—actually conjectures—about the human psyche.

The "saintliness" you speak of for controlling magical power occurs at points along the way. And yes, it does allow us to control that power. But at no time do we become so 'holier than thou' that we dispense blessings upon those that others may see as 'less fortunate' than ourselves. The Mystical States of Attainment are the end of Magic: not the beginning of it. And certainly very few of us sought Magic in the beginning to attain such states. Make no mistake about it: almost all of us initially sought Magic because we were incapable of dealing with life on its terms. It was only after we began the Path and continued, regardless of the personal inner obstacles and external impediments, that we saw 'something else.' A 'something' which lies over our personal horizons of self-gratification and indulgence. Then—and truthfully, only after having attained to some satisfactory level of personal gratification and indulgence—did that 'something' else beckon to us, and lead us in the ultimate Path to which Magic serves as the Gateway.

We—all of us who have struggled, clawed, and crawled our way along the magical path—are intensely REAL, HARD WORKING individuals in the extreme. We have come from—what is now referred to in oh, such a politically correct, sociably responsible way—"dysfunctional families," having been bombarded to the extreme by so-called "psychologically impaired" parental and social influences. But—and this is the quality that makes us different from those who have used such negative influences as excuses for laziness, dependence, and to commit crime—we persisted, uncovered what we found to be the Truth, and continued until we found the Light at the end of the tunnel.

Make no mistake about it. That "Light" is just that: a Divine Light wherein all of the pain and anguish does not simply melt away as so many of the contemporaries and their psychology-spouting cronies would have you believe. But rather, those negativities are TRANSFORMED by this Light into something of such beauty, that our lives are fulfilled in ALL ways—and that includes the material. And by the way, this is not to mention the deepest emotions we experience from having finally and honestly forgiven ourselves and all those who have wronged us throughout the years. There are no words for this personal purging of hate and anger, and for the depth of love and peace we experience as a result of its dawning upon us. We learned what the phrase, "When hating someone else, dig two graves," truly means. Know then, that Magic is for ALL who have the COURAGE to face who and what they are at this moment, take themselves in their own two hands, and determine to tread that Path that has been called, "The most grueling discipline ever conceived of by the mind of man." The Path of Magic.

There are no easy routes to Salvation. And by "Salvation," I do not mean that emotional sense of 'righteousness' that is *sold* by churches, temples, or synagogues, or by that host of so-called "magical orders" and "secret societies." I am speaking of an inner spiritual freedom and cleanliness; something so pervasive and complete, that the errors of your past life are actually transformed by an Event that leaves no part of you untouched. You cannot 'buy' such by paying your church, Order, or synagogue dues, attending their religious rituals, or being members of their inner societies that give begrudged alms to the community, while holding back the bounty for their own extravagances and comforts. No. It is a matter of each of us becoming accountable for our own spiritual progress, and doing something about it. Something for which we take the "blame or the fame" as the saying goes. Be guided accordingly.

As to the outcome for the INDIVIDUAL? As in all things in life, this depends EXCLUSIVELY on the individual; on the lengths he will take, the devotion he will give, and upon the links he makes with his own Divinity within as he treads the Path. All in all, one cannot ask for more in life: to be able to write one's own ticket, and then use it to get to where one wants to go.

As to your concern with psychoanalysts, their 'sayings,' so-called theories and conjectures? Based upon those whom I met and knew throughout my life, and from the writings of such that I have studied for well nigh 35 of my 43+ years in Magic, I will attempt to answer your question regarding them in two parts.

First: why is it that for the simplest so-called 'psychic disturbance' or psychological phenomenon, any randomly chosen 12 different 'Schools of Psychological Thought'—will produce as many different answers? Can you imagine if, say, gravity had as many explanations that determined 'how' it worked? And why? In short, *these people have no science that can define anything with predictability, repeatability, and which is capable of independent verification.*

Second: In order to shore up their own negative views they reduce human existence to a purely mechanical, chemical phenomena, including the complexity of the brain itself. Yet those same 'intellectuals' cannot explain the workings of the brain with any more clarity and certainty than if they advanced the idea that the skull was filled with cotton wadding! Yes, there are those psychoanalysts of another era that I admire, and whose work are (at the very least) inspiring, as they encourage us to look within to study our own nature and complexity; that nature and its inherent complexity that the mechanistic psychologists and psychoanalysts of today have reduced to a handful of interacting chemicals: the works of Roberto Assagioli, William James, and to

Howlings from the Pit

some extent, even select writings of Carl Jung, to name those I am thinking of. The writings of Assagioli and James have great value here.

Listen to no "naysayer". Be your own man (or woman), chart your own course, make the inevitable errors, continue to learn, and hold no one accountable but yourself for where you are in life at this moment, where you want to go, and for your finally getting there—or not. This is how the man or woman of Honor lives and dies: not according to the prevailing whims of an insane society that is slowly but surely killing itself with every passing day. These are hard core words of Truth; the only Truth that can truly—and once and for all permanently—set you free.

QUESTION: In your article "The Magical Chamber" you mention that the altar is "that basic design taken from *The Book of the Sacred Magic of Abramelin the Mage*. In The Book it says "the altar, which should be made of wood, ought to be hollow within after the manner of a cupboard, wherein you shall keep all the necessary things." That is helpful but still a bit vague. Before I read this, at first I pictured something similar to a small podium that you would sit at on the floor; but now I am thinking it may be something you stand at.

ANSWER: Imagine if you will, two cubes, each made of ¾" thick plywood, and having 18" finished sides. Imagine these two cubes stacked one atop the other, and secured in place by four 4" × ¾" bolts (the bolts are placed inside the two cabinets, such that the bottom of the upper cabinet is secured to the top of the bottom cabinet.) Now imagine a burnished solid brass handle on the front face of each cabinet, and a 12" brass hinge securing the front face of each cabinet to one of the sides, such that each cabinet can be opened and closed easily (a simple brass latch with eyehook keeps the face of each cabinet closed until access to the interior is needed.) Finally, add four 2" diameter coaster-wheels to the bottom cabinet, such that the entire assembly can be moved above the Magical Chamber with a single push of one hand. This is my interpretation of the cabinet Abramelin described, and which is simple to make. It is also an Altar you can stand in front of.

One thing: NEVER, and I repeat, NEVER, have anyone build this or any critical magical structure or Impedimenta for you!

(The only exception to this rule, which many grimoires allow, applies to the Sword. It can be purchased or forged. If the latter, it must be done by you.) Such is your job, as is its design. If the Abramelin Operation demands the most intense effort from you over an extended period of time—as does all Old System Magic.

QUESTION: When I have decided which room I want as my temple is there a ritual I must perform to "make it official"?

ANSWER: There is a ritual procedure I use in such cases that may be of help to you. It is simple and straightforward, but has proven extremely effective. It assumes you have a ritual or ceremonial vestment of the type described below, an Altar erected in the center of the room, and a candle snuffer. The rest of the material is easily obtainable.

Purchase 9 white, unscented candles; 9 new candle holders; a new unglazed earthen bowl; a new box of table salt; fresh, clean mountain spring water (a few ounces will do); and a box of new wooden sulfur-less matches.

Enter your new Magical Chamber and don your pure white, ritual linen vestment. Place one of the white candles in each quarter of the universe, and one in each sub-quarter in such a way that the positions of the candles outline a Circle 9 feet in diameter. Place the 9th candle at the center of your Altar. Light the candles in the following order: rotating clockwise, first light those in the quarters. Begin in the East, continue through the North, and then move back to the East. Next, light the candles in the sub-quarters, beginning with that in the SE, moving to the SW, then to the NW, on to the NE, and conclude by returning to the East. Move clockwise within the circle of candles to the West of the Altar, facing East, and light the 9th candle there.

While facing East, add some water to the bowl. To this, add ½–1 oz. of table salt. From your position behind your Altar (still facing East) dip your right hand into the saltwater, remove it along with a quantity of the liquid, and asperge toward the East, turning clockwise through the directions of the compass until you are facing East once more. While you are asperging, say the following:

> "Thou shalt purge me with Hyssop, Oh, Lord, and I shall be clean! Thou shalt wash me, and I shall be whiter than snow!"

Make the Sign of the Cross (equal-armed to indicate the equilibration of the four Elements) in the air, in each quarter and sub-quarter. Begin doing this from your position behind your Altar, again facing East (make the Sign of the Cross in the quarters and sub-quarters in this one circumambulation.) As you make this Sign, recite some Prayer of Dedication you feel is appropriate to your purpose. *This prayer must be composed by you and no one else*, i.e., it must not be taken from any book of any kind. Be highly focused on the words you speak, and on their meaning.

Extinguish the candles in the quarters first, beginning in the East and finishing in the North. Return to the East, move to the SE and extinguish the candle in that sub-quarter first. Then extinguish those in the remaining sub-quarters, always moving desoil.

Remove your ritual or ceremonial vestment, take each of the white candles and their holders, and destroy them: make certain they can *never* be used again by anyone. Take the saltwater outdoors, and while facing East, pour the mixture on the ground, reverently. Finally, destroy the bowl totally. Your Magical Chamber has now been asperged, and is properly consecrated to Magic.

QUESTION: Is there any ritual or practice that you have found that will increase a person intelligence or learning ability, so that the person could comprehend written and verbal information better? If not anything to improve memory? Would you recommend any Sephiroth for doing either of these in conjunction with Regardie's *The Art of True Healing* technique?

ANSWER: Most certainly, you could and should create and 'charge' a Talisman of Mercury for these purposes. Mercury rules all matters of communication—including those matters of our internal communication with ourselves—intelligence in particular (both general and specific, e.g., the increase of one's general intelligence, as well as the improvement of one's verbal and written skills.) Mercury takes the correspondence of the Sephirah, Hod, and its color is orange. You should of course, learn all you can about this planet's Kabbalistic nature, and incorporate these ideas and the specifics of your intentions into the talismanic design.

I take it your reference to *The Art of True Healing* was made because you intend to charge the device by the Middle Pillar Ritual. In that case, you would use the properties of Mercury as Regardie gives in that little treatise, turn your aura orange (at the end of the formulation of the ovoid of white light surrounding you) and vibrate the Divine Name assigned to the planet/Sephirah. As the Mercurial forces of the universe converge upon your (now) orange auric ovoid, you would direct those forces into the Talisman, while concentrating on the specifics you wish to bring about within yourself from the talismanic influence.

Be certain to place the charged Talisman in a piece of asperged and consecrated white linen—not silk. The linen does not have to be dyed orange: you will find that a pure white linen is best in all magical matters.

QUESTION: In your book, *Ceremonial Magic,* you mention in Axiom Six that the magician should not wish for wealth. I take this to mean that in the line of your charge that reads "I therefore charge thee to bring unto me (name your desire here)..." I should not install the word "wealth" or the phrase "great wealth" at the end of this line. On the one hand you say this would be too general and on the other hand I certainly do not wish to be as specific as the friend you mention, so what if I were to install the phrase "x (x as in unknown, meaning I am not mentioning the amount as I type this) amount of dollars" or to make an effort to close loopholes "x amount of American dollars in denominations of (such and such)." Would this kind of wording get the results I am looking for?

ANSWER: If I understand your general query, the charge to be given would be something on the order of:

> "And thou shalt insure the delivery unto me of material, worldly wealth in such abundance that shall delight me and be made use of by me as I so see fit to use, and in whatsoever way I desire to use it. Further, thou shall always see to it that regardless of the material wealth needed by for an issue that I choose to undertake, that wealth shall come into my possession in any and all ways that hurt neither man nor beast, nor violate the lands in any way nor cause any grievances onto any thing."

You should consider the above as a template and adjust it to your own particular requirements. It works as you will find out if you use it. Be warned though, that unless you are very skilled in Evocation to Physical Manifestation, you will not escape the Slingshot Effect. Yes, the more experience you have and consequently the more complete the physical manifestation of the demon, the greater your control and command, the less the Slingshot Effect will be. *But it will still be, and that is the important point to remember.* You *cannot* escape Cause–Effect no matter how hard you try. Remember, as I have said so often before, "Something for nothing does not exist in this business." You will pay for what you get. The only question is "How much will you pay?"

QUESTION: Seeing as you seem to feel ritual has to be done by the book, how do you feel about Agrippa's comments on astrological magic: i.e., that planets should be in their sign of rulership, term etc.; basically that electional astrology should be used to determine the proper time of ritual.

How far can one go with that? I find it almost possible to find the right timing where for example Jupiter is essentially dignified and has no bad aspects and the moon is not void of course and the midheaven is well aspected and it goes on and on. One rotten bad apple in the chart makes me have serious doubts about the ritual and that is not a good thing. Do you feel planetary days and hours are good enough? I used to do OK with just that but now the more I read the more confused I get.

ANSWER: What you do need is *Ceremonial Magic and the Power of Evocation* and *Kabbalistic Cycles and the Mastery of Life*. The first will explain the relevance of Agrippa's works in relation to Old System Magic—you have an incorrect view of it as you expressed it here. The second book will give you a method of using Kabbalistic Cycles—which incorporate astrological influences—that will work 100% of the time.

We all want 'guarantees' in everything we do in life. This is perfectly understandable. The two books I mentioned above—particularly the *Kabbalistic Cycles and the Mastery of Life*—will give you just that—as much as is humanly possible. Later, the *Kabbalistic Handbook for the Practicing Magician* will give you greater insight into Old System Magic and even into the magic of the Golden Dawn.

QUESTION: I'm seeking to understand the distinction you make between "Imaging" and "Visualization". You say that New Thought did not originally teach visualizing, right? But, according to Kabbalistic theory, doesn't a "thoughtform" have to be placed in the astral so that it can materialize? And, wouldn't that require creating a specific image in the mind? New Thought seems to emphasize "treatments". I understand these to be long affirmations where one seeks to fully identify with Source before stating what's desired. Is that right? Is this also meant to nullify any contrary ideas in the Subconscious Mind? And, is that why they didn't emphasize visualization, because it is " The Word" that creates?

ANSWER: A "Treatment" (abbreviated form of the phrase, "prayer treatment") is a definite movement of the mind, in a definite direction, so created and released from consciousness as to accomplish a definite purpose. Yes, they can use Affirmations, but in and of themselves they are thoughts which must pass through a process which enables the purpose they contain within them to be made manifest in the world of form.

They can identify with the Source, but that depends on the 'type' of process you are using when working with New Thought or "Higher Mysticism". Meaning, there are 'mechanical' ways of working New Thought that do not entail 'connecting' with the Source and they work just as well. Mysticism—both Higher Mysticism and "High Mysticism" are infinitely more complex than any form of magic, Old System Magic included. Thus, it is not a simple matter. I know of no stand alone book that teaches all of it or even a large part of it. It is something which requires many years of study.

An "Affirmation" is a statement, spoken in the present tense, used to declare a desire. It may or may not be true for you at the moment you say it, in which case, the content of your spoken words will fail to materialize. There are ways of attenuating such spoken words in order to make them acceptable to your emotional perceptions and therefore to your subconscious mind.

"Visualization," as it is used today, denotes an elaborate process of mentalizing in which a highly specific picture of that which you desire is to first be constructed in your mind before it is 'released' to the Universe for fulfillment.

"Imaging" on the other hand—the word I insist on—is that process in which a generalized yet complete image is constructed within the mind and then energized in such a way that it creates a complex 'frequency' with an 'amplitude' that is much, much greater and more acceptable to the Universe.[1]

---

[1] The distinction between these two ideas is subtle yet important. Dr. Lisiewski states that the overly detailed and exact nature of the 'visualization' process in modern occult practices creates such an elaborate and detailed image that is chokes out the materialization of other, and thereby possibly better, outcomes. The more general, yet clear processes of 'imaging' allows for possible outcomes that are within the established range of the mental image created. To paraphrase an Eastern proverb, we must create an image that is neither too tight, nor too loose, but just right. In addition, one does not visualize demons or angels in Medieval magic, they call upon them and witness the form they appear in. Hence, in *The Fourth Book of Occult Philosophy* we are given a list of possible forms for each of the angles of the seven planets—no one form will be used all the time—just as we do not wear the same clothes every day. This notion is somewhat further complicated by Medieval and Renaissance source that state unequivocally the power of the human mind is supreme and is in complete agreement with New Thought, Hindu and Buddhist Tantras, and Classical Magic. As stated earlier, Jakob Boehme called the Imagination, the inner power to create, the divine power in man. This was a power the swelled up from deep inside, a passion, and both created images and forms, as well as was stimulated by them. This power of imagination was for Boehme to be used to bring man closer to God, and Divine Harmony, "Faith is partaking if the substance of God...an introduction of the substance of God into one's soul by means of Imagination...thereby the soul becomes clothed in the substance of God." This power also effected the material world, "Love is the creative Imagination, which...manifests the good. 'Imagination makes substance.' By living in the Kingdom [of Heaven] inwardly, I create it outwardly. I become the channel through which divine light streams into the... world."

"Imagination is like the sun. The sun has a light which is not tangible; but which, nevertheless, may set a house on fire; but the imagination is like a sun in man acting in that place to which its light is directed. Man is that what he thinks. If he thinks fire, he is fire; if he thinks war, then he will cause war; it all depends merely on that the whole of his imagination becomes an entire sun; i.e., that he wholly imagines that which he wills. Man is a twofold being, having a divine and an animal nature. If he feels, and thinks, and acts as divine beings should act, he is a true man; if he feels and acts like an animal, he is then an animal, and the equal of those animals whose mental characteristics are manifested in him. An exalted imagination caused by a desire for the good raises him up; a low imagination caused by a desire for that which is low and vulgar drags him down and degrades him. The spirit is the master, imagination the tool, and the boy the plastic (PLAS'TIC, a. [Gr. to form.] Having the power to give form or fashion to a mass of matter; as the plastic hand of the Creator; the plastic virtue of nature.) material." by Theophrastus Paracelsus who also states:

"The magical is a great hidden wisdom, and reason is a great open folly. No armour shields against magic for it strikes at the inward life of spirit of life. Of this we may rest assured, that through full and powerful imagination only can we bring the spirit of any man into an image. No conjurations, no rites are needful; circle making and the scattering of incense are mere humbug and jugglery. The human spirit is so great a thing that no man can express it; eternal and unchangeable as God Himself is the mind of man; and could we rightly comprehend the mind of man, nothing would be impossible to us upon the earth. Through faith the imagination is invigorated and completed, for it really happens that every doubt mars its perfection. Faith must strengthen the imagination, for faith establishes the will. Because man did not perfectly believe and imagine the result is that arts are uncertain when they might be wholly certain."

To be clear, the process of "visualization" as it is called was clearly used in certain mystical practices, even of the Roman Catholic Church. The Jesuit manual, *The Exercises of St. Ignatius* being the most famous and cited in modern magical circles; even the Rosary was accompanied by distinct images that were to be visualized as the prayers were being said, although that practice appears to have all but died out by the later half of the Twentieth Century. Boehme even stated that when praying we must earnestly visualize ourselves standing before God, and with God all around us. This is no different from the process used in Tibetan yoga when visualizing the "Buddhafield" or "Awakened World" of the various deities used. So, we have clear evidence of the process of creating mental images for mystical purposes, but we do not find the process anywhere stated within the process outlined in the grimoires. The process of visualization, creation of elaborate and precise images, creates an obstacle for many students, as once created, they become an end of themselves, and failure to 'let them go' and be receptive to the Divine influence they are designed to be a conduit for is a common experience. To quote Tulku Rinpoche on this matter, "Training in all-encompassing purity is training in what is. Based on this one can apply [esoteric visualization] practice authentically. Without this, visualization practice become just 'brick-laying' or mental labor." Further on he state, "The authentic way of practicing…is to allow the visualization to unfold as the natural state of [the relaxed and natural mind]." This process of letting our inner images becoming 'brick-laying' would be known to Boehme as *phantasia*, and in modern terms as day-dreaming. For a complete and thorough overview of the role of imagination and visualization in Hermetic and occult practices during the Classical, Medieval, and Renaissance periods, see: *The Art of Memory* by Frances A. Yates.

Afterword

by David Rankine

My first encounter with Dr Lisiewski was through his book, *Ceremonial Magic and the Power of Evocation*. It was immediately clear to me on reading this book that I had in my hands a work by a true old school magician who was well versed in both the philosophies and practices of the grimoires. The book is a treasure trove of practical advice and philosophical explanations based around the hugely significant early fourteenth century grimoire, the *Heptameron*.

The *Heptameron* has turned up repeatedly in my own research, and I have discussed its influence as a foundation stone of the tradition on the most significant grimoires including the *Goetia* and the *Key of Solomon* in my works with Stephen Skinner.[1] The *Heptameron* formed the basis for the conjurations of the four demon princes of the cardinal points found in the cipher grimoire called *Clavis Inferni* (The Key of Hell), which Stephen and I translated and published as *The Grimoire of St Cyprian: Clavis Inferi*.[2] It is also to be found in less well known texts, such as the material in Sloane MS 3824, where it is combined with material drawn from the sixteenth century German mages Trithemius and Agrippa, and Goetic demons and fairies.[3]

After reading *Ceremonial Magic and the Power of Evocation* and being suitably impressed, I began a fruitful correspondence with

---

[1] See *The Goetia of Dr Rudd*, Skinner & Rankine, 2007, and *The Veritable Key of Solomon*, Skinner & Rankine, 2008. Stephen Skinner first published the facsimile *Heptameron* in 1978, and later edited the first complete modern English edition: Abano, Peter de, Heptameron, or the 'Magical Elements' in *Agrippa, H C. Fourth Book of Occult Philosophy*, revised, Ibis Press/ Nicolas-Hays, Berwick, 2005.
[2] *The Grimoire of St Cyprian: Clavis Inferni*, Skinner & Rankine, 2009.
[3] See *The Book of Treasure Spirits*, Rankine, 2009.

Dr Lisiewski. It transpired that while I was reading his books, he was likewise reading the *Sourceworks of Ceremonial Magic* series produced by Stephen Skinner and me. The contents of both our publications has provided us with plenty of material to discuss the grimoires and old school magic and find many points of shared opinion and experience.

From his writings, it is clear that Dr Lisiewski is one of the rare few authors writing today who fully grasps the material he discusses. Not only does he grasp it, but his decades of practice, experience and contemplation of the material mean that he can wield it in the manner it was created for. Make no mistake, the grimoires are by their very nature challenging. They demand the best from the practitioner, in the discipline, application and dedication they need to apply to achieve results. All the qualities, in fact, which a scientist (such as Dr Lisiewski) applies to his work.

In Dr Thomas Rudd's seventeenth century writings, he paraphrased a line from the earlier *Arbatel* (which was bound with the *Heptameron* in the *Fourth Book of Occult Philosophy*), stating *"He that is a true Magician, is brought forth a Magician from his Mother's Womb; and whoso is otherwise, ought to recompense that defect of Nature by Education."*[1] This attitude, whilst likely to be extremely unpopular in the mediocrity of modern society, reflects a view of magic which sees it is a gift and a calling. By reading this book you are choosing to use that gift or follow that calling.

It is important to appreciate that the instructions contained in this book are based on both experience and sound magical principles. So when e.g. the author explains the use of the blasting rod in chapter four, and the power of the magnetic end caps to attract and repel demons, he is also continuing a tradition of the apotropaic use of magnetic iron found in the ancient world, such as the magnetic iron rings given to initiates of the mysteries of Samothrace.[2]

Another key area of practice stressed by Dr Lisiewski and finally given the consideration it deserves is that of suffumigation. The use of fragrant incenses to attract spiritual creatures, and conversely unpleasant fragrances to banish unwanted atten-

---

[1] *The Keys to the Gateway of Magic,* Skinner & Rankine, 2005.
[2] *The Goetia of Dr Rudd,* Skinner & Rankine, 2007, p.81.

tion is seen throughout the grimoires, and as such is a crucial part of the process of evocation, as Dr Lisiewski makes very clear. He vividly illustrates the point made in the *Key of Solomon*, where the chapter *Concerning Burning Incense and of Perfumes* states:

"*There are several sorts of incense you can burn, as well as fumigations and perfumes which are made for the Spirits. Those which give off a sweet smell are used for attracting Good Spirits. Those which give off a bad smell, on the contrary, are used to drive off harmful Spirits.*"[1]

Not only are the instructions contained in these pages on practices firmly rooted in efficacy and experience, so too is the philosophy expounded as part of the same process. As the author stresses, mysticism and magic are inseparable, as are practice and philosophy. Magical practice expands the mind, and the accompanying magical philosophy makes this process harmonious and part of the process of reification undertaken by the mage. In this the reader is well served by the seamless blending of philosophy in the practical descriptions of the practices and actions necessary for progress.

This is in many ways the first book of its kind, which is solely dedicated to providing efficacious and valuable direction on how to perform the magic of the grimoires. In this Dr Lisiewski is to be congratulated. His no-nonsense attitude is entirely appropriate to the grimoires, and is wonderfully exemplified by his comment that *"There are no shortcuts to Heaven. But there are to Hell."* This statement encapsulates the practice of old school grimoire magic perfectly, and is a good example of how a simple sentence can contain layers of meaning which speak to different people in different ways as they progress on their personal journey.

As well as describing grimoire magic, this could also describe Dr Lisiewski himself. As a writer he takes no prisoners, expressing his perceptions with scientific precision and backing them up with experience. This is the only way to progress, and it is not easy or gentle. The old school grimoire path is often harsh and challenging, and by its nature will filter out the numerous

---

[1] *The Veritable Key of Solomon,* Skinner & Rankine, 2008, p.346. There is a whole treatise on the use of suffumigations in magic in Stephen Skinner & Don Karr. *Sepher Raziel: Liber Salomonis,* 2010, Chapter on 'Tractatus Thymiamatus' of Suffumigations, p.185.

poseurs and wannabes unwilling to dedicate themselves to its pursuit. Only those who light and feed the flames of their will can hope to know the divine bliss and wonder which reward those of true heart and intent. Now in this book those worthy seekers have the benefit of a roadmap which cuts through illusory landscapes and glamours to the burning heart of magic.

MORE BOOKS FROM JOSEPH LISIEWSKI

CEREMONIAL MAGIC & THE POWER OF EVOCATION
by Joseph C. Lisiewski, Ph.D.

Introduced by Christopher Hyatt, Ph.D. & S. Jason Black

Ceremonial Magic lays bare the simplest of Grimoires, the Heptameron of Peter de Abano. Its Magical Axioms, extensive Commentaries, copious notes, and personal instructions to the reader make this a resource that no serious student of Magic can afford to be without. The world of evocation and personal gratification are well within your grasp!

ISRAEL REGARDIE & THE PHILOSOPHER'S STONE
by Joseph C. Lisiewski, Ph.D.

Introduced by. Mark Stavish

Dr. Lisiewski delves into the hitherto unknown role Israel Regardie played in the world of Practical Laboratory Alchemy: not the world of idle speculation and so-called "inner alchemy," but the realm of the test tube and the Soxhlet Extractor. For the first time Dr. Regardie's private alchemical experiments are revealed as is his intense interaction with Frater Albertus of the Paracelsus Research Society and later, with the author himself.

MORE BOOKS FROM JOSEPH LISIEWSKI

KABBALISTIC CYCLES & THE MASTERY OF LIFE
by Joseph C. Lisiewski, Ph.D.

Foreword by Christopher S. Hyatt, Ph.D.

This groundbreaking book reveals a new system of occult cycles that gives you complete Control over your own life. The Kabbalistic Cycles System explains heretofore hidden universal laws known to but a few. The knowledge of these strange cycles— and the detailed, step-by-step explanation of their derivation and use—will place you light years beyond those who would maintain a stranglehold over you.

KABBALISTIC HANDBOOK FOR THE PRACTICING MAGICIAN
by Joseph C. Lisiewski, Ph.D.

Foreword by Christopher S. Hyatt, Ph.D.

For the practicing Magician, there is no more crucial working knowledge than the Kabbalah. This complex structure serves as the backdrop against which the magician's thoughts, ideas, ritual and ceremonial work are placed, and is the archetype which breathes life into secret occult practices. Yet, none of the numerous books on 'Qabalah' give those 'on-the-spot' attributions, correspondences and key concepts in a 'user-friendly' style. Until now.

The *Original* Falcon Press

Invites You to Visit Our Website:
http://originalfalcon.com

At our website you can:

- Browse the online catalog of all of our great titles
- Find out what's available and what's out of stock
- Get special discounts
- Order our titles through our secure online server
- Find products not available anywhere else including:
    – One of a kind and limited availability products
    – Special packages
    – Special pricing
- Get free gifts
- Join our email list for advance notice of New Releases and Special Offers
- Find out about book signings and author events
- Send email to our authors
- Read excerpts of many of our titles
- Find links to our authors' websites
- Discover links to other weird and wonderful sites
- And much, much more

Get online today at http://originalfalcon.com